David Lamb is Lecturer in Philosophy at the
University of Manchester

D0850319

Hegel and Modern Philosophy

HEGEL
AND
MODERN PHILOSOPHY

Edited by David Lamb

CROOM HELM
London • New York • Sydney

© 1987 David Lamb
Croom Helm Ltd, Provident House,
Burrell Row, Beckenham, Kent BR3 1AT

Croom Helm Australia, 44–50 Waterloo Road,
North Ryde, 2113, New South Wales

Published in the USA by
Croom Helm
in association with Methuen, Inc.
29 West 35th Street
New York, NY 10001

British Library Cataloguing in Publication Data

Hegel and modern philosophy.
   1. Hegel, Georg Wilhelm Friedrich
   I. Lamb, David, *1942*–
   193   B2948
   ISBN 0–7099–4168–4

Library of Congress Cataloging in Publication Data

   ISBN 0–7099–4168–4

Typeset by Photoprint, Torquay, South Devon
Printed and bound in Great Britain by Mackays of Chatham Ltd, Kent

Contents

Acknowledgements   vi

Introduction   vii

1. Hegel's Historical Phenomenology and Social Analysis   1
   Bernard Cullen
2. Hegel and Feminism   30
   Susan M. Easton
3. On Becoming   56
   Anthony Manser
4. Sense and Meaning in Hegel and Wittgenstein   70
   David Lamb
5. Hegel on Political Economy   102
   Christopher J. Arthur
6. Marx's Hegelianism: An Exposition   119
   Michael George
7. The Actual and the Rational   143
   Sean Sayers
8. Hegel, Marx and Dialectic   161
   Joseph McCarney
9. Hegel and Religion   189
   John Walker
10. The Difference Between *Begrifflicher Spekulation* and Mathematics in Hegel's Philosophy of Nature   226
    Wolfgang Neuser
11. Hegel's *Habilitationsthesen*: A Translation with Introduction and Annotated Bibliography   249
    Norbert Waszek

Index   261

Acknowledgements

The editor would like to thank various members of the Hegel Society of Great Britain for comments and advice throughout this project, and participants in the 'Hegel Panel' of the Political Studies Association where several of the papers included here had their first airing. A special note of thanks to Joe McCarney who, for several years, has organised Hegel seminars where many of the topics covered here have been discussed. Thanks also to the following: the editor of *Clio* for the use of material from 'Hegel and Wittgenstein on Language and Sense-Certainty' by D. Lamb in vol. 7, number 2, 1978, which appears here in an expanded form in the chapter titled 'Sense and Meaning in Hegel and Wittgenstein'; the editors of *Radical Philosophy*, number 38, 1984, for the use of material from Susan M. Easton's paper 'Functionalism and Feminism in Hegel's Political Thought', and the editors of *Politics* vol. 5, 1985 for the use of material from Susan M. Easton's 'Slavery and Freedom: Towards a Feminist Reading of Hegel', which has been developed further and incorporated into the chapter in this collection on 'Hegel and Feminism'.

Introduction

For the greater part of this century the philosophical writings of Hegel have been either badly misunderstood or totally neglected. But during the past twenty years there has been a tremendous revival of interest in Hegel, which is partly due to interests in Marxism and Continental philosophy and partly a reaction against what was perceived as the dullness of the linguistic and analytic philosophy which has dominated English-speaking philosophy. Many who turned to Hegel saw him as a challenge; both difficult to comprehend but impossible to ignore Hegel seemed to have something to say about almost every branch of philosophical inquiry. The flood of exegesical texts and English translations has continued since the 1960s, and the setting up of the Hegel Society of Great Britain in 1979 was an acknowledgement of the fact that Hegelianism is to have a prominent position in philosophy for many years to come. But what is of great significance in the Hegel revival is the actual diversity of research interests which led scholars to Hegel's philosophy. It is certainly impossible to single out one strand of his work as being accountable for this growing interest. For some philosophers it is his social and political philosophy that explains the attraction, others seek insights in his metaphysics, his philosophy of nature, philosophy of religion, or philosophy of history.

It is this very diversity of interests which underlies the selection of papers included in this volume. No attempt has been made to show that contemporary Hegelians belong to a school or have anything in common beyond the fact that an interest in Hegel is reflected in their current philosophical research. The reader who expects a final and definitive statement about Hegel's philosophy will not find it in this collection. For the purpose in bringing together this wealth of current research has not been to present a detailed exegesis of a philosopher who has been long dead, but rather to demonstrate the life and vitality of an Hegelian tradition and its influence upon those who are grappling with some of the issues that dominate contemporary philosophy.

Thus in the first paper Bernard Cullen argues that contemporary social philosophy is enriched with an appreciation of Hegel's insights in *The phenomenology of spirit*, and maintains that 'our attempts to understand the complexities of human society and culture today can hope to succeed only within the framework bequeathed to us by Hegel'. Susan Easton, in the second paper, approaches recent issues in feminist social and political philosophy from an Hegelian standpoint. Rejecting some of the standard feminist criticism of Hegel's analysis of the family (namely his alleged endorsement of the public-private distinction, and alleged reductionism and functionalism) she explores the possibility of an Hegelian understanding of women's potential freedom.

In the paper by Anthony Manser, attention focuses on Hegel's logic. As Manser points out Hegel's *Science of logic* represents a radical attempt to change the very nature of philosophy but, whilst many commentators have written about the initial dialectic of being, nothing, and becoming, none have taken Hegel's remarks about becoming seriously enough and have consequently misunderstood one of the most essential features of his attempt to replace traditional metaphysics with dialectical logic. There have been other attempts to transform the nature of philosophy. One of the more recent attempts has been attributed to Ludwig Wittgenstein whose radical approach to problems of language and meaning is compared with Hegel's philosophy in the following paper by David Lamb.

In a detailed examination of Hegel's socio-economic philosophy Christopher J. Arthur looks at the role of political economy in Hegel's *Philosophy of right* and argues that Hegel's emphasis on social forms is highly relevant to the contemporary attempt to develop economics as a social science.

The three papers by Michael George, Sean Sayers and Joseph McCarney indicate the extent to which an understanding of the relationship between Hegelianism and Marxism is relevant today. Michael George interprets Marxism as a construction upon foundations laid by Hegel and consequently takes issue with commentators who have attempted to rewrite Marxism without reference to its Hegelian heritage. According to Sean Sayers both Hegel and Marx were advocates of a scientific and realistic method, but it was only by means of a rejection of Hegel's conservative system that Marx was able to develop a method which was both scientific and critical. Joseph McCarney raises the question of how the social sciences can be conceived of as being dialectical and argues that progress in this direction can be achieved only through an appreciation of Marx's methodological debt to Hegel.

Hegel's contribution to the philosophy of religion is an

important feature in the revival of Hegelian philosophy, and the relationship between his views on philosophy and his views on religion has been a subject of considerable debate. Pitting himself against those philosophers who separate the religious elements from Hegel's epistemology and metaphysics, John Walker provides a convincing case that 'Hegel's view of philosophy as itself a religious activity is of crucial relevance to his philosophy as a whole' and that 'far from being an anachronism' the religious character is one of the main reasons why that philosophy continues to be relevant.

Whilst Hegel's contribution to the philosophy of religion has been recognised and progress continues in the application of his method to the social sciences, the significance of his philosophy of nature for contemporary philosophy of science has, until very recently, been virtually ignored. Wolfgang Neuser's examination of how Hegel saw the role of mathematics in the natural sciences therefore marks a significant step in the recognition of benefits to be derived from an Hegelian approach to the philosophy of science.

The appendix to this collection is a translation of Hegel's *Habilitationsthesen* together with an introduction and annotated bibliography by Norbert Waszek.

David Lamb
Department of Philosophy
University of Manchester

1

Hegel's Historical Phenomenology and Social Analysis

Bernard Cullen

FOR FRITHJOF BERGMANN

The present world and the present form and self-consciousness of spirit contain within them all the stages that appear
to have occurred earlier in history . . . What spirit is now, it
has always been; the only difference is that it now possesses
a richer consciousness and a more fully elaborated concept
of its own nature . . . Those moments that spirit appears to
have outgrown still belong to it in the depths of its present.
Hegel, Introduction to *Lectures on the philosophy of world
history* (1830)[1]

In the first part of this essay, I propose to offer a reading of
Hegel's *Phenomenology of spirit*. This does not pretend to be the
only legitimate reading; especially with a text as tantalising and
as rich and complex as the *Phenomenology*, I am always suspicious
of commentators who claim to have discovered 'what Hegel really
meant' (or any other philosopher, for that matter). I hope, all the
same, that mine is what Werner Marx calls an 'immanent' rather
than an 'assimilative' account:[2] I have not attributed to Hegel
what is not in the text, and I have no particular philosophical axe
to grind, except to articulate my own conviction that our
attempts to understand the complexities of human society and
culture today can hope to succeed only within the philosophical
framework bequeathed to us by Hegel. Not, of course, that Hegel
had all the answers. However, while the Hegelian synthesis — of
subjectivity and objectivity, humanity and nature, finiteness and
infinity — has been fruitfully supplemented by subsequent
thinkers, it has not, in my view, been superseded. In part II, I

1

shall indicate some of the ways in which contemporary social analysis can learn from Hegel's insights.

Because of its short compass, my account is partial, and much of considerable significance is, inevitably, omitted. Nevertheless, I hope to present a coherent synopsis of a very long and often baffling book, and to highlight a unifying thread that runs through it.[3] The central theme of the *Phenomenology* is that human reason *can* attain knowledge of the spirit that permeates all of reality; but this can only be achieved through a philosophical consideration of all the forms that spirit has assumed throughout history. To look at it from a slightly different perspective, the *Phenomenology* is an account of the history of self-consciousness — i.e. of the ways in which people have understood themselves and their relations to other people, to nature and to the divine — culminating in the 'absolute' knowledge that is attainable today.

I have argued elsewhere that Hegel's primary motivation to write an all-encompassing system of philosophy was his anguish in the face of the social and political fragmentation around him.[4] This ubiquitous bifurcation (*Entzweiung*) was parallelled by a growing estrangement of human beings from the ground of their being in nature. When the instrumental reason of the Enlightenment introduced a radical cleavage between human society and nature, society was left suspended as if in mid-air. In his solution to this problem, Rousseau assumed the universal possibility of a social reciprocity that has its juridical equivalent in the idea of a social contract: according to this understanding, all dissymmetry and inequality in status, functions and powers is abolished, so that each member of the community is recognised as a homogeneous unit, with equal access to the realm of the rights and duties that are presupposed by all forms of collective life.

Hegel took Rousseau to task for the formalism of his social contract theory (see *PG* 316–23, *PS* 355–63, on absolute freedom and terror)[5] and for his failure to recognise (as Montesquieu and Herder had done) the concrete reality of the spirit of a people expressing itself in its art, its religion, its political and economic institutions. According to Hegel, an underlying unity can be rediscovered beneath this manifold of spiritual/cultural universes. Each time the philosopher enters in thought into another historical period, it becomes self-sufficient and excludes the other forms of life that have preceded it or will succeed it: India, Greece, Rome, the Middle Ages, the Enlightenment are so many worlds, the richness and originality of which must be acknowledged. There can, therefore, be no lapidary affirmation valid for the whole range of human societies that might permit any thinker to overcome their heterogeneity. For Hegel, concepts such as freedom, nature, the will are themselves the products of a certain stage in the development of what he calls spirit (*Geist*); and they certainly may not be accepted unquestioningly when one's thought is confronted with the vast sweep of world history.

Hegel's overriding aim is to examine in thought the being of this spirit, and to grasp the process through which modern society strives to become adequate to it. Spirit, actualised in different ways in different societies, has not heretofore been accessible to thought; but it is because spirit has now *explicitly* become what it has always been implicitly that philosophical science is finally able to achieve adequate knowledge of its object.[6] The inadequacy or the bias of earlier philosophical doctrines was due not so much to blindness or intellectual laziness, but to the incompleteness of spirit itself; and it is because of the maturing of spirit that we can now embark upon the transcendence of the division between knowledge (phenomena) and faith (noumena) instituted by Kantian Criticism, that still characterises the modern world. This 'ripening' process is not the product of mere reflection. It involves the whole unfolding of universal history; and it is in this fundamental connection between the ultimate success of philosophical discourse and the becoming of spirit that the radical novelty of Hegelianism is evident: a single reading of the facts of experience is only now conceivable because spirit has deepened its own content, since the totality of its virtualities could only be developed with the passage of time. Hegel elaborates on this theme in the final chapter of the *Phenomenology of spirit*, entitled 'Absolute Knowledge (*Das absolute Wissen*)'. In it he discusses the relation between his *Science of logic* (finally published in 1812–16), which is adumbrated in this final chapter, and the phenomenological dialectic described in the preceding chapters. He underlines the interpenetration and mutual modification of philosophical science and the historical and natural reality out of which it was developed. According to Hegel, the philosopher can know and know absolutely; but it has become possible, at a specific point in history, for a particular person (Hegel himself) to come to know and to write down the content of the *Science of logic* only because of the unfolding of the course of human history, that is, the effective development of spirit. For a better understanding of how Hegel

,arrived at this conclusion, we should refer back to the Preface (written in early 1807, and a summary of Hegel's philosophical project in its own right), in which he defines the purpose of the *Phenomenology*.

I

Hegel insists that human reality is fundamentally historical: 'Spirit is never at rest but is engaged in constantly progressive movement (*in immer fortschreitender Bewegung*), (*PG* 14, *PS* 6). He describes the transition from one form[7] of spirit to another: spirit matures (*reift*) slowly and quietly into its new shape, like a child in the womb, and then 'there is a qualitative leap (*ein qualitativer Sprung*), and the child is born' (*PG* 14, *PS* 6). Although spirit dissolves almost imperceptibly the structure of its previous world, 'this gradual crumbling that left unaltered the face of the whole is cut short by the sunrise which, in a flash, all at once reveals the features of the new world' (*PG* 15, *PS* 7). The Roman world succeeded the Greek city-state, and was itself in turn replaced by the medieval Christian world: the becoming (or the 'maturing' or 'ripening') of spirit can best be understood as a long succession of incomplete forms that gave rise to each other, negated each other, or sometimes co-existed on the basis of different principles, while the meaning of the totality of the process was never fully grasped.

But the emergence of a new form of spirit takes on today a significance quite different from any it could possibly have had in previous epochs:

> Our time (*Zeit*) is a time of birth and transition to a new epoch (*Periode*). Spirit has broken with what was hitherto the world of its existence and imagination (*Daseins und Vorstellens*), and is about to submerge it in the past, and in the work of its own transformation. (*PG* 14, *PS* 6)

Our era is different, because for the first time this meaning underlying everything that has existed can be recognised as genuine knowledge, the very object of science. Of course Hegel does not prove this thesis in the Preface (nor can I), since such a demonstration is only available in the *Phenomenology* as a whole.

The ultimate aim of the work, however, is defined quite unambiguously: 'To lead the individual from his uneducated (*ungebildeten*) standpoint to knowledge' (*PG* 24, *PS* 16).

And this is to be accomplished by examining 'the universal individual (*das allgemeine Individuum*), the world spirit, in its formative education (*Bildung*)' (*PG* 24, *PS* 16).[8] While 'the universal (or general) individual' is humankind in general, the individual to whom Hegel is directing the *Phenomenology* is you or me. In the course of our own experience, we will have integrated into our existence all the moments of the development of spirit; which means that we will be in a position, using Hegel's terminology, to apprehend the true not as an objective *substance* but as a *subject*.

This formula involves both phenomenology and ontology: individuals must dissolve the exteriority of the thing-like object, must abolish the rigidity of substance and recognise in what is other than themselves their own handiwork. The *Phenomenology* is an account of this abolition of exteriority. By the end of the seventh chapter (that is, just before the eighth and final chapter on 'absolute knowledge'), we have arrived at the content of the absolute, albeit in an inadequate form, that of the Christian religion. And in the final chapter, Hegel abolishes all duality between the thing-like object — in this extreme case, God — and human self-consciousness. But this overcoming of all dualism is possible only because the disparity between being and thought is only one moment (or aspect) of a history, the one true subject of which is spirit.

This is not simply a modification of classical metaphysics governed by the traditional definition of truth. Whether one claims that knowledge must conform to the objects (empiricism), or, on the contrary, that the objects must be governed by our knowledge (rationalism/idealism), one is still assuming the duality and mutual indifference of being and knowing. But the object that presents itself to the individual as an immutable and unchangeable 'nature', out there, is so only because it has not yet been grasped in a properly scientific way. But this delay is not a simple accident due to contingent factors. According to Hegel, the delay exists only because the object itself has not reached its full development. And furthermore, if an object has now become an object of scientific knowledge, it is because it is moving towards its completed form, the sign of that completion being the knowledge itself.

The complexity of such a dialectic obviously transforms the very notion of error. The definition of truth as the adequation of the intellect to the thing is a proposition empty of meaning when non-truth refers to the non-fulfilment of being. Not that speaking of error is a meaningless act; but in this case, it has a purely technical meaning, internal to a discourse that has already been constituted. A judgement is recognised to be false when it is revealed that the content to which it refers does not exist. Presence, therefore, is the only norm against which what is stated can be measured. But what is presence apart from that discourse in which it is contained? Being is not the fixed and immutable entity that reflection alone can decompose or dissociate (in the chemistry sense); being is what discourse brings into existence *and* what has enabled that discourse to be held in the first place.

Reality articulates itself in discourse, but only to take over discourse itself. Discourse — that is, the totality of its manifestations — is a moment (or aspect) of being itself. The word is not external to what exists; it is the supreme incarnation of it. The dichotomy between subjectivity and objectivity postulated by all traditional theories of knowledge is seen, ultimately, to be illusory. The two histories, the history of the object and the history of the subject, coincide in their mutual transformation. Any effort, therefore, to describe the real as an objective given is necessarily inadequate; it is not a question of objectifying but of receiving and reintegrating. We are not to affirm a particular philosophical theory and reject all the others but, for the first time in the course of universal history, we are to confront all the discourses, all the philosophical theories, that the human mind has produced.

If the incompleteness of knowledge always refers back to the incompleteness of that historical reality of which it is knowledge, the notion of a completed science prompts two questions. In what form does it lead that which exists to fulfilment? And what is it in being that permitted it to come into existence? These questions help to elucidate the development of the *Phenomenology of spirit* on three levels. The object is appropriated and transformed into a subject according to three quite distinct processes. And the *Phenomenology* itself has three main stages:

a. The first five chapters (more than half the book) survey the emergence and development of subjective spirit (i.e. of particular forms of subjectivity or individual consciousness), which goes beyond the realm of individuality and opens up to the world of spirit.

b. Chapter VI (which corresponds to the stage of objective

spirit) presents a survey and analysis of the various forms or shapes of spirit, the successive cultural formations in history: the Greek city-state, the Roman world, feudal society, the French Revolution, which has heralded the rational (*vernünftig*) modern state. These are so many moments that have brought spirit to the fullness of its development. However, these earlier forms of consciousness are only what Hegel calls '*Abstractionen*' (*PG* 239, *PS* 264).

c. Finally, Chapters VII and VIII deal with absolute spirit: that is, the forms of discourse that people have adopted and through which the totality of being has been expressed: art, religion, and philosophy. Science proper only becomes possible, the content of knowledge can only be adequately expressed, after the completion of this triple movement. And each one of these processes calls forth the process that succeeds it.

Subjective spirit

The first five chapters of the *Phenomenology of spirit* describe the slow progress of individual consciousness leading from the appearances that are initially given to it to the very heart of Hegelian 'spirit'.[9] Since the world that the individual confronts is only the totality of the manifestations of his own activity, knowledge of the object is, therefore, just as much its suppression. Accordingly, this dialectic has first and foremost a negative signification: it is perceived by the subject as the brutal destruction of its own certainties. It appears to have no rigour and indeed seems quite chaotic. The object of experience is not given as the necessary product of the development of self-consciousness but as a content that one just stumbles upon, that appears out of the blue. It is in this respect that Hegelian description has often been compared to the essential character of psychoanalytic experience: what appears to be revealed at the end of the process as the ultimate law of consciousness has the same kind of strangeness as that which subjects can say about themselves in analysis. No intentional design can exhaust what comes into existence. It thus becomes apparent that individuals are nothing outside of an order of which they are part.

They can indeed affirm their own (partial) independence by abandoning one attitude for another; but they will depend just as much as ever on what is outside of them, which continues to elude them. Through the plurality of possible attitudes can be discerned an order that determines the vantage points from which those attitudes become intelligible. But consciousness does not recognise itself in this truth and submits to it as to a strange and archaic law. It hangs on then to what it is or what it thinks it is; it is unsure of its whole world; its inadequacy to the universal reality of which it is part is unveiled.

> Natural consciousness will show itself to be only the concept (*Begriff*) of knowledge, or in other words, not to be real knowledge. But since it directly takes itself to be real knowledge, this path has a negative significance for it, and what is in fact the realization of the concept counts for it rather as the loss of its own self (*Verlust seiner selbst*); for it does lose its truth on this path. The road can therefore be regarded as the pathway of doubt (*des Zweifels*), or more precisely as the way of despair (*der Verzweiflung*). (*PG* 56, *PS* 49)

This tragic phenomenon appears on a number of levels. In one sense, spirit has developed through innumerable individual dramas that are like the foam on the surface of its movement. Stoicism became dominant in the heyday of the Roman world; the unhappy consciousness (*das unglückliche Bewußtsein*) depends upon the institutionalisation of the duality endemic to the Christian world-view. The tragedy, then, is a real tragedy, insoluble in itself, since individual alienation is only the microcosmic reproduction of a more all-embracing alienation, the alienation of an incomplete form of spirit. The incompleteness of self-consciousness refers back to its base, the incompleteness of history.

The modern individual, who lives in a world in the process of completion, may of course fail to recognise this, and adopt Stoicism, scepticism or Christianity; but these forms are by now out of phase with what exists, since the work of universal history serves as their substructure and sooner or later makes it impossible to maintain them. These same forms of spirit, understood in their original form, appear as examples of the tragedy of the individual consciousness, unable to forge a world in accordance with its desires and unable to overcome the alienation of spirit. But spirit was not reduced to any one of its phases. Through the multiplicity of plans and individual tragedies, spirit cleared a path for itself; and the discourse of the philosopher now recognises and proclaims that the history of spirit is approaching the end and that individuals can now recognise in what is initially given to them externally the guiding law of their own evolution.

In this sense, the alienation of modern individuality is ready to be reabsorbed and to be reduced to the level of a moment that has been superseded. Furthermore, the cultural forms that emerge from the past and to which I can now refer are no longer rooted in the soil that produced and nurtured them: they are now items in the cultural memory. In an extremely important text, Hegel articulates the being of the modern world as a manifestation of spirit that is more advanced than other, earlier, ones; and specifies the relation between the modern individual and earlier cultural formations:

In the universal individual every moment displays itself as it gains concrete form and a shape of its own. The particular individual (*das besondre Individuum*) is incomplete spirit, a concrete form in whose existence (*Dasein*) one determination (*Bestimmtheit*) predominates, while the others are present only in blurred outlines (*in verwischten Zügen*). In the spirit that is on a higher level than another, the lower concrete existence has been reduced to an inconspicuous moment; what used to be important (*die Sache selbst*) is now but a trace; its form is shrouded and becomes a mere shading (*Schattirung*). The individual whose substance is the more advanced spirit (*der höher stehende Geist*) runs through this past just as one who takes up a higher science goes through the preparatory data (*Vorbereitungskenntnisse*) he has long since absorbed, in order to bring their content to mind; he recalls these memories to the inward eye, but has no lasting interest in them for their own sake. The individual must also pass through the formative stages (*Bildungsstuffen*) of universal spirit so far as their content is concerned, but as forms that spirit has already left behind, as stages on a way that has been prepared and levelled ... In this respect, formative education (*Bildung*), considered from the point of view of the individual, consists in his acquiring what thus lies at hand, devouring his organic nature, and taking possession of it for himself. But, considered from the side of

> universal spirit as substance, this is nothing but its own
> acquisition of self-consciousness, the bringing about of its
> own becoming (*Werden*) and reflection into itself. (*PG* 24–25,
> *PS* 16–17)

When we adopt the role of the Stoic or the sceptic or 'the
unhappy consciousness' of Christendom (see *PG* 116–131, *PS*
119–138), we are not, despite appearances, guided solely by the
content of those forms of spirit. If it were concretely possible
today to transform a particular stage in the history of consciousness into a self-subsistent moment, if it were even conceivable
that the imaginary level on which self-consciousness can live
could be permanently cut off from the becoming of spirit, then the
individual would only have to make a choice from among several
possible attitudes. But this is by definition not the case:
individuals are not as they see themselves, but are always more
than they themselves can articulate. The level upon which the old
worlds are evoked is an indication that spirit has definitively left
them behind, even though the individual subject may not yet
realise it.

> Consciousness is explicitly the concept (*Begriff*) of itself.
> This means that consciousness goes beyond the limits, and
> since these limits belong to itself, it goes beyond itself. For
> the particular individual, the beyond (*das Jenseits*) is also
> established for consciousness. (*PG* 57, *PS* 51)

This 'beyond' is, from the outset, the real driving power of the
dialectic of self-consciousness. Even when they recognise themselves in Greek or Roman or medieval Christian forms of spirit,
modern individuals remain part of the totality of contemporary
society. Even though they fail to recognise the essence of that
society, they are always driven beyond this misreading of their
own world, towards what is implied by the totality. The object
experienced by consciousness is not isolated, but presents itself in
relation to a norm that is both outside the object and within self-
consciousness. This is why Hegel says that both the object and its
yardstick lie within self-consciousness.

> Consciousness seems incapable, as it were, of getting
> behind the object to examine it not as it exists for
> consciousness, but as it is in itself; and so also cannot test its

own knowledge by that criterion. But the distinction between the in-itself and knowledge exists already in the very fact that consciousness knows an object at all ... Should comparison between these two moments show that they do not correspond to each other, it would seem that consciousness must modify its knowledge to make it conform to the object. But in the modification of the knowledge, the object itself modifies itself for it also, for the knowledge that was present was essentially a knowledge of the object. As the knowledge changes so also does the object, since the object essentially belonged to this knowledge. So for consciousness, that which it previously took to be the in-itself is not an in-itself, or it was only an in-itself for it (i.e. for consciousness). Since consciousness thus finds that its knowledge of an object does not correspond to its object, the object itself does not stand up to the test either; in other words, the yardstick for testing (*der Maßstab der Prüffung*) is modified when that for which it was to have been the yardstick fails to pass the test; and the testing is not just a testing of knowledge, but also a testing of the yardstick of knowledge. (*PG* 59–60, *PS* 54–55)

The duality between spirit and what is known by spirit (a duality essentially present in the phenomenological dialectic, as in all kinds of knowledge) *can* be overcome in so far as the object of knowledge is no more than the externalised form of spirit: this modification of knowledge as it adjusts to an outside reality also involves the transformation of that reality as it (the reality) progresses towards full knowledge of itself. Phenomenological critique consists in highlighting the gap between how a given situation is described and the actual being of spirit. This gap is opened up each time that a particular modern individual identifies himself or herself with one or other of the forms of spirit that has been superseded: the self-identification of a particular individual today as, for example, a Platonist or a Christian can only be understood on the 'ideological' level. Since these earlier forms of spirit do not fully account for the reality of the individual subject, the subject withdraws from that reality; and the principle that really governs it (i.e. the 'maturing' of spirit through history) is not yet apparent to the subject. The substance (i.e. the object of consciousness) is thus perceived as the polar opposite to subjectivity, and takes on the appearance of a fixed natural given, although it continues to live within the same reality as the active individual subject. The individual can appropriate the whole range of spiritual or cultural worlds that human activity has brought into existence, but this involves not just knowing but also retrieving. The human subject is not yet fully aware of all that humanity has accomplished, but just because it has been accomplished, subjects will never be able to reduce themselves simply to the sum of what they know. Gradually, with the development of its knowledge and learning, consciousness comes to a full understanding of the historical dimension that ultimately governs it.

Objective spirit

The second stage of the *Phenomenology* (Chapter VI, 'Spirit') presupposes the acceptance of such a historical dimension; and also that history can become an object of knowledge. Individual subjects have come to recognise themselves in the substance of the objective world. They are now able to read there the work of human negativity, and the stages of their past evolution are now going to be described on a higher level. In the earlier sections of the book, only that in the movement of spirit which was apparent to consciousness was described, but the transformation from one form of spirit into another, as described, was unreal: subjectivity was depicted as deceptively fluid, while the work of history is in fact slow and difficult. The upshot is that there can be no simple one-to-one correspondence between the two levels: the unhappy consciousness is not Christianity, but merely one of the forms of the internalisation of the Christian world. In the same way, the dialectic of the lord (*Herr*) and the bondsman (*Knecht*) (see *PG* 109–116, *PS* 111–19) does not capture the reality of the clashes between lords and bondsmen that have occurred throughout history. In this latter case, oppressors and oppressed, aristocratic consciousnesses and dependent consciousnesses demonstrate certain social and cultural characteristics, and certain common features gradually come to light through the consideration of conflicts between them: the initial confrontation between two self-consciousnesses, the demand for recognition that emerges from such a confrontation, the acceptance of the ultimate risk (of death) in the course of the struggle, and the differentiation into lord and bondsman. But these characteristics must not be thought of as necessary moments in the genesis of human society. The *Phenomenology* is not intended to be an anthropology, in that sense. Hegel's insistence that spirit is a primary entity with respect to all the individual specifications that might intervene rules out the possibility of any chronological or logical anteriority between the descriptions in the first section and those in the second.

Particular consciousness is now in a position to derive, from consideration of the historical material available, the significance of its own existence, only because spirit has attained a certain stage of development:

> Spirit is herewith self-supporting, absolute, real being. All previous forms of consciousness are abstractions (*Abstractionen*) of it. They are so because spirit analyzed itself, distinguished its own moments, and dwelt a while on each of them. This isolating of these moments presupposes spirit itself and subsists therein; in other words, the isolation of moments exists only in spirit, which is existence itself (*die Existenz*). Thus isolated, the moments have the appearance of really existing as such; but that they are only moments or vanishing quantities (*Größen*) is shown by their advance and retreat into their ground and essence; and this essence is just this movement and resolution (*Auflösung*) of these moments. (*PG* 239, *PS* 264)

The completion of the itinerary of consciousness (as depicted in the first five chapters) does not signal the birth of spirit, or real society, but the possibility of coming to know spirit. The attitudes that have made this possible are so many 'models' or 'paradigms' by means of which consciousness can understand in thought its relation to the outside world. Each of these attitudes in turn demonstrates that the divergence between the inside world (of consciousness) and the outside world has not been fully bridged. But this duality is eventually overcome, and the unity of being-in-itself and being-for-itself is revealed.

The phenomenological dialectic implies an overlap of the different levels. It begins with the cleavage between subject and object, between the individual and the outside world, between consciousness and the object of consciousness, between thought and what is thought. This cleavage should first of all be understood as a historical phenomenon. Although it has existed, to all intents and purposes, since the beginning of time, modern culture (to wit, bourgeois society) has brought this opposition to a peak. But if our society has exacerbated the rupture, the form it has taken depends on the very nature of what is thus divided into its subjective side and its objective side, namely spirit.

The dialectic proceeds, therefore, on several levels. Before their ultimate identity is revealed, the relation between subjectivity and its object can be on three levels: (i) where the object is primary with respect to the subject; (ii) where the simple otherness of subject and object is transformed into a simple correlate of self-consciousness, thus bringing about, at this level, the identity of knowledge and the object of knowledge; (iii) finally, the simultaneous maintenance of the two realities and their difference (i.e. the identity of identity and difference). To this threefold relation corresponds the division in the *Phenomenology* into consciousness, self-consciousness and reason (*Vernunft*). This covers the entire range of logical possibilities.

The content of the external object has two essential characteristics: it is multiple and heterogeneous and it presents itself both explicitly and implicitly. The multiplicity of objective reality corresponds to the formalism exercised by the subject who analyses objective reality down into its component parts: in this way, everything (a stone, a table, a living thing, a person, a work of art) is treated as an object that is felt, perceived, thought. But the multiplicity corresponds also to the plurality of the orders of reality that enable different levels to be distinguished: there is a succession of metaphysical levels rising from inanimate nature to the animate world and to culture. The fusion of these levels defines the very life of spirit. As the external objective world presents itself to consciousness, therefore, a range of relations becomes possible. But at the same time, each time subjectivity strives to think the object that is in the outside world, it is compelled to go back to the object; because, without even fully articulating it, subjectivity derives from the substantial universe within which it lives the concepts, the experiences, the theories that enable it to consider in thought what is initially foreign to it. This process brings to light the equivalence of the two realms (subject and object) hitherto considered antithetical.

In the *Phenomenology*, the objects of experience follow one another according to a particular sequence, so that the other person and cultural relations do not appear until Chapter IV. But while the type of relation to the objective world depicted in each successive form of spirit can be carried along and can also apply in any succeeding form, the inverse is not the case. This is why Hegel's work depicts phenomenological progress.

This eventual identity of the objective world and the means of understanding it in thought accounts for the final synthesis of subject and object. This synthesis is only possible when everything that formerly presented itself as ungraspable inertia is newly animated by a primordial dynamism that defines it as its own self-becoming. The history of spirit itself can now be retraced; and thus Chapter VI leads us from the Athenian city-state to the French Revolution, the Terror, and the Napoleonic state, through successive manifestations of spirit in history, or objective spirit.

This is not, of course, a complete history of humanity; nor even a full history of these epochs. Hegel singles out for attention only those particular aspects that are directly relevant to the matter under consideration. In the immense variety of forms deposited and sedimented by time, self-consciousness has come to recognise the work of spirit's self-actualisation, as the latter developed the full range of its potentialities. In going back again over the stages of this development, self-consciousness is reconstituting its own reality. But why could spirit not hitherto be known, since it has always existed? Because, writes Hegel, the acorn is not the oak; or in his own terminology, the concept is not the whole:

> Its first appearance is only its immediacy (*Unmittelbarkeit*) or its concept (*Begriff*). Just as a building is not finished when its foundation has been laid, the achieved concept of the whole is not the whole (*das Ganze*) itself. When we wish to see an oak with its powerful trunk and its spreading branches and foliage, we are not content to be shown in its place an acorn. Thus science (*Wissenschaft*), the crown of a world of spirit, is not complete in its beginnings. (*PG* 15, *PS* 7)

The potentialities of spirit have only been actualised in a haphazard way; this resulted in profound dissymmetries that have distorted the true nature of reality:

> But the actuality (*Wirklichkeit*) of this simple whole [that is, spirit] consists of those various forms that have become its moments, and that will now develop and give themselves

shape anew, but in their new element, in their newly acquired meaning. (*PG* 15, *PS* 7)

The 'new element' to which Hegel refers is his own philosophical system; 'their newly acquired meaning' is their place in that system. Spirit can now be known, after many centuries when it could not be known, because a universal state (or a fully rational state) is currently in course of actualisation: that is, a state the institutions of which demonstrate the very being of spirit and in which spirit becomes self-conscious. Not only can the modern state now be known, in a way in which, for example, feudal society could not be known by its members; but we now have the benefit of a relatively full understanding of earlier societies or cultural formations, because they can now be seen in the context of the development of spirit overall.

Hegel then proceeds to examine each of the historical periods mentioned, as an articulation of a particular kind of dominant dissonance or contradiction. Thus, for example, the Greek *polis* is presented as the first attempt at the universalisation of a human community which, striving to wrench itself from the immediacy of natural life, tried to make its social rules conform to laws of reason. This attempt did not succeed because the new concept of political organisation could not become a reality. This was so because the nascent state conflicted with the institution of the family (or the clan) out of which the new state had painfully emerged. This institution of the family is the concrete manifestation of the principle of subjectivity, which remains outside the realm of political activity and constitutes its permanent limit. Hegel illustrates this conflict with a thinly veiled analysis of the *Antigone* of Sophocles, which underlies most of Chapter VIA on 'True spirit, the ethical order (*die Sittlichkeit*)'. He interprets the emergence of the Greek city-state as the passage from the primacy of the divine law to the primacy of human law, from customary law to written law, from actions based upon ties of kinship to those derived from the abstract criteria of political organisation. (This is also the principal theme of the *Orestes* of Aeschylus, with which Hegel was familiar.) In the *Antigone*, the full might of state authority is ultimately powerless against a young girl's refusal to accept the dictates of *realpolitik* as the supreme values.

The play demonstrates that the old archaic order still retains its power and that no recourse to 'reasons of state' (however justified) can overcome it. The conflict between Creon (who represents the state) and Antigone (who represents the family, not the individual as in the modern play by Anouilh) revolves around the depth of meaning bestowed upon death. In one sense, the death of any citizen is a contingent event that could happen to anyone, especially anyone involved in political or social struggles; it remains external to that struggle and does not modify its content significantly. But in another sense, as a moment in the life of a family, such a death is a fundamentally significant and necessary milestone, which is accepted and which becomes a link in a non-temporal chain against which the demands of history and politics fall on deaf ears. Thus people can be model citizens, can work for the good of the city, can risk their lives in defending the state; but deep down (especially when death intervenes), they do not belong to this public, civic world at all. The appearances, the accidental aspects of their existence may be devoted to public life; but when death strikes, their spiritual home is with their family, who will receive their body and will strip their death of all its inessentials — death in some cause or another, in one manner or another, against this or that enemy — and return them directly into that ontological continuity maintained by the religion of their ancestors. It matters little to Antigone that Eteocles was struck down while defending the city and that Polynices, his brother, was a traitor to the city. As far as she is concerned, they are both her brothers, and they are both entitled to a proper funeral, in accordance with tradition.

Creon, of course, sees Antigone first and foremost as a threat to public order. But Hegel does not come down on one side or the other. When a conflict such as this appears in the course of the development of spirit, it cannot be resolved simply by accepting one side of the conflict and rejecting the other. The potentially disastrous conflict between the two principles will only be overcome (*aufgehoben*) following great upheavals in the world of society and culture. In a fundamentally important way, however, the conflict is never negated, but the two poles are retained, in suspension, in higher (and historically later) forms of society.[10]

Absolute spirit

And so, spirit proceeds, from one formation to another, towards full consciousness of its own being. Absolute knowledge is knowledge of all those forms assumed by spirit in the course of its development up until now. This ultimate knowledge is attained in the third and final section of the *Phenomenology* (Chapters VII and VIII), devoted to the various forms of discourse people have adopted to characterise the human condition: art, religion, and philosophy.[11] Hegel considers the similarities and the differences among these forms of discourse, each with its own means of expression; but he emphasises that, beneath the diversity of languages, spirit is present in its entirety in each; and this can now be known. But for this to come about, everything that was implicit in spirit when it first emerged had to be actualised in history; and spirit has gathered into itself all that it has been, with none of its earlier forms left external to it.

Thus the dialectic, in which the individual has been caught up as both active subject and quarry, had to run through the long line of cultural formations in history. The Hegelian philosophical structure implies that whatever emerges henceforth will only be comprehensible by using the categories of which the structure is composed. Not that individual subjects are no longer free to think: they may wish to dwell in specific moments of the phenomenological genesis of spirit; they may wish to reformulate their relation to substance in a new language. However, any new formations will have the same logical texture as the formations already recounted. Philosophy is essentially historical, because what being is is inseparable from how being has expressed itself. In the preface to his *Science of logic*, Hegel expresses the relation of his phenomenology of spirit to his mature philosophical system thus:

This spiritual movement . . . is the absolute method of knowing, as well as the immanent soul of the content itself. I contend that only this self-construing method will enable philosophy to be an objective, demonstrated science. It is in this way that I have tried to depict consciousness in the *Phenomenology of Spirit*. Consciousness is spirit as concrete knowledge, involved in external appearance (*in der Äußerlichkeit befangenes*); but the progress (*die Fortbewegung*) of this object, like the development (*die Entwicklung*) of all natural and spiritual life, rests solely on the nature of the pure essentialities (*Wesenheiten*) that constitute the content of logic. Consciousness, as spirit in its appearance (*der erscheinende Geist*) [i.e. as phenomena], which in its progress frees itself from its immediacy (*Unmittelbarkeit*) and its external concrete form (*Konkretion*), attains to the pure knowledge which takes as its object those same pure essentialities as they are in and for themselves. They are pure thoughts, spirit thinking its own essence (*der sein Wesen denkende Geist*). Their self movement is their spiritual life and is that through which scientific philosophy (*die Wissenschaft*) constitutes itself and of which it is the exposition.[12]

However, the full content of spirit can only be grasped in thought and become the object of knowledge when all the possibilities have become actualised realities. And this poses the problem of the relation between scientific philosophy (*Wissenschaft*) and history (or between necessity and contingency), which Hegel confronts in the concluding pages of the *Phenomenology*. Absolute knowledge has been made possible by the prodigious work of universal history, to which it is inseparably linked. But despite these profound links, a gap still persists between the two levels. Hegel was clearly aware of this gap, and this accounts for the tragic tone of the last few pages of the *Phenomenology*, and the sudden appearance of the notion of sacrifice:

This sacrifice (*Aufopferung*) is the externalization (*Entäusserung*) in which spirit displays its process of becoming spirit in the form of free contingent happening, intuiting its pure self as time outside of it, and equally its being as space. (*PG* 433, *PS* 492)

For I shall never be able to actualise in my own existence the totality of the moments of spirit's becoming. I am a member of a specific society, I participate in a specific culture. My contingent incarnation is the very condition of philosophical knowledge: this is why Hegel writes that although history is the externalisation of being in time, it is also the overcoming of that externalisation. The return to the immediacy of existence (*Dasein*) is a necessary step in the growth of philosophical knowledge; but it is a step that can never be successfully undertaken, since this world towards which the philosopher returns is necessarily limited, particular and contingent. The philosopher recognises in each of the many pre-Hegelian forms of discourse an essential truth, because genuine philosophical reflection is at a level on which the totality of human discourses can be articulated. But between what the philosopher knows and what the philosopher is there intervenes a definitive and irreducible gap. Absolute knowledge involves not presence, but recollection of what has been internalised. (The word Hegel uses, *Erinnerung*, which commonly means memory or recollection, also has the etymological connotation of 'internalisation'.) Spirit comes to know itself as spirit by remembering itself; but this recollection of the past is knowledge and not life. Even though I may recall the ancient Greek or Roman citizen, I realise that I am neither one nor the other: I can never recapture, for example, that immersion in the world of nature that was typical of the early Greeks. Spirit knows itself completely, but it can only *exist* in one particular guise; and it recognises the gap between the necessity of knowledge and the contingency of history. Hegel concludes the *Phenomenology* thus:

> The goal, absolute knowledge, or spirit that knows itself as spirit, has for its path the recollection (*Erinnerung*) of the spirits as they are in themselves and as they accomplish the organization of their realm. Their preservation, from the point of view of their free existence (*Dasein*) appearing in the form of contingency (*Zufälligkeit*), is history, but from the point of view of their philosophically comprehended organization (*ihrer begriffnen Organisation*), it is the science of the knowledge of appearances (*die Wissenschaft des erscheinenden Wissens*) [phenomenology]. The two together, comprehended history, form the recollection (*Erinnerung*) and the Golgotha (*Schädelstätte*) of absolute spirit, the actuality, truth and certainty of its throne, without which it would be lifeless and solitary. Only —
> from the chalice of this realm of spirits
> foams forth to him his infinitude
>
> (*PG* 433–4, *PS* 493)

II

I now propose to sketch, in the most schematic fashion, just some of the most important implications for social analysis of Hegel's historical phenomenology. These can be considered under two headings: what to look for; and how to proceed.

The most striking characteristic of Hegel's philosophy, a simple affirmation that underpins his whole system, is his insistence that 'The true is the whole (*Das Wahre ist das Ganze*)' (*PG* 19, *PS* 11). This entails not only that all the different aspects of contemporary culture and society (for example, art, economic life, political institutions, religion, political mythology, philosophy) are essentially interrelated, but also that there is continuing interplay among the different levels of self-consciousness that have been sedimented as human experience has become more differentiated through history.

My introductory quotation expresses perfectly Hegel's conception of the cumulative manner in which spirit has matured through history: 'Those moments that spirit appears to have outgrown still belong to it in the depths of its present.' One of the best illustrations of this point is his account of the conflict between Antigone and Creon. This moment in the history of European self-consciousness illustrates the conflict between the old customary practices that grew out of the communal soil and the edicts devised by the abstract reason of the ruler. As history moved on and the latter gained the upper hand, the former were not extirpated, but *aufgehoben*, that is, superseded but conserved in a subordinate, or even repressed, role: 'In the spirit that is on a higher level than another [in this case, more sophisticated political societies, and eventually our own bourgeois society], the lower concrete existence [that is, customary practice] has been reduced to an inconspicuous moment; what used to be important is now but a trace' (*PG* 24, *PS* 16).

Antigone represents the most basic form of 'natural *Sittlichkeit*', that is, the set of rules, customs (*Sitten*) and practices that are grounded in the traditions of a community. Hegel illustrates the status of these primitive rules by quoting from the play of Sophocles:

> The distinctions in essence itself [namely, the rules and practices] . . . *are*, and nothing more . . . Thus, the *Antigone* of Sophocles acknowledges them as the unwritten and infallible (*untrügliches*) law of the gods:
>
> 'They are not of today or yesterday, but everlasting,
> And no one knows from whence they came.'
> (*PG* 235–6, *PS* 261)[13]

For Hegel, natural *Sittlichkeit* emerges from a community as unreflective spirit. It is not itself rationally grounded, but it is this

Sittlichkeit that reason then proceeds to work on and to differentiate into higher forms of *Sittlichkeit*: for example, civil society and the fully actualised modern state.[14] But the structures and demands of a society based upon ties of kinship persist within the more advanced, more centralised state run by the pragmatic Creon. Hegel does not portray this as the heroic martyrdom of good and right by the tyranny of evil and wrong. He quite correctly sees the tragedy as a struggle between two passionately held principles, each of them good and right in its own way; and he does not betray his own sympathies. The important element, for our present discussion, is Antigone's determination to honour her brother with appropriate burial rites (thereby protecting his soul), despite the acknowledged fact that he was a traitor who tried to overthrow the government, and despite the fact that she is betrothed to Creon's son. The earlier form of self-consciousness has not been left behind in the development of spirit into a 'higher' form of social organisation.

Even this most basic 'natural *Sittlichkeit*' is present today at the heart of what is still, in effect, bourgeois society. The general principle that emerges from Hegel's description is that human beings — be they individuals, groups, or whole communities — operate on different levels at any one time. Each one of us has several different levels of response to any situation; and different levels advance and recede depending on the circumstances. In our sophisticated, technologically advanced society, dominated by the analytical and instrumental rationality of the Enlightenment[15] (what Hegel calls *Verstand*, or understanding), the pre-rational or sub-rational level often comes to the fore. Hegel's conception of reason as *Vernunft* — which encompasses these different levels of human response to situations — points to a kind of social depth psychology. The rationalism of analysis is impotent (and certainly unimpressive in its results) when faced by the bomb placed by terrorists in a crowded restaurant, the emotional power of the demonstrations at the Greenham Common cruise missile base, the jingoism that was rampant in Britain at the time of the Falklands/Malvinas adventure, or the nexus of motivations of those prepared to starve themselves to death for a cause, and the extraordinary depth and breadth of the public response.

Such situations typically appear utterly irrational to those outside the community within which they occur. To grasp their meaning, we have to look not just at the persistence of powerful family and kinship ties and the atavistic importance bestowed upon death rites, but at other non-rational factors such as shame, pride, the satisfaction of honour, the need for recognition, the sense of belonging to a place:[16] in short, everything that comes into the category of the symbolic and the mythic. Hegel discusses the significance of symbols in the section of his chapter on objective spirit entitled 'the struggle of Enlightenment with superstition'. In many ways (especially in the conduct of the social sciences) we are still under the spell of the Enlightenment. But Enlightenment thinking cannot possibly grasp the significance of, for example, seemingly irrational behaviour motivated by racial prejudice or religious conviction, or even a slap that symbolises an insult.[17]

At one time, our behaviour and our discourse were almost entirely symbolic; in some societies they still are. And although the development of a scientific method based on mathematics signalled a steady erosion of the symbolic, parallel to the sublimation of *Sittlichkeit* in general, the symbolic often rises to the surface: not just in political contexts, such as the response to hunger-striking prisoners, but in the everyday decision to buy a particular model of car or a jacuzzi (as a status symbol). Even the very example Hegel gives — the primeval compulsion to give the dead (no matter whom) a proper burial in holy ground — is bursting with political significance in many parts of the world today.

It is important to note that to emphasise the significance of the symbolic, the mythic, the bonds of kinship, and so on, is not to glorify them. Myths and symbols are often enriching, but just as often destructive (and one person's enrichment is often another person's destruction); families (especially in the husband-wife relation that Hegel does appear to glorify) are often oppressive and cruel to each other. But they are there, they are integral components of *Dasein*, and they are deeply significant. Many (especially Marxists) have tried to change the world. Perhaps they have failed because they have not really understood it. To be effective, political action must be informed by a deep appreciation of the many factors that motivate people to do the baffling things they do; and Hegel's model, of forms of self-consciousness that have been surpassed but not obliterated, provides clues as to some of the things we should be looking for when analysing a complex social situation.

Once a wide range of potentially significant factors has been identified, how are we to go about investigating social phenomena? Perhaps Hegel's most important lesson in this respect is that social research must never be reductionist: since social situations are essentially multi-dimensional, it is unlikely that human behaviour could ever be explained by reference to a single causal factor. This is the chief inadequacy of orthodox Marxism: Marx was correct to highlight the importance of economic factors, but there is no convincing reason to claim that 'the economic' or 'the material' is universally basic. Hegel included these factors in a nexus of explanatory factors (both ideal and material), all manifestations of the *Zeitgeist* (the spirit of the age). Hegel and Marx should be seen as complementary, not as rivals. What *should* be analysed is the dialectical interaction between one's self-conceptualisation and one's economic and social relations.

This dialectical analysis of social and political life can never be carried out by the quantitative method of positivist analysis that came to prominence in the seventeenth century and continues to dominate the social sciences.[18] Hegel was already underlining the inadequacies of this method in 1807:

> The scientific regime bequeathed by mathematics — with its explanations (*Erklärungen*), divisions, axioms, sets of theorems, its proofs, principles, deductions, and conclusions from them — is already seen by current opinion to be rather old-fashioned . . . Truth is its own self-movement, whereas the method described above is the mode of cognition that remains external to its material. (*PG* 35, *PS* 28)

At most, 'the tabulating understanding (*der tabellarische Verstand*)' can offer a table of contents, but no content: 'Scientific cognition, on the contrary, demands surrender to the life of the object, or, what amounts to the same thing, confronting and expressing its inner necessity' (*PG* 39, *PS* 32). The whole *Phenomenology* is the story of the dichotomy between the knowing subject and the object of knowledge. The barriers between subject and object are eventually broken down as the subject is seen to be part of the objective world and the objective world becomes known as living subject. Dialectical analysis, therefore, must enter into the life of the situation under investigation, must become immersed in it. Furthermore, Hegel's whole account of the struggle of self-consciousness for recognition rejects the notion that the individual is the basic ontological entity: individuals, therefore, cannot be the unit of social investigation, but can be understood only in the context of their social situation, which they themselves have helped to create.[19] Human interaction cannot be studied as we would observe water freezing in a laboratory bottle: in other words, there can be no physics of social life.

Finally, I should like to dispose of the old canard that Hegel's theory of absolute knowledge meant that Hegel thought he knew everything. Hegel, of course, believed no such thing. It must be remembered that Hegel's main quarry in the *Phenomenology* was Kant, who had insisted that genuine knowledge of the 'things-in-themselves' (the noumena) is unattainable. Hegel claimed to show, in his *Phenomenology*, that the 'things-in-themselves' could indeed be known; in other words, that 'absolute knowledge' (and not just phenomenal knowledge, or partial knowledge) can be attained. So Hegel's notion of the 'absolute knowledge' in which the *Phenomenology of spirit* culminates is not an embarrassing flourish which we can discreetly jettison. As a recent commentator has put it, 'the "absolute" is not an optional extra'.[20]

Absolute knowledge is the goal towards which the whole *Phenomenology* is moving: 'Of the absolute [*von dem Absoluten*, that is, an adjective used as a noun] it must be said that it is essentially a result, that only at the end is it what it truly is; and that precisely in this consists its nature, to be the actual (*Wirkliches*), the subject, the spontaneous becoming of itself' (*PG* 19, *PS* 11). So the dialectic of self-conscious spirit of the earlier analysis is unconvincing when cut off from its *telos*; and the last chapter read on its own makes little sense without the preceding book, which is its content. But to say that human life can be known is not to say that it is transparent. On the contrary, it is certainly opaque and ambiguous. In the last chapter of his book, Hegel himself is certainly aware of the tragic gap between the ambition of absolute knowledge and its realisation. And in our day, just as we think our increasing knowledge will afford us complete dominance over nature, non-human nature hits back at us with a powerful vengeance, and threatens a complete withdrawal of co-operation with us. We are, after all, only human. Although the 'things-in-themselves' are, in principle, knowable, the goal of absolute knowledge is probably asymptotic, a goal towards which we may (and should) strive, but which none of us is likely to reach.

Hegel's *Phenomenology* is the story of the peregrination of the human spirit through history *and* a description of the multilayered human self-consciousness that has resulted. One of its most important lessons is that *everything* is important in trying to understand the human condition, and that we do not often behave in accordance with the dictates of Enlightenment rationality. The holistic framework that Hegel bequeathed has been modified and strengthened by the insights of thinkers as diverse as Marx, Freud, Heidegger, Sartre, Lévi-Strauss, Gadamer, Habermas and Ricoeur. Quite a shopping-list; but even those that appear to be quite opposed to Hegel have important contributions to make to the overall enterprise: a historical structuralism, for example, is not necessarily contradictory. In the meantime, there's nothing wrong with being unashamedly eclectic. The task of synthesising the thought of these writers (and others) in a new neo-Hegelian social theory is a job for another day.

Notes

An earlier version of this article was read to the Political Thought Conference at New College, Oxford in January 1983. I am grateful to the participants for some incisive comments. My thanks also go to Terry Sullivan, and to John Gruchala. I owe a special debt to my teacher Frithjof Bergmann, whose infectious enthusiasm first excited my fascination with Hegel's *Phenomenology*.

1. *Lectures on the philosophy of world history, Introduction: Reason in history*, trans. H.B. Nisbet (Cambridge, 1975), pp. 150–1.
   Other recent analyses of the *Phenomenology* include C. Taylor, *Hegel* (Cambridge, 1975), pp. 127–221; R. Norman, *Hegel's phenomenology* (Brighton, 1976); M. Westphal, *History and truth in Hegel's 'Phenomenology'* (Atlantic Heights, N.J. and Brighton, 1978); R.C. Solomon, *In the spirit of Hegel* (New York and Oxford, 1983). Recent German scholarship is represented by O. Pöggeler, 'Zur Deutung der *Phänomenologie des Geistes*', and other articles in *Hegels Idee einer Phänomenologie des Geistes* (Freiburg, 1973); W. Marx, *Hegel's Phenomenology of Spirit: A commentary on the Preface and Introduction* (New York, 1975); H.-G. Gadamer, *Hegel's dialectic* (New Haven and London, 1976), pp. 35–74. The classic French analyses are by J. Hyppolite, *Genèse et structure de la Phénoménologie de l'Esprit de Hegel* (Paris, 1946); and A. Kojève, *Introduction to the reading of Hegel* (New York, 1969, an abridged trans. of the 1947 French edition). One of the most influential of all, of course, has been Karl Marx's critical analysis of Hegel's dialectic, especially of the final chapter of the *Phenomenology* (Paris manuscript, 1844), in *Early Writings*, ed. and trans. T. Bottomore (London, 1963), pp. 195–219.
2. W. Marx, *Hegel's Phenomenology of Spirit*, pp. xii–xiv.

3. W. Kaufmann documents Hegel's frenetic scramble to complete the book in 1806, against a background of social and personal chaos, in his *Hegel* (Garden City, N.Y. and London, 1965), pp. 110–14, 315–19.

4. *Hegel's social and political thought* (Dublin and New York, 1979), pp. 1–55, esp. 49.

5. For quotations from the *Phenomenology*, I have used the historical-critical edition by W. Bonsiepen and R. Heede, *Gesammelte Werke*, Band 9 (Hamburg, 1980); the preferred English version is by A.V. Miller, *Phenomenology of spirit* (Oxford, 1977). These are cited in the text as *PG* and *PS* respectively, with page references. Although, for the most part, my translations are based on Miller's version, I have altered it freely, to give a more literal rendering of the original German; I have also found helpful the translation of the Preface by W. Kaufmann, in his *Hegel*, pp. 363–459.

6. Hegel usually refers to his own philosophical system as science (*Wissenschaft*), which has a much wider reference than the English word 'science'.

7. Hegel seems to have used the words *Gestalt, Gestaltung* and *Form* quite interchangeably, and I have rendered them equally interchangeably as 'form', 'formation' or 'shape'.

8. *Bildung* is almost impossible to translate. It does mean 'education', but not just what goes on in schools and colleges. I have tried to suggest its wider connotation of growing maturity with expressions such as 'cultural formation'. Similarly, *ungebildet* means 'uneducated', but also 'uncivilised' or (in this case) 'naïve'. *Selbstbewußtsein* means 'self-consciousness' as knowledge of self, with none of the connotation of embarrassment that the English word carries. Incidentally, Charles Taylor seriously distorts Hegel's position by systematically personalising spirit (*Geist*) as 'he', and by identifying *Geist* with God. Hegel's *Geist* is certainly greater than humankind, since it encompasses nature as well: to this extent, Taylor is correct to refer to *Geist* as 'cosmic spirit'. But humankind ('the universal individual') is *self-conscious* spirit, since nature cannot be self-conscious, and Hegel's *Geist* has little affinity with the transcendent God of Christianity.

9. Hegel does not really offer an epistemology, or theory of knowledge, in the sense familiar in philosophy since Descartes and Locke. In fact, his introduction and first three chapters — on sense-certainty (*die sinnliche Gewißheit*), perception (*die Wahrnehmung*), and force and understanding (*Kraft und Verstand*), respectively — constitute a devastating critique of the whole epistemological project since Descartes. Richard Norman is very good on this, especially his chapter on 'The Dilemma of Epistemology', in *Hegel's phenomenology*, pp. 9–27. He also quotes, in this connection, Hegel's favourite philosophical joke, from the *Lesser logic* (§ 10): 'To seek to know before we know is as absurd as the wise resolution of Scholasticus, not to venture into the water until he had learned to swim.'

10. Indeed, Hegel reworks this section of the *Phenomenology* in his *Philosophy of right* (1820), where the conflict represented by Antigone and Creon reappears as an analysis of the place and significance of kinship in the modern rational state. Merold Westphal analyses this section of the

Philosophy of right (§ 158–61) in 'Hegel's radical idealism: family and state as ethical communities', in Z.A. Pelczynski (ed.), *The state and civil society* (Cambridge, 1984), pp. 77–92.

11. The charge has often been brought — and not just by his detractors — that Hegel contended that the history of philosophy (if not the world) was brought to a close by him. Hegel's pretensions to completeness notwithstanding, it is important to repeat his remarks towards the end of his lectures on the history of philosophy: 'This is the standpoint of the present time (*der jetzigen Zeit*), and the series of spiritual formations is for the present (*für jetzt*) concluded with this. At this point I bring this history of philosophy (*diese Geschichte*) to a close' (Haldane and Simson trans., vol. III, p. 552). This clearly reveals Hegel's open mind with respect to the forms of spirit that might appear after him.

12. *Wissenschaft der Logik*, ed. G. Lasson (Leipzig, 1932) vol. I, p. 7; *Science of logic*, trans. A.V. Miller (London and New York, 1969), p. 28.

13. Hegel goes on to confuse the demands of the 'infallible law of the gods' with sisterly affection. We can safely draw an embarrassed veil over his gratuitous and often offensive discussion of the peculiar ontological status of sisters, and womankind in general.

14. Cf. Aristotle, *Nic. Ethics* II, i: 'Moral virtue comes about as a result of habit (*ethos*).'

An outstanding contemporary reappraisal of this Aristotelian concept of moral practices is Alasdair MacIntyre's *After virtue*, 2nd edn (London and Notre Dame, 1984): 'By a "practice" I am going to mean any coherent and complex form of socially established cooperative activity through which goods internal to that form of activity are realised in the course of trying to achieve those standards of excellence which are appropriate to, and partially definitive of, that form of activity' (p. 187). Would it be impertinent to suggest that the profound pessimism that emanates from this book could well be mitigated by grounding virtue, in the contemporary world, within the Hegelian framework here proposed?

15. According to Enlightenment rationality, says Hegel, 'everything is useful' (*PG* 304, *PS* 342); or, as Marx put it, everything (including another person) is a commodity.

16. For an excellent discussion of 'honour offended' and the resulting 'duel to the death' between lord and bondsman, see H.-G. Gadamer, *Hegel's dialectic*, pp. 64–71.

17. See *PG* 309, *PS* 347–8, for Hegel's discussion of the symbolism of fasting.

18. This tendency approaches its apotheosis (and tips over into the absurd) with the development of computerised data banks and statistical analysis. See, for example, the voluminous work of J.D. Singer, such as his 'Variables, indicators, and data in macro-political research', in K. Deutsch (ed.), *Methods of political behavior research* (New York, 1980), which concludes with the clarion-call to colleagues to take on 'the important and challenging work in indicator construction and data generation [sic]' that will hasten the day when 'we will begin to turn out what the discipline and the world need most: the complete social scientist'.

19. For an interesting account of the Hegelian contribution to what he

calls 'the interpretive approach to social analysis', see P.J. Steinberger, 'Hegel as a Social Scientist', in *Amer. Pol. Sci. Rev. 71* (1977), pp. 95–110.

20. Gillian Rose, in *Hegel contra sociology* (London, 1981), p. 42. The author presents her impressive book as an 'attempt to retrieve Hegelian speculative experience for social theory' (p. 1).

2
Hegel and Feminism

Susan M. Easton

Introduction

A timely aspect of the revival of Hegel's work has been the examination of his ideas by feminists identifying the masculinist assumptions underpinning the history of political thought. However, the initial reaction of feminism to Hegel's writings has been to align him with other major figures in Western political thought, including Plato, Aristotle, Hume, Rousseau and Mill in a biological, reductionist tradition. This feminist response to Hegel will be critically examined. We shall begin by outlining feminist objections to Hegel's analysis of women and the family, which centre on the public-private distinction, and then move on to an appraisal of evidence of anti-reductionism in his writings. It will be argued that even with the *Philosophy of right* — the object of sustained feminist critiques[1] — Hegel challenges rather than endorses reductionism. Finally the possibility of an Hegelian understanding of women's potential freedom will be explored.

Political philosophy, according to Moller Okin in *Women in Western political thought*, consists of 'writings by men, for men, and about men'.[2] Although the frequent references to the generic term 'mankind' by political philosophers might suggest a concern with 'the human race as a whole', she argues that 'we do not need to look far into their writings to realise that such an assumption is unfounded.[3] Instead a sharp distinction is drawn between men and women with women's destiny being perceived as biologically determined which leads to 'the prescription of a code of morality and conception of rights for women distinctly different from those that have been prescribed for men.'[4] This distinction, she claims, underpins the history of political thought: 'Philosophers who, in laying the foundations for their political theories, have asked "What are men like?" "What is man's potential?" have frequently, in turning to the female sex, asked "What are women for?".'[5] In answering this question, they have seen biological differences between men and women as 'entailing all the other, conventional and institutional differences in sex role which the family, especially in its most patriarchal forms, has required'.[6]

Hegel's commitment to such a 'functionalist' or reductionist view of the family as a necessary and natural institution, argues Moller Okin, is expressed in his treatment of the male head of the family as its only political representative and the fact that he 'disposed of the female half of the human race.'[7] Women are denied any distinct identity in his political thought and are cut off from public life. Moreover, his view of marriage as resulting from 'the free surrender by both sexes of their personality' is over-optimistic, she notes, since the surrender of the man's personality is 'more symbolic than real.'[8] The significance and pervasiveness of the reductionist view should not be underestimated, she concludes, since 'the continuing oppression of women is ideologically supported by the survival of functionalist modes of thought'.[9]

A similar interpretation of Hegel is offered by Elshtain in *Public man, private woman*, where she points out that 'like the inhabitants of Orwell's *Animal farm*, . . . the inhabitants of Hegel's conceptual universe are ethically significant but some are more significant than others'.[10] Excluded from the public sphere, women are 'defined by the family: the family is a woman's beginning and her end'. For the man, 'the family is that ethical relationship which serves as the basis of all others including citizenship'[11] and he alone can become a real citizen. For Hegel, women are confined to the level of the household while the public world remains the 'locus of human action':

> Although there is no public-private split in Hegel's account in the sense of a radical separation of one sphere from the other, the public and the private *are* differentiated and ordered as higher and lower . . . The reciprocal, if asymmetrical, relationship between spheres requires connecting links or mediations. These are provided by males in their roles as brothers, husbands, fathers and property-owners.[12]

Hegel's political theory is rooted in teleological assumptions regarding male and female nature, which he distinguishes in terms of 'the analogue of form and matter whereby the male provides the human form during mating and the female serves as a vessel within which the male-created *homunculus* incubates'.[13] She concedes that 'within the constraints of his presumptions on male and female natures, Hegel positions women as near to the universal as his perspective allows',[14] but inevitably, given this starting-point, he denies women any *intrinsic* value or significance within the family, in contrast to the value placed on the lives of men as citizens. Without their slender connection to the universal through males, they would possess no ethical significance. Elshtain is critical of Hegel not simply for excluding women from the universal but also because he is indifferent to 'the realities of economic power and the manner in which a predatory civil society vitiates the possibilities for a just public order'.[15]

Elshtain's dissatisfaction with Hegel's treatment of women extends to the work of Simone de Beauvoir who employs Hegelian concepts in analysing women's oppression. Pointing to similarities between the work of de Beauvoir and Shulamith Firestone, Elshtain notes that women, for de Beauvoir, can achieve transcendence only by rejecting their female identities. Similarly, Genevieve Lloyd in her critique of de Beauvoir argues that we should 'expect some oddities in any attempt to apply the relations of recognition between Hegelian selves and others to understanding the condition of women. And some of the puzzling features of de Beauvoir's analysis . . . do seem to derive from the underlying maleness of the original Hegelian confrontation of consciousnesses.'[16]

Hegel's remarks in the *Philosophy of right* on the fundamental differences between men and women have attracted criticism because he appears to contrast men and women in terms of a distinction between rationality and feeling, which he uses to exclude women from the public domain. Hegel's work has therefore been seen by a number of commentators tracing the origins of patriarchal attitudes and practices, as committed to the biological reductionism characteristic of Western political thought in so far as he confines women to the private sphere on the basis of assumed natural characteristics.[17] Certainly, Hegel's analysis of the differences between men and women in the *Philosophy of right* does provide grounds for this interpretation. Men, he argues, are 'powerful and active', characterised by the 'self-consciousness of conceptual thought' while women are 'passive and subjective', their knowledge and volition taking the form of 'concrete individuality and feeling'.[18] Contrasting the rationality of men with the feelings and opinions of women, Hegel likens women to plants:

> The difference between men and women is like that between animals and plants. Men correspond to animals, while women correspond to plants because their development is more placid and the principle that underlies it is the rather vague unity of feeling. When women hold the helm of government, the state is at once in jeopardy, because women regulate their actions not by the demands of universality but by arbitrary inclinations and opinions. Women are educated — who knows how? — as it were by breathing in ideas, by living rather than by acquiring knowledge. The status of manhood, on the other hand, is attained only by the stress of thought and much technical exertion.[19]

Women, he continues, 'are not made for activities which demand a universal faculty such as the more advanced sciences, philosophy, and certain forms of artistic production', but instead have 'happy ideas, taste and elegance'.[20]

Hegel infers from this that 'man has his actual substantive life in the state, in learning, and so forth, as well as in labour and struggle with the external world and with himself so that it is only out of his diremption that he fights his way to self-subsistent unity with himself' while woman, in contrast, 'has her substantive destiny in the family'.[21] While men do engage in family life at the level of feeling, this forms only part of their existence, whereas for women it represents the limits of their self-realisation. A woman 'surrendering her body' before or outside marriage therefore loses her honour while for a man this would not follow.[22] However, the family does constitute a sphere of ethical activity for women, one in which their sexuality is contained and which is complete only with the arrival of children. Hegel argues firmly for monogamous marriage and for its indissolubility. Divorce should not be granted on 'the mere whims of hostile disposition or the accident of a purely passing mood' but only when 'the estrangement is total.'[23]

Clearly, Hegel's arguments here render him an unpromising candidate for inclusion within feminist theory. His view that women's sexuality needs to be controlled and that their destiny is primarily reproductive would seem to suggest a commitment to biological reductionism. But does Hegel's account of the family in the *Philosophy of right* provide unqualified support for a reductionist interpretation? Or are there grounds for a feminist reading of the *Philosophy of right* and of Hegel's work as a whole? Can his work contribute to an understanding of the oppression of women in advanced industrial societies? In answering these questions it will be necessary to consider his formulation of the public-private distinction in the *Philosophy of right*, his analyses of tragedy and of slavery in *The phenomenology of mind* and his historical studies in his *Lectures on the philosophy of world history*.

Anti-reductionism

Anti-reductionism I: Philosophy of right

A closer examination of the *Philosophy of right* reveals a tension between Hegel's conservative reductionism and a more progressive anti-reductionist standpoint. Unlike the reductionist political theorists with whom he is often identified, Hegel distances his account of marriage and the family from approaches which focus on biological needs, which reduce the relationship between men and women to a natural biological basis. For Hegel the family provides a means of escape from the subjectivism of the state of nature through an institutional commitment to an ethical universal. Instead of grounding his conception of the family in the biological dimensions of human existence, he describes the family as an institution which offers a means of transcending them. Marriage constitutes a partnership between men and women, the ethical aspect of which is irreducible to either the biological necessity of precreation or the sexual passions of the individuals. The ethical bond of marriage has a universality which surpasses the sexual relationship contained by it. It is this emphasis on the ethical dimension, rather than the appeal to biological needs, which underpins his arguments for monogamy and for diversity in the selection of marriage partners.

For Hegel, the value of marriage is precisely that it compels its members to transcend their individuality, in a relationship whose ethical aspects constrain the contingency of physical impulse. As he notes in the *Philosophy of right*, in marriage 'the sensuous moment, the one proper to physical life, is put into its ethical place as something only consequential and accidental'.[24] In this way the sexual union is transformed into a union at the level of mind or self-consciousness: in renouncing their individuality, the partners attain self-consciousness. Unlike his predecessors, Hegel is not concerned to drive a wedge between passion and reason but to designate the limits of passion within an objective ethical framework. Contrasting the 'ethico-legal' love, on which he believes marriage should be based, with 'the transient, fickle and purely subjective aspects of love,'[25] he is highly critical of those who focus solely on passion:

> But those works of modern art, dramatic and other, in which the love of the sexes is the main interest, are pervaded by a chill despite the heat of passion they portray, for they associate the passion with accident throughout and represent the entire dramatic interest as if it rested solely on the characters as *these individuals*: what rests on them may indeed be of infinite importance to *them*, but is of none whatever in itself.[26]

This contingency can only be transcended, as he comments in his *Philosophy of mind*, when the 'bodily conjunction is a sequel to the moral attachment'.[27] Hegel's attempt to draw together passion and reason lies in marked contrast to de Beauvoir's radical distinction between immanence and transcendence. As Lloyd points out, transcendence for de Beauvoir and Sartre entails a denial of women's biological lives: 'It is as if the female body is an intrinsic obstacle to transcendence, making woman "a prey of the species"'.[28]

Hegel also challenges the Kantian view of marriage which sees it as a contract between two individual atoms: 'In this view,' says Hegel, 'the parties are bound by a contract of mutual caprice, and marriage is thus degraded to the level of a contract for reciprocal use.'[29] Although marriage may begin at the level of contract, it moves beyond this, for in a contractual relationship the parties are related to each other as individual atoms, while in a genuinely ethical bond, this particularity is transcended. Any attempt to subordinate marriage to some other end, whether contract or sexuality, is ruled out by Hegel. He objects to arranged marriages which indicate 'scant respect' for women and marriages based on wealth or political gain. For Hegel, the

35

distinguishing feature of the family is that it lies outside the realm of possessive individualism and thus provides a counter to the fragmenting forces of civil society as it forces individuals to move beyond subjectivity. The family, says Hegel, is 'the first precondition of the state'[30] and it is only within the state that we find 'the *self-conscious* ethical substance, the unification of the family principle with that of civil society':[31] 'The same unity, which is in the family as a feeling of love, is its essence, receiving however, at the same time, through the second principle of conscious and spontaneously active volition the *form* of conscious universality.'[32]

Hegel's critique of possessive individualism in relation to the family may also be seen as part of the general anti-reductionist direction which he takes in the *Philosophy of right*. To the extent that Hegel rejects possessive individualist ideas of 'natural' self-interest, greed and avarice, and portrays marriage as a means of transcending these dispositions, he moves further away from biological reductionism than the other figures in Western political thought with whom he is identified by the orthodox feminist interpretation. His conception of the family as excluded from the realm of self-interest and standing opposed to it is paralleled by his concern with the poverty and class conflict arising from the individualism of the emerging bourgeois society.[33] Families constitute, for Hegel, a living refutation of the state of nature in the sense that marriage introduces an ethical universal which supersedes individual desires. This is not to devalue women's biological existence but to subvert it from its prime position as the principal determinant of their social and political lives.

Emphasis on the family as a means of superseding nature is also evident in *The phenomenology of mind* where he argues that women transcend the particularism of a specific relation to one individual and to his immediate needs within the family: 'the woman's relationships are not based on a reference to this particular husband, this particular child but to a husband, to children *in general* — not to feeling, but to the universal.'[34] Her ethical life 'has always a directly universal significance for her, and is quite alien to the impulsive condition of mere particular desire'.[35]

In this text, Hegel clearly defines the family in terms of the universality of the ethical bond:

in order that this relationship may be ethical, neither the

individual who does an act nor he to whom the act refers must show any trace of contingency such as obtains in rendering some particular help or service. The content of the ethical act must be substantial in character, or must be entire and universal . . . [36]

Anti-reductionism II: Antigone

A challenge to the reductionist interpretation of Hegel and grounds for a feminist reading of his work may also be found in Hegel's analysis of *Antigone*. Although Hegel sees Antigone as guided by love, this does not mean, for Hegel, that she is governed by subjective emotions, but rather that she rationally analyses the consequences of her actions in relation to ethical principles and acts in full knowledge of those consequences. In doing so, she moves beyond contingency towards the universal. The hallmark of tragedy for Hegel is precisely this quality of self-reflection. It is important that the ethical consciousness recognises its guilt: 'Because of our sufferings we acknowledge we have erred'[37] says Antigone, and for Hegel this acknowledgment signifies 'the return to the ethical frame of mind, which knows that nothing counts but right.'[38] The only ethical decision Antigone can take is to disobey Creon and bury her brother, yet her actions are marked not by subjectivity but by a highly rational appreciation of the effects of her action. Hegel points out that the 'ethical consciousness is more complete, its guilt purer, if it knows beforehand the law and the power which it opposes, if it takes them to be sheer violence and wrong, to be a contingency in the ethical life, and wittingly, like Antigone, commits the crime'.[39] It is significant that when Hegel defines tragedy he focuses on tragic heroines with the capacity and desire for self-reflection. Instead of reducing woman's nature to mere particularism, as the reductionist interpretation suggests, he stresses the way in which she moves beyond contingency. What we find in tragedy 'are *self-conscious* human beings, who know their own rights and purposes, the power and the will belonging to their specific nature, and who know how to state them'.[40] They do not express merely the external aspects of their lives but 'make the very inner being external, they prove the righteousness of their action, and the "pathos" controlling them is soberly asserted and definitely expressed in its universal individuality, free from all accident of

37

circumstance, and the particular peculiarities of personalities'.[41]
Love, as represented by Antigone, is not devalued to subjectivity
but rather signifies its opposite for Hegel: love constitutes
redemption, redemption from the subjectivity of individualism of
the self and of the society. In the *Phenomenology* he argues that in
returning to 'the ethical frame of mind', the agent 'surrenders his
character and the reality of his self . . . His being lies in belonging
to his ethical law, as his substance'.[42] The ethical bonds of love
incorporate individuals into the wider unity of the family and
destroy their individuality. They also protect the individuals from
the contingency and inevitability of death: death in the natural
world is lonely and finite but the network of ethical duties and
generalised responsibilities within the family ensure the transcendence of the particularity of existence. In his discussion of
Hegel's work on tragedy, Bradley refers to the 'strange double
impression which is produced by the hero's death. He dies, and
our hearts die with him; and yet his death matters nothing to us,
or we even exult. He is dead; and he has no more to do with death
than the power which killed him and with which he is one'.[43] But
this is not so strange when we recall that for Hegel the 'blood-
relationship . . . supplements the abstract natural process by
adding to it the process of consciousness, by interrupting the work
of nature, and rescuing the blood-relation from destruction'.[44] He
adds:

> The family keeps away from the dead this dishonouring of
> him by the desires of unconscious organic agencies and by
> abstract elements, puts its own action in place of theirs, and
> weds the relative to the bosom of the earth, the elemental
> individuality that passes not away. Thereby the family
> makes the dead a member of a community which prevails
> over and holds under control the particular material
> elements and the lower living creatures, which sought to
> have their way with the dead and destroy him.[45]

This is epitomised for Hegel by Antigone who, in burying her
brother, protects him from death and dishonour and rescues him
from subjectivity. Hegel finds *Antigone* particularly compelling as
he sees the relationship between brother and sister as the purest
ethical relationship, being based on common blood but marked
by an absence of sexual desire. .

Love is also redemptive in shielding the individual from the positivity of society. In his early theological writings, Hegel had defended Mary Magdalene for refusing to succumb to the expectations of her society but 'through sin' experiencing love and developing consciousness. He poses the question:

> Would anyone say it had been better for Mary to have yielded to the fate of the Jewish life, to have passed away as an automaton of her time, righteous and ordinary, without sin and without love? Without sin, because the era of her people was one of those in which the beautiful heart could not live without sin, but in this as in any era, could return through love to the most beautiful consciousness.[46]

Hegel saw love in his early work, as Lukács notes, as 'the highest point of existence; it alone can overcome all that is dead and positive in the world.'[47] When analysing *Antigone*, Hegel can therefore perceive the justification for Creon's desire to maintain the authority of the state, but at the same time he recognises the ethical superiority of Antigone and the way of life she upholds. The tragedy can be understood, as Lukács says, in terms of a conflict between tribal society, represented by Antigone, and the emerging forces which would lead to its demise:

> What is striking about Hegel's view of the *Antigone* is the way in which the two poles of the contradiction are maintained in a tense unity: on the one hand, there is the recognition that tribal society stands higher morally and humanly than the class societies that succeed it; and that the collapse of tribal society was brought about by the release of base and evil human impulses. On the other hand, there is the equally powerful conviction that this collapse was inevitable and that it signified a definite historical advance.[48]

In Hegel's essay on *Natural law*, for example, tragedy is analysed in terms of the conflict between man and citizen, 'a collision of spirit with itself'.[49] Hegel recognises that 'the beautiful solution achieved by the civilisation of antiquity had to perish'[50] and that this is compensated to some extent by the progressive nature of the gestating new order. But he also realises, as Lukács points out, that:

> the type of man produced by this material advance in and

through capitalism is the practical negation of everything great, significant and sublime that humanity had created in the course of its history up to then. The contradiction of two necessarily connected phenomena, the indissoluble bond between progress and the debasement of mankind, the purchase of progress at the cost of that debasement — that is the heart of the 'tragedy in the realm of the ethical'.[51]

Consequently, Hegel sees tragedy disappearing with the development of modern society predicated on individualism, being replaced by romantic art concerned with the 'boundless subjectivity' of passion rather than the clash of ethical principles. His sympathy for the protagonists in *Antigone* had rested on the fact that both Antigone and Creon, in following one ethical principle, brought about the destruction of another, and for Hegel, as Bradley observes, 'the more nearly the contending forces approach each other in goodness, the more tragic is the conflict'.[52]

We can see, then, that while Antigone's choices are governed by love, Hegel does not perceive love as mere subjectivity but rather sees subjectivity as alien to tragedy. His focus on the ethical bonds of love in *Antigone* does not suggest a reductionist view of women: drawing attention to the 'feminine' quality of love does not in itself entail a reductionist position provided it is clear that this quality is not biologically based. It is significant that in defying the patriarchal authority of the state, Antigone's actions are determined by an authentic relation of love rather than sexual or economic motives or by blind obedience to authority.

Anti-reductionism III: Hegel's historical studies

Hegel's historical studies reveal an awareness of the cultural mediation of gender roles which presents a challenge to reductionist theories. In his *Lectures on the philosophy of world history*, for example, he identifies a range of patterns of behaviour, including a state of women in the Congo ruled over by a woman who renounced the love of her son, pounding him in a mortar and smearing herself with his blood.[53] The women survived by plundering and eating human flesh. Prisoners of war were used as slaves or husbands, and male offspring were murdered, often together with their fathers. Hegel's aversion to these women, however, seems to be due less to a fear of women in control, than to the lack of respect for humanity which he sees as characteristic of these societies. Lying between the full participation of women in public life in the Congo, and the privatisation of Western cultures, is the tribe in Dahomey which Hegel describes as engaging in a communal way of life. Here, he observes, women fight alongside the king and children are brought up communally, distributed among the villages at birth and sold by the king when of marriageable age. Each man has to take the woman he is given and when presenting himself for marriage, the suitor is first given a mother to maintain, and only subsequently, if his behaviour is satisfactory, is he given a wife. While Hegel's discussion of these examples may rely more on travellers' tales than scientific research, none the less his awareness of these variations does highlight the difficulty of attributing to him a reductionist standpoint.

The treatment of women in different cultures and its effects is also considered by Hegel in his historical writings. The repression of women's imagination in the medieval period and its conse-quences in 'the ghastliness of witchcraft',[54] for example, is contrasted with the Bacchanalian festivities in which Greek women were able to give full expression to their imagination:

On the one hand witches, on the other maenads; in the one case the object of phantasy is a devilish grimace (*Frazze*), in the other a beautiful vine-bedecked God; in the one socialized satisfaction of envy, of the desire for revenge and hate, in the other nothing but purposeless pleasure often verging on raging madness; in the one progress from individual attacks of insanity to total and enduring derange-ment of the mind; in the other withdrawal into ordinary life; in the first case the age did not consider this displaced madness as an illness but a blasphemous outrage which could be atoned only with the funeral pyre, in the second the need of many female phantasies and temperaments was something holy, the outbreak of which gave (occasion for) holidays, something which was sanctioned by the state and thereby given the possibility of being innocuous.[55]

Hegel also draws attention to the links between particular family types and the forms of the state. Monogamy, for example, he sees as a corollary of Christian states, 'since this is the only form in which both partners can receive their full rights',[56] although he points out that the relationship between children and parents can include slavery and allow children free property ownership. The patriarchal family, where the 'head of the family . . . is the will of the whole; he acts in the interests of the common purposes, cares for the individuals, directs their activity towards the common end, educates them, and ensures that they remain in harmony with the universal end',[57] is seen as characteristic of Oriental cultures. Tracing the uneven development of individualism through ancient society, he shows how the state gradually takes on an abstract existence, apart from the head of the family. Attitudes towards sexuality in different cultures are also contrasted.[58] In Jewish culture, for example, he notes that sex is spoken of freely, while in Oriental cultures, women are seen as separate from society. They cannot be likened to objects, so there cannot be a relation of lordship and bondage between men and women but only one of seclusion. Their physical separation embodies this image and consequently it constitutes a dishonour to talk of women. Hegel's historicisation of gender roles is therefore difficult to reconcile with the reductionist interpretation of his work.

Slavery and freedom

In seeking to explain and transcend the subordination of women in advanced industrial societies, Hegel's *Phenomenology* is arguably the most significant text, offering a rich harvest of concepts for feminist theory.[59] Its analysis of the dynamics of domination and subordination in the master-slave dialectic raises issues which lie at the heart of the feminist critique of patriarchy. In so far as he construes the move from slavery to freedom in terms of a movement away from nature or biological constraints, towards self-consciousness — a conception of freedom which is also central to certain strands of contemporary feminist thought — Hegel's work on slavery offers insights into the supersession of women's subordination and provides further affirmation of an anti-reductionist stance. Consciousness and labour as the preconditions of the transformation of oppressive social relationships play a central role in Hegel's political thought but are equally essential dimensions of feminist political theory. He also sheds light on the power of ideologies by pointing to the extent to which the slave may accept his or her slavery.

Hegel postulates a distinction between two modes of consciousness: 'The one is independent, and its essential nature is to be for itself; the other is dependent, and its essence is life or existence for another. The former is the Master, or Lord, the latter the Bondsman'.[60] For Hegel, self-consciousness exists only to the extent that it is acknowledged or recognised by another, but here emphasises that the master's recognition is dependent upon the consciousness of the bondsman: 'for, just where the master has effectively achieved lordship, he really finds that something has come about quite different from an independent consciousness. It is not an independent, but rather a dependent consciousness that he has achieved'.[61] The master, relying on the slave, becomes dependent, while the slave, in working for the master, achieves independence through the acquisition of knowledge in productive labour. For Hegel the master represents a purely transient stage in the history of spirit while the significant movement in human development springs from the consciousness of the servant, because the servant meets the two preconditions of freedom, namely fear and service. Fear of the master is significant insofar as it imposes discipline and thus constitutes 'the beginning of wisdom'.[62] Without this initial fear of the master, freedom is impossible.

The slave has the possibility of confronting freedom through fear and service, while the master's relation to the world is mediated by, and contained in, the desire for the object, but this satisfaction of desire is seen by Hegel as evanescent. The master remains trapped within his own egotism: experiencing neither fear nor labour, he perceives in the slave only his immediate will and receives from him the formal recognition of an unfree consciousness. But for the slave, the experience of fear according to Hegel is the first moment of freedom. Fear, combined with service or labour, constitutes the necessary precondition for the development of self-consciousness: 'Without the formative activity shaping the thing, fear remains inward and mute, and consciousness does not become objective for itself'.[63] In serving the master, the slave loses his 'individual self-will' and goes beyond the immediacy of appetite. His divestment of self and 'fear of the lord' mark, for Hegel, the beginning of knowledge and the movement to universal self-consciousness. Freedom is attained 'solely by risking life'[64] when consciousness, which has 'tottered and shaken', is combined with struggle. The fear and service of slavery contain, for Hegel, the possibility of freedom beyond subjectivity. Self-consciousness passes through the slave rather than the master, dependent on the slave for recognition and trapped by desires which lack substance and objectivity.

The importance of work for Hegel is that in labour the worker moves beyond immediate instinctual life, flees the darkness of nature and becomes truly human. Hegel does not idealise the labour-process — in contrast to many of his contemporaries — but rather acknowledges the drudgery of mechanistic labour. However, he does characterise the labour-process as a means of enhancing self-consciousness and says that in working upon an object the worker externalises his self-consciousness and makes it permanent: 'precisely in labour where there seemed to be merely some outsider's mind and ideas involved, the bondsman becomes aware through this re-discovery of himself by himself, of having and being a "mind of his own".'[65] In fashioning the object the worker 'makes himself into a thing' by expressing the objective laws of work as independent of individual desires. By placing labour between his desires and their fulfilment, he moves away from nature towards sociality.

The slave's proximity to freedom thus rests on his engagement in purposive rational labour, whereas the master remains limited by his desire for the object. While the master's desire is ephemeral, the slave's labour fosters the development of self-consciousness. His desires embrace those of the master as well as his own, forcing him to move beyond the immediacy of his own will. For Hegel the feeling of the worthlessness of egotism and the 'habit of obedience' of the slave is a necessary stage in the growth of self-consciousness. In satisfying the needs of others, the slave moves beyond nature towards a genuinely human existence, as he enters into relations with others and becomes part of the division of labour.

It is precisely this dimension of slavery as *potential* consciousness which eats away at the heart of the master-slave relation and the system of slavery arising from it, ultimately leading to its destruction. But in stressing potential rather than actual consciousness, Hegel attributes a degree of responsibility for slavery to the slave rather than the master; 'To adhere to man's absolute freedom', he says, 'is *eo ipso* to condemn slavery. Yet if a man is a slave, his own will is responsible for his slavery, just as it is its will which is responsible if a people is subjugated'.[66] Unless the slave struggles to win his freedom, he deserves his servitude, since slavery demands its own negation. A slave is subject to an ethical imperative to free himself. Hegel applies this argument specifically to the history of nations but his account of the responsibility for slavery could also be seen as relevant to the history of women's exploitation. There is no 'absolute injustice' in slaves remaining slaves, argues Hegel, for if they do not risk their lives to gain freedom, their slavery is deserved: 'he who has not the courage to risk his life to win freedom, that man deserves to be a slave'.[67] Slavery, as a system of social relationships, cannot survive unless the slave accepts and is at home in his slavery.

A further justification of slavery for Hegel lies in the fact that slavery may be appropriate to a particular phase of social development and in that sense 'just': 'Slavery and tyranny,' he says, 'are, therefore in the history of nations a necessary stage and hence *relatively* justified'.[68] Referring to the slaves' hostility to the efforts of English reformers to abolish slavery, he argues that slavery is accepted as natural by the slaves. While slavery is seen as an absolute injustice by Western reformers, it is the typical legal relationship of a society in which a low value is placed on human life and this evaluation of human life is internalised by the slaves themselves. It is entirely consistent, for Hegel, with the state of nature characteristic of primitive societies. If a man can sell his wife, parents and children into slavery, this demonstrates a contempt for life in general as well as his own and signifies an absence of morality. Taking a broader historical perspective, Hegel sees slavery as part of the transition from the state of nature to a genuinely ethical existence. It arises in a world where 'a wrong is still right',[69] where wrong has some validity and constitutes a necessary moment in the progression towards a higher stage of development. Only when a society reaches maturity may it realise its freedom and eliminate slavery. Where a society is undeveloped we should expect to find slavery, says Hegel. Even in Greece this 'relative injustice' may be found, since in that culture freedom was not based on the idea of a rational self-consciousness.[70] Only if self-consciousness apprehends itself, through thought, as human does it free itself from contingency and move into the realm of morality and ethical life. Rational reflection is what distinguishes the slave's unfreedom from freedom, and thus it was the Greek slaves resisting their slavery, and not the citizens, who grasped this and sought to attain their 'eternal human rights'.[71]

If we consider the implications of Hegel's analysis of slavery for an understanding of social change, and, specifically, changes in the position of women, his standpoint may seem at first sight to be rather pessimistic. He attributes responsibility for slavery to the slave and seems to suggest that the slave enjoys his slavery. He also treats slavery as appropriate to particular forms of life, as a necessary stage in social development and therefore inevitable. Both arguments may appear to be antithetical to the likelihood of a radical change in women's lives, yet precisely because Hegel attributes slavery to the will of an individual or people, he opens up the possibility of a dramatic change in social relationships through the power of rational reflection. Recent work within feminism has examined the ways in which women may embrace patriarchal ideas or ideologies of domesticity and resist change.[72] Attention has also been paid to the low self-esteem in which many women hold themselves, placing a low value on their own needs and on their lives generally. Yet in neither case does this preclude the possibility of change. Furthermore, Hegel's account of slavery is an historical account which presupposes the potentiality for changes in relationships of domination and subordination, given certain changes in the way of life in which these relationships are grounded.

Hegel's acknowledgement of the slave's identification with his slavery is combined with an awareness of the tensions inherent in any relation of oppression. The dominance of the master over the slave and the slave's acquiescence are neither stable nor eternal. Rather, the relation is one of constant struggle in which the master's authority, from the beginning, may be negated. This may be illustrated by Hegel's observations on slavery in certain African cultures in his *Lectures on the philosophy of world history*. A system of despotism based on force, patriarchal authority and an arbitrary will is inherently weak, says Hegel, for the despot is always in danger of being challenged by his subjects: 'thus even such despotism as this is not completely blind; the peoples of Africa are not just slaves but assert their own will too'.[73] Slavery, as a system of social relations, can never be secure for 'the sword really hangs above the despot's head day and night' and, like his subjects, the despot is vulnerable to the lack of respect for human life.[74]

The movement towards self-consciousness is built into the master-slave relation and incorporates the possibility of freedom for the master as well as the slave. The emancipation of the slave furthers the interest of the master since, as Hegel notes in the *Phenomenology*, only when the slave realises his freedom does the master move beyond immediacy. This idea is applied to colonial relations in the *Philosophy of right* where he points out that 'Colonial independence proves to be of the greatest advantage to the mother country, just as the emancipation of the slaves turns out to the greatest advantage of the owners'.[75] Hegel's arguments concerning responsibility for slavery and its appropriateness do not therefore entail a static model of the master-slave relation. Rather, he offers a dynamic model which sees that relationship as characterised by a fundamental tension which may ultimately tear it apart. Applying Hegel's analysis to the position of women, we find that the acceptance of patriarchal ideologies is matched by examples of women's resistance to their exploitation. In struggling against their subordination women at the same time precipitate a qualitative improvement in social relations for men who are also constrained by those ideologies.

Furthermore, Hegel is optimistic that when the slaves begin to resist, the system of slävery will perish: 'if a nation does not merely imagine that it wants to be free but actually has the energy to will its freedom,' he says in the *Philosophy of mind*, 'then no human power can hold it back in the servitude of a merely passive obedience to authority.'[76] One can infer from this that the very fact of struggling together is as important for women as the formal freedoms thereby obtained and is inseparable from them, since collective resistance ensures the growth of consciousness. Because freedom constitutes the human essence for Hegel, he emphasises that the slave has an absolute right to free himself and essential to this transition to freedom is rational self-consciousness. While attributing slavery to the will of the slave, Hegel none the less envisages a complete reversal of the master-slave relation given the will for change and consciousness of the potential for freedom:

> it is only as thinking intelligence that the will is genuinely a will and free. The slave does not know his essence, his infinity, his freedom; he does not know himself as human in essence; and he lacks this knowledge of himself because he does not think himself. This self-consciousness which apprehends itself through thinking is essentially human, and thereby frees itself from the contingent and the false, is the principle of right, morality and all ethical life.[77]

He contrasts this reflective self-consciousness with appeals to

47

'feeling, enthusiasm, the heart and the breast', which are absorbed in 'instinctive desire' and 'particularity'.[78] For freedom to be obtained, the slave has to move beyond his own individuality, as well as that of the master, to grasp 'the absolutely rational in its universality which is independent of the particularity of the subjects'.[79] Hegel's identification of the freedom of the slave with reflective self-consciousness, and of the need to move beyond feelings to reason, points clearly to the importance of rational reflection for women as a means of transforming their position.

Moreover, while Hegel gives an historical analysis of slavery, this does not commit him to a total relativism which would rule out criticism of particular forms of life. While attracted to the liberal ideals of the French Revolution, for example, Hegel recognised the limitations of the emerging bourgeois society as well as the shortcomings of the liberal theories used to understand and justify the new order. Like Marx and Engels, he was well aware that the progressive aspects of liberal capitalism were accompanied by greed, egotism and self-interest, which would lead to the 'creation of a rabble of paupers'.[80] He notes that 'At the same time, this brings with it, at the other end of the social scale, conditions which greatly facilitate the concentration of disproportionate wealth in a few hands'.[81] Hegel did not allow his acknowledgement of the progressive aspects of liberal capitalism to become an apologia for that society. Rather, he saw poverty and class conflict as inevitable features of that mode of production. It is therefore difficult to accept Elshtain's argument that Hegel ignores the 'realities of economic power'.[82] While Elshtain postulates that individualism 'may arguably be the *only* means available to the woman to attain an identity other than a thoroughly privatised one',[83] Hegel draws attention to the pathological effects of a social structure governed by the pursuit of self-interest. Although Hegel did not develop his understanding of the labour-process into an extensive critique of the division of labour of the kind Marx and Engels subsequently elaborated, none the less such a critique is implicit in his teleology. The connections he drew between freedom and necessity, consciousness and labour, constituted a significant advance on earlier theories and bequeath to feminist theory a firm foundation on which to construct an investigation into the development of the division of labour and ways of transcending it.

By showing how slavery is 'natural' or appropriate to

particular stages of development, for example, Hegel points to the necessity of a *fundamental* change in social relationships if slavery is to be eliminated. The implication here for women is that radical improvements in their position will not be achieved by piecemeal changes. What is needed is a transformation of the social structure which generates inequalities and leads to their privatisation. Nor will these inequalities be removed by an appeal to moral principles since their subordination is linked to the needs of capital for a reserve army and its own reproduction. Hegel's comments on the 'relative justification' of slavery anticipated Marx's argument in the *Critique of the Gotha programme* that 'Right can never be higher than the economic structure of society and the cultural development conditioned by it.'[84] Marx's observations on justice have led some commentators to argue that the extraction of surplus value cannot be seen as unjust since it is an essential feature of capitalism and the labourer freely exchanges his labour-power for wages.[85] 'Exploitation' is thus a 'natural' feature of capitalist society appropriate to that stage of development and should not be seen in moral terms. It follows from this that it is mistaken to see Marxism as a moral theory aimed at removing injustice: the 'injustices' it analyses are a necessary part of that mode of production and will not be dissolved by a moral critique but only by a radical change in the economic and social structure. Similarly it could be argued that the subordination of women will be overcome only by a challenge to the division of labour which forms the heart of the system of oppressive social relations and the source of slavery.

Hegel's quasi-relativist view of morality does not preclude the possibility of advancement, however, since he suggests that the move away from slavery towards freedom, although dependent on consciousness, is nevertheless inevitable and reflects the growth of reason in the world. His analysis of slavery consequently provides a rich source of concepts for feminist theory. His political thought is also of particular interest insofar as it offers an understanding of freedom and enslavement from a standpoint which transcends individualism.

A comparison may be drawn between the status of women in advanced industrial societies and slaves in ancient society in the sense that both societies are characterised by their dependence on the unpaid labour of a service class. Domestic labour for both women and slaves is unwaged, low status and unsatisfying, consisting of repetitive tasks performed for other members of the household. It is physically separated from other spheres of production and is seen as exclusively the responsibility of a particular group, constituting the defining role for those who perform these tasks. Many women, like slaves, live and work within the household of the oppressing social group, divorced from public life, in a relationship which is universalised. As Delphy says:

> While the wage labourer depends on the market (on a theoretically unlimited number of employers), the married woman depends on one individual. While the wage labourer sells his labour power the married woman gives hers away. Exclusivity and non-payment are intimately connected. Providing unpaid labour within the framework of a universal and personal relationship (marriage) constitutes a relationship of slavery.[86]

Women, like slaves, provide an indeterminate amount of domestic and personal services in return for their maintenance, but this cannot be construed as an exchange relationship since their rewards are not calculated on the basis of the amount of work completed. Fluctuations in living standards do not reflect variations in the work-load. Unlike wage-contracted labourers, wives cannot easily change their employers. At best, they can seek a wealthier husband to whom they offer the same services. The marriage contract can be seen as affording a means of extracting unlimited labour-power from wives. The relationship between husband and wife is similar to that between master and slave since, in both cases, there is an obligation to maintain the labour-power of the service class. Patriarchal exploitation, sanctioned and facilitated by this contract is, according to Delphy the 'common, specific and main expression of women'.[87] It is universal in so far as the majority of women marry at some point in their lives.

This is not to deny that there are differences between the position of women and the slaves of antiquity, both in terms of the nature of the relationship to the head of the household and the level of development of the productive forces. But while it could be argued that the marriage contract is based on reciprocal affective ties, this could be seen as exacerbating women's subordination, in binding them more tightly to an exploitative relationship and also in subjecting them to a further set of expectations in relation to the performance of affective roles as well as the execution of routine domestic tasks.[88] Moreover, the existence of such a service class is anomalous within the context of an advanced mode of production, governed by the cash nexus, and cannot therefore be accounted for simply in relation to the needs of capital. An explanation must be sought within the deeper structures of patriarchy.

Domestic labour poses problems for feminism which may be illuminated by Hegelian insights into the tensions implicit in the master-slave relation. Although engagement in the labour process for Hegel is the key mechanism for the growth of self-consciousness, he also recognises the limitations of a way of life marked by routine and repetition and sees acceptance of such routine as tantamount to death.[89] Domestic labour is the only sphere of employment where drudgery is combined with isolation. Taken separately these factors may inhibit the growth of consciousness; together they present a formidable obstacle to change. Where women are engaged in service occupations outside the home, the monotonous aspects of labour are counteracted by contact with others, but the atomised nature of the domestic mode of production militates against the formation of self-consciousness. Hegel also points to the extent to which the slave may accept his slavery and resist liberation. His analysis of the master-slave dialectic in the *Phenomenology* is therefore followed by a description of the modes of false consciousness attributed to the slave unwilling to resist the bonds of slavery, namely Stoicism and Scepticism. These rationalisations of unfreedom lead into Hegel's account of the Unhappy Consciousness where the slave taking refuge from the master submits to a transcendental God. This phenomenon of false consciousness confronts all liberation movements and, for this reason, feminists have begun to examine women's resistance to change, their commitment to dominant reproductive ideologies and the needs which the family may be perceived to meet. The limited aspirations of women and the marginal value they themselves place on their labour-power have also become significant areas of investigation precisely because they are as strong a barrier to freedom as the material conditions of exploitation.[90]

At the same time, Hegel sees labour and subordination as essential to the development of self-consciousness. The realisation of freedom incorporates awareness of freedom and the practical accomplishments of freedom, and both are grounded in the fear and service of slavery. Insights into women's subordination and their potential for liberation may therefore be lost if Hegel is dismissed too readily as a biological reductionist. The orthodox feminist view which identifies Hegel's work with the public-private distinction of mainstream political thought fails to take account of the strongly anti-reductionist strand in his writing and loses the significance of his analysis of slavery for an understanding of women's oppression. Since, for Hegel, the fear and service of slavery place the slave closer to freedom than the master imprisoned by sensation and desire. Women, because of their subordination, could be seen as nearer self-consciousness than the men who depend on their labour-power and recognition. In using their biological and personal needs and desires as a means of oppression, the latter are less free than the women who are forced to move beyond the immediacy of desire into the realm of rational reflection, to confront their own subordination and exploitation through consciousness and action.

Moreover, this domination is dehumanising and limiting for both master and slave, men and women, in so far as men are confined by patriarchal modes of thought. While men stand in a relation to women governed by dependency and the gratification of physical needs alone, the growth of their own self-consciousness is truncated. They remain tied to the sensual world, using the gratification of physical needs and the control of reproduction as a means of oppression.[91] Although the master receives recognition from the slave he can, within the existing power relationship, never be sure that the recognition is genuine. It is for this reason that Hegel sees the liberation of the slave as furthering the interests of the master, as Camus observes:

> The master, to his detriment, is recognized in his autonomy by a consciousness which he himself does not recognize as autonomous. Therefore, he cannot be satisfied and his autonomy is only negative. Mastery is a blind alley. Since, moreover, he cannot renounce mastery and become a slave again, the eternal destiny of masters is to live unsatisfied or to be killed.[92]

Notes

1. See, for example, S. Moller Okin, *Women in Western political thought*

(London, Virago, 1980); G. Lloyd, 'Public reason and private passion', *Politics, 18*, 2, p. 25, 1981; 'Masters, slaves and others', *Radical Philosophy, 34*, Summer 1983; J.B. Elshtain, *Public man, private woman* (Oxford, Martin Robertson, 1981); S. Harding and M.B. Hintikka, (eds), *Discovering reality, feminist perspectives on epistemology, metaphysics, methodology and philosophy of science* (Dordrecht, Reidel, 1983).

2. S. Moller Okin, *Women in Western political thought*, p. 5.

3. Ibid., p. 5.

4. Ibid., p. 9.

5. Ibid., p. 10.

6. Ibid., p. 9.

7. Ibid., p. 197.

8. Ibid., p. 341.

9. Ibid., p. 293.

10. J.B. Elshtain, *Public Man*, p. 174.

11. Ibid., p. 174.

12. Ibid., p. 176.

13. Ibid., p. 175.

14. Ibid., p. 177.

15. Ibid., p. 179.

16. G. Lloyd, 'Masters, slaves and others', p. 5.

17. See S. Moller Okin, *Women in Western political thought*, pp. 6, 197, 283–4, 341; G. Lloyd, 'Public reason and private passion', pp. 31–4; J.B. Elshtain. *Public man.*, pp. 170–83.

18. G.W.F. Hegel, *Philosophy of right (PR)* (Oxford, Clarendon Press, 1952), trans. T.M. Knox, § 166.

19. Ibid. § 166 Addition.

20. Ibid.

21. Ibid. § 166.

22. Ibid. § 164 Addition.

23. Ibid. § 176.

24. Ibid. § 164.

25. Ibid. § 161 Addition.

26. Ibid. § 162.

27. G.W.F. Hegel, *Philosophy of mind*, (PM) (Oxford, Clarendon Press, 1971), trans. W. Wallace and A.V. Miller, § 519.

28. G. Lloyd, 'Masters, slaves and others', p. 8.

29. G.W.F. Hegel, *PR* § 161 Addition.

30. Ibid. § 201 Addition.

31. G.W.F. Hegel, *PM* § 535.

32. Ibid., 535.

33. See Hegel, *PR* and L. Davidoff, 'The rationalisation of housework' in D.L. Barker and S. Allen (eds), *Dependence and exploitation in work and marriage* (London, Longman, 1976), pp. 121–51, for an analysis of the way in which the family was perceived as resisting the encroachment of the market in late eighteenth and nineteenth century England.

34. G.W.F. Hegel, *The phenomenology of mind (PG)*, (London, Allen and Unwin, 1931), trans. J. Baillie, p. 476.

35. Ibid., p. 476.

36. Ibid., p. 469.

37. Sophocles, *Antigone*, 926.
38. G.W.F. Hegel, *PG*, p. 491.
39. Ibid., p. 491.
40. Ibid., p. 737.
41. Ibid., p. 737.
42. Ibid., p. 491.
43. A.C. Bradley, 'Hegel's theory of tragedy' appendix to A. (in *Oxford Lectures on Poetry*, (Indiana University Press, Indiana, 1961), pp. 69–95), and H. Paolucci, *Hegel on tragedy* (New York, Harper and Row, 1962), p. 385.
44. Hegel, *PG*, p. 471.
45. Ibid., p. 472.
46. G.W.F. Hegel, *Early theological writings* (Tübingen, 1907), ed. H. Nohl, p. 293.
47. G. Lukács, *The young Hegel* (London, Merlin Press, 1975), p. 121.
48. Ibid., p. 412.
49. Ibid., p. 403.
50. Ibid., p. 404.
51. Ibid., p. 408.
52. A.C. Bradley, 'Hegel's theory of tragedy', p. 384.
53. G.W.F. Hegel, *Lectures on the philosophy of world history* (*LPWH*), Introduction (Cambridge University Press , 1975), trans. H.B. Nisbet, appendix on Africa, pp. 173–190.
54. G.W.F. Hegel, 'Fragments of historical studies', *Clio*, 1977, vol. 7, no. 1, p. 123.
55. Ibid., p. 123.
56. Hegel, *LPWH*, p. 113.
57. Ibid., p. 198.
58. G.W.F. Hegel, 'Fragments of historical studies', pp. 117–18.
59. G.W.F. Hegel, *PM*.
60. Ibid., p. 234.
61. Ibid., pp. 236–7.
62. Ibid., p. 238.
63. Ibid., p. 239.
64. Ibid., p. 233.
65. Ibid., p. 239.
66. Hegel, *PR* § 57 Addition.
67. Hegel, *PM* § 435 Zusatz.
68. Ibid. § 435 Zusatz.
69. Hegel, *PR* § 57 Addition.
70. Hegel, *PM*, § 433 Zusatz.
71. Ibid. § 433 Zusatz.
72. See, for example, A. Dworkin, *Right-wing women, the politics of domesticated females* (London, Women's Press, 1983).
73. Hegel, *LPWH*, p. 187.
74. Ibid., p. 187.
75. Hegel, *PR* § 248 Addition.
76. Hegel, *PM* § 435 Zusatz.
77. Hegel, *PR* § 21.
78. Ibid. § 21.

79. Hegel, *PM* § 435 Zusatz.

80. Hegel, *PR* § 244.

81. Ibid. § 244.

82. J.B. Elshtain, *Public man*, p. 179.

83. Ibid., p. 181.

84. K. Marx, 'Critique of the Gotha programme', in *Basic writings on politics and philosophy* (London, Pelican, 1963), ed. L.S. Feuer, p. 160.

85. See, for example, A. Wood, *Karl Marx*, (London, Routledge and Kegan Paul, 1981); M. Cohen, T. Nagel and T. Scanlon, (eds), *Marx, justice and history* (Princeton, University Press, 1980); S.M. Easton, *Humanist Marxism and Wittgensteinian social philosophy* (Manchester, University Press, 1983).

86. C. Delphy, *Close to home: a materialist analysis of women's oppression* (London, Hutchinson, 1984), p. 71.

87. Ibid., p. 74.

88. According to R.E. Dobash and R. Dobash, in their study of wife abuse, *Violence against wives* (New York, Free Press, 1979) these multiple expectations arising from the marriage contract constituted the significant factors in transforming women into 'legitimate' objects of violence. Jealousy and possessiveness as well as a perceived inadequate performance of domestic tasks were predominant precipitating causes of abuse in the cases they examined.

89. Hegel, *PR* § 151 Addition.

90. P. Hunt, 'Cash-transactions and household tasks: domestic behaviour in relation to industrial employment', *Sociological Review, 26*, 1978, pp. 555–71.

91. This point is illustrated by *The draughtsman's contract*.

92. A. Camus, *The rebel* (London, Peregrine, 1962), p. 110.

3

On Becoming

Anthony Manser

The opening moves of Hegel's *Science of logic* are compressed; in three short paragraphs we are faced with an argument in which being, nothing and becoming[1] are merged into each other:

> Pure being and pure nothing are, then, the same; the truth is, not either being or nothing, but that being — not passes — but has passed over into nothing, and nothing into being . . . Their truth is therefore this movement, this immediate disappearance of the one into the other, in a word, becoming; a movement wherein both are distinct, but in virtue of a distinction which has immediately dissolved itself. (*SL* 95)[2]

Admittedly this brief introduction of the terms is followed by some twenty pages of 'Observations', but these are not formally a part of the argument, but rather glosses and attempts to forestall objections. Becoming is given two further paragraphs and a separate 'Observation' at the end of the chapter. This is preceded by a discussion of being and nothing in the previous section 'With what must science begin?', though what is said there is bracketed off by the concluding words of that section: 'This consideration is so simple that the beginning as such requires no preparation or further introduction, and this preliminary discussion was not so much intended to deduce it as to clear away all preliminary matters'. (*SL* 90) The first chapter, or rather the argument of the first chapter, concludes with an equally rapid move from becoming to determinate being: 'Becoming, then, taken as transition into the unity of being and nothing, which exists because it is, or has the form of, the one-sided immediate unity of these moments, is determinate being'. (*SL* 119)

Many commentators seem puzzled by what Hegel says of 'becoming'; some have ignored it altogether, treating the union of being and nothing simply as determinate being. None, as far as I am aware, have seen the argument of the first chapter of the *Science of logic* as central to the whole Hegelian enterprise, as a vital element in his attempt radically to change the whole nature of philosophy. One strand in this is the substitution of logic for the old metaphysics, a point which is often mentioned but seldom taken seriously. The problem is what this means in such a context. Here I can only give a truncated answer, but one which I hope will justify my concentration on the concept of becoming in this paper. Metaphysics had been regarded as the 'Queen of the Sciences', the study which revealed the unchanging ground of the changing world of appearances, a ground which was superior because it was unchanging and permanent. This idea had its reflection in politics, e.g. in Plato's *Republic*, with the attempt to provide a blue-print for a state which would likewise be immune from change. Hegel's state certainly does not possess that characteristic; it is driven by an inner dialectic; even if he does think that something like the Prussian constitution of the early 1800s is the best so far available, he admits that it contains problems that it is incapable of solving, e.g. the problem of the creation of a pauperised rabble. Judgments about constitutions are necessarily provisional. This, I take it, is the meaning of the famous passage from the *Philosophy of right*: 'When philosophy paints its grey on grey, then is a form of life grown old, and with grey on grey it cannot be rejuvenated but only understood; the Owl of Minerva only begins her flight when dusk is falling.'

The substitution of dialectical logic for metaphysics is equivalent to taking history seriously, at every level of intellectual activity. It involves the replacement of a metaphysical foundation by an end, absolute mind or spirit. This, I would argue, though not in this paper, is not merely the displacement of the same kind of foundation that older philosophers had used to a position at the conclusion of the historical process. A crude teleology argues for an end which is equally the source of all that happens, albeit one that lies in the future. For Hegel, the shape of the absolute end could not be clearly discerned from the present, even though some of its logically necessary features might be discernible. There was no backward causation, and in that sense teleology in the old style was an illusion.

Such a change also alters the way philosophy is to be regarded, and Hegel expresses radical views on this as well. In the *Lectures on the history of philosophy* he says the view of each philosophy refuting the ones that went before looks on the History of Philosophy as: 'a battlefield covered with the bones of the dead, a kingdom not merely formed of dead and lifeless individuals, but of refuted and spiritually dead systems, since each has killed and buried the other'.[3] He, on the contrary, wishes to stress that to study any philosophy is to become acquainted with Philosophy as such.[4] This could be expressed by saying that Philosophy is not a realm of being, but of becoming.

So the failure of commentators to take 'becoming' seriously enough is not a trivial error, but a deep one. It leads inevitably to a falsification of Hegel's aims and a misunderstanding of the role which he gives to Philosophy and hence to a difficulty in understanding the form of his own philosophy, which is thought to be the ultimate system instead of a stage in the advance of the subject. The 'Owl of Minerva' passage in the *Philosophy of right* is one expression of this. Such a view deprives philosophy of its old Platonic ideals, but gives it a non-metaphysical foundation, which is constituted by the efforts of prior philosophers. From our position we can see the necessity of one system being replaced by another, but it would never have been possible to predict the next system on the basis of the one that preceded it. I am aware that these remarks are only programmatic and need to be backed by argument. I believe they can be, but now I must turn to one necessary stage of such an argument, the role of becoming in the *Science of logic*, for if this is grasped it will be easier to understand the radical transformation of philosophy that Hegel undertakes.

To begin it is perhaps best to look at how some commentators have dealt with becoming; McTaggart writes:

> For these reasons I believe that the course of the dialectic would become clearer if the name of Becoming were given up, and the Synthesis of Being and Nothing were called Transition to being Determinate (Uebergang in das Dasein). This follows the precedent set by Hegel in the case of the last category of Measure . . . '[5]

McTaggart's suggested change of name implies that Hegel has been careless in his nomenclature. He does not even ask why Hegel believed 'becoming' an appropriate word to use, or why he thought a stage to be necessary between being and nothing on the one hand and determinate being on the other.

Charles Taylor, like McTaggart, also wants to eliminate 'becoming', implying in his account of the opening dialectic that it can be ignored: 'The upshot of this first dialectic of being and non-being is thus the synthesis of the two in *Dasein* or Determinate Being.'[6] However, on the next page he does discuss becoming, though criticising its introduction as illegitimate:

> But the derivation of Becoming here is not as solid as that of *Dasein*. This is the first, but not the last place in the *Logic* where Hegel will go beyond what is strictly established by his argument, because he sees in the relation of concepts a suggestion of his ontology: here the universality of movement and becoming in the relation of Being and Non-Being. But of course as probative arguments these passages are unconvincing. They fail, as strict conceptual proof, however persuasive they are as *interpretations* for those who hold Hegel's view of things on other grounds.[7]

Taylor's main argument against the validity of introducing becoming is that Hegel is dealing with Kantian categories, so that what has to be shown is that things cannot be thought in certain categories unless other categories also apply:

> And this is what we do show when we establish that *Sein* (Being) can only be applied as *Dasein* (Determinate Being), whereas we have not yet shown the objective necessity of Becoming. This will come when we examine *Dasein* further and see that it is prey to contradiction and hence movement.[8]

However, he does regard becoming as essential to Hegel's ontology, since '*Geist* can only be embodied, and yet the embodiments are all inadequate, and hence disappear to give place to others.'[9] This would seem to apply at a later stage of Hegel's argument. The question of whether Hegel's 'Concepts' are Kantian-type categories will not be discussed here, for there are other reasons to doubt Taylor's view. It seems that he is suggesting that the becoming that is the subject of the first chapter of the *Science of logic* is tantamount to the normal concept of change. If it were so, then it might legitimately be claimed that the establishment of ordinary objects was necessary before bringing it in to the picture. However, given Hegel's emphasis on the fact that it is the pure concepts of being and nothing that are under discussion, it is likely that it is 'pure' becoming which is here at issue. I agree that the notion is problematic, but it seems that Hegel does take care, in the 'Observations', to avoid a reading like that of Taylor. If pure being can be conceived, then, perhaps, it may not be impossible to conceive pure becoming; at least the attempt should be made before it is decided that it has no place.

M.J. Inwood, the most recent British commentator, is equally convinced that there is something wrong with the first chapter of the *Science of logic*, though his diagnosis of the error is different to that of Taylor:

> To speak of the concept of being *becoming* that of nothing is to run together our thinking and the concepts about, or in terms of which, we think. Concepts may of course be closely associated with each other without being identical. The concepts of a husband and a wife, for example, are intimately linked. When we think of, or in terms of, the one we automatically think of, or in terms of, the other. But neither of these concepts becomes or passes into the other. Any movement involved is that of our thinking, following the conceptual pathways provided. It is illegitimate therefore to derive the concept of becoming from those of being and nothing, or indeed from any other two concepts, solely in virtue of the fact that there are conceptual routes from one to the other. Concepts and their interrelationships are static in a way that our thinking is not.[10]

The passage seems to involve a resolute refusal to contemplate what is actually going on in the first chapter of the *Science of logic*. There it is obvious that the concepts 'being' and 'nothing' are not just any connected pair, but play a special role in philosophy. In everyday thought they are not 'intimately linked' as 'husband' and 'wife' are; in their case it is impossible to define one of the pair without also defining the other; that every husband has a wife could be considered an analytic *a priori* truth. In philosophical tradition, pure being could exist, and be understood, without 'nothing', which is why Hegel has to argue for their identity. And it is obvious that he expects his argument to be resisted by commonsense and his conclusion to be found striking. He is aware that what he is doing goes against a great deal of philosophising. More important is the failure to grasp what Hegel is trying to do in the argument; Inwood seems to think that he 'derives' one concept from another; I will say more about this later.

Thus three distinguished Hegelian commentators, two of them contemporary, have difficulty in grasping his arguments about, and the meaning he gives to 'pure becoming'. It is also significant that their objections differ from each other; they do not agree on the nature of the mistake in the first chapter. Hence it is necessary to examine the text to see if it is possible to produce a better interpretation.

Hegel's starting-point, it seems to me, is the unsatisfactory nature of the traditional concept of 'being'. Historically it was thought of as the unchanging ground of change. But if that were the case, the problem arises of how change could come about. If there is to be a dialectic process, or even a temporal one, then being cannot be static. If dialectic essentially involves contradiction, then the starting-point must itself be 'dialectical' or suitable for the operation of dialectic. The same applies to temporality; real time cannot arise from a timeless system. If being is what it is and nothing more, there is no way in which it could change. Similarly, determinate being cannot consist of self-subsistent entities, of 'substances' which depend on nothing outside of themselves in order to exist, for then changes in them would be inexplicable; in Hegel's words:

> Being would not be absolute beginning if it were in any way determined; for if it were, it would be dependent on something else, would not be immediate, would therefore not be the beginning. But if being is indeterminate and therefore the true beginning, it lacks whatever could transform it into an other . . . Parmenides, equally with Spinoza, will not admit progress from being, or the absolute substance, to the negative or finite. (*SL* 107)

There is no way in which time could get a foothold in a static realm of being. In so far as pure being and nothing are considered, there is no room for time. It is possible to make a heroic move and say that time is unreal, though that leaves still the problem of how the illusion itself could arise. It is a consequence of such thinking that one is obliged to accept a Kantian position, in which time is an order imposed by the human mind on appearances of timeless things-in-themselves. If we start from a position of one, or some, necessarily static entities, then time is contradictory, for what is at one moment is not at another. (This is not to deny that there are non-temporal contradictions, e.g. mathematical ones.)

Hegel's attack on metaphysics is directed against the view of it as a super-science which puts us in contact with that which lies behind the veil of appearance, for 'there is nothing behind the curtain except that which is in front of it'. Philosophy, or logic, which is the heir to the old metaphysics, has to deal with an actual world. Hegel is attempting to revolutionise the old conception of philosophy, including that of Kant, and this attempt has to be taken seriously. Here I am not claiming that he is right, only that before we can decide whether he is, we must first grasp what it is that he is claiming. It is easy to make him into just another metaphysician, and there have not been wanting philosophers, both Anglo-Saxon and European, who have done precisely this. And if he is a metaphysician, there are grounds for saying that he is a confused one.

For it does seem *prima facie* nonsense to say that becoming is the unity of being and nothing, and I have previously argued for such a position. One reason why Hegel's argument is hard to grasp is that we tend to think of becoming as a change in some pre-existing determinate entity. The bud becomes the flower; an identifiable object becomes a different one, equally identifiable without reference to its origin. And yet the flower *was* the bud. Objects in nature are constantly changing, though it may only be when the change has reached a certain magnitude that we say the original object has become something else. At this point of the discussion it is tempting to invoke Heraclitus and maintain that all things are in a state of flux. There is no doubt that Hegel, in this opening chapter, had in mind the historical move from Parmenides to Heraclitus, and I suppose it would be possible to read the chapter as advocating the views of the latter in preference to those of the former. However, Hegel could not here be asserting 'all things are in a state of flux' for that presupposes the existence of things, which are first examined in the second chapter at the level of 'Determinate being'.

Failure to grasp what is meant by 'becoming' arises from insufficient attention to Hegel's words, a failure which my earlier criticisms exemplified and which, I think, also affects the three commentators I have cited. However, there is a genuine problem.

Though it may make sense to say 'being is', or, perhaps, 'nothing is not', it is impossible to say 'becoming is' (or 'is not') for that would make it into a static entity; the right mode of expression would seem to have to be 'becoming becomes'. It is hard to see this as meaningful, even if 'being is' is found acceptable. Indeed, it does violence to language, which is why I used to regard the discussion as nonsensical. However, it should be remembered that Hegel expressly admits that language is misused in the context of philosophy; he discusses the notion under the heading of the 'speculative proposition'. 'The paradoxical and bizarre light in which many aspects of modern philosophy appear to those unacquainted with speculative thought is frequently due to the form of the simple judgment when it is used to express speculative results.' (*SL* 103) Given the way in which simple propositions are normally understood, there is a tendency to take being or becoming as the subjects of the propositions in which they occur, and the predicate as expressing the properties which belong to them. This is a mistake when dealing with speculative propositions: 'The nature of the judgment or proposition, which involves the distinction between subject and predicate, is destroyed by the speculative proposition, and the identical proposition into which the former turns contains the counter-thrust against this relation.'[11] In normal discourse both the utterer and the hearer know to what the subject term refers, and give or obtain information from the predicate. In the speculative proposition this priority of the subject is overturned:

> In a proposition of this kind one begins with the word God. This is by itself a senseless sound, a mere name; only the predicate says what he is and fills the name with content and meaning; the empty beginning becomes actual knowledge only in the end.[12]

These remarks must be understood if Hegel is to be. The claim is that in philosophy the problem lies not in what is said about the subject, but in its identification. Hence it is impossible to verify a philosophic proposition by inspecting the subject to see if it does possess the claimed predicate. The subject is, in any case, not the kind of entity which can be pointed to. Verification here involves providing arguments, which is why the truth in philosophy must be the whole. In everyday matters it is possible to grasp a fragment of truth, an isolated fact, because the subject can be identified and the predicate checked without considering any other matter. In philosophy we cannot do this.

Hence the problems which arise when we are faced with propositions like 'being is'. This looks as if it gave us information about 'being'; in Hegel's words, 'it is intended to take being . . . as that which is simply other than nothing' (*SL* 104). We, however, immediately think of concrete examples where there is a difference between being and nothing — there is a distinction between there being drink in the bottle and there being nothing in it. This, however, is a case of determinate being, in which Hegel agrees that there is an important difference, though one that is not of philosophical interest. If we talk of pure being and pure nothing, then the possibility of citing any difference has already been ruled out. In the case of pure being, because it has been a traditional concept in philosophy, we may manage to gain some idea of what Hegel is getting at.

It is not so easy to see what 'pure becoming' might mean, which is why McTaggart thought that there could not be such a concept. It may be that we have been corrupted into accepting pure being as a philosophical term, and as long as we think of it along traditional lines we will find it hard to make sense of pure becoming, which consists of both pure being and pure nothing:

> Becoming is the unseparatedness of being and nothing, not the unity which abstracts from being and nothing; rather becoming as the unity of being and nothing is this determinate unity in which there *is* being as well as nothing. But each, being and nothing, in so far as it is unseparated from its other, is not. They *are*, therefore, in this unity, but only as disappearing and transcended. From the independence (which they were primarily imagined as possessing, they fall to the status of *moments*, which still are distinct, but at the same time are transcended. (*SL* 118)

The final sentence reveals that being, the ostensible subject of the chapter, has lost its traditional status and become a mere 'moment'. As such it can hardly be considered the foundation on which every existent thing rests.

The temptation then is to say that in becoming we have a new entity which itself can serve as a metaphysical foundation. There are several reasons for rejecting this suggestion. First, becoming turns out to be determinate being, not as it were an independent entity, and that it is permanent is denied in the following section, entitled 'Transcendence of Becoming'. Second, and perhaps more important for our purposes, this suggestion would be foreign to the whole drive of the *Science of logic*.

To take these points in order; the next section begins: 'The equipoise of arising and passing away is, first, becoming itself. But this equally collapses into static unity . . . Becoming is a baseless unrest which collapses into a static result.' (*SL*118–9) A static entity could hardly be 'becoming'. Hegel is here wrestling with the problem of how to express thoughts which are, we might say, radically opposed to our commonsense ideas in a language which is designed to accommodate such ideas, is indeed structured by them. A philosopher, faced with the failure of one suggested foundation, typically tries to provide another which will escape the difficulty which destroyed the former. To say all things are in a state of flux looks as if it were a better suggestion, precisely because it is founded on a criticism of the original one. Hegel's object is more radical, to show that the whole procedure is wrongly conceived.

This leads us to the second point; what is under discussion cannot become clear until the whole system has been grasped. Far from there being a fundamental proposition or set of propositions on which the rest of the system is based, it is the system as a whole which is the foundation for each of the propositions which comprise it. It is for this reason that we discover, at the end of the *Science of logic*, that the whole system is a circle, a figure which is continuous, does not start at a particular place. Applied to a system, the implication is that each proposition is determined by its relation to all the rest. In the words of the Introduction to the *Science of logic*:

> But not only the scheme of philosophic method, but also the very concept of philosophy in general belongs to the content of Logic and in fact constitutes its final result; what Logic is, cannot be set out beforehand — on the contrary this knowledge of what Logic is can only be reached as the end and consummation of the whole treatment of the subject. (*SL* 53)

The question then seems to be whether there is a good reason to use the word 'becoming' rather than any other. One possible answer is that Hegel uses it because historically the first philosophical attempt, that of Parmenides, involved the existence of being and the non-existence of nothing, a position which Heraclitus denied by making 'becoming' fundamental. Hegel says this in the *Encyclopaedia*, though it would seem unlikely that his reason is just historical. There is a philosophic point being proposed, and it is connected with the need to bring time into the picture. If the universe were fundamentally static, founded on changeless being, then time would, as I said above, seem to be an illusion. However, Hegel says in the *Lectures on the history of philosophy*:

> The advance requisite and made by Heraclitus is the progression from being as the first immediate thought, to the category of becoming as the second. This is the first concrete, the absolute, as in it the unity of opposites.[13] Thus with Heraclitus the philosophic Idea is to be met with in its speculative form; the reasoning of Parmenides and Zeno is abstract understanding. Heraclitus was thus universally esteemed a deep philosopher and even was decried as such. Here we see land; there is no proposition of Heraclitus which I have not adopted in my Logic.[14]

He also explicitly credits Heraclitus with the introduction of time into philosophy:

> It is because Heraclitus did not rest at the logical expression of becoming, but gave to his principle the form of the existent, that it was necessary that time should first present itself to him as such; for in the sensuously perceptible it is the first form of becoming. Time is pure becoming as perceived, the pure Notion [concept], that which is simple, and the harmony issuing from absolute opposites; its essential nature is to be and not to be in one unity, and besides this it has no other character. It is not that time *is* or *is not*, for time *is* non-being immediately in being and being immediately in non-being: it is the transition out of being into non-being, the abstract notion, but in an objective form, i.e. in so far as it is for us. In time there is no past and future, but only the now; and this is, but is not as regards the past; and this non-being, as future, turns round into being.[15]

It should be noted that time is the sensuous form in which

becoming appears to us, i.e. that becoming is more abstract and more fundamental than time, and, it would seem to follow, than change. By the same token it must be logically prior to determinate being, the realm of objects which do change.

But this does not yet enable us to grasp what becoming is. If I were to give a characterisation of it, I would be tempted to say 'It is not being that becomes but rather the becoming itself that becomes and thus constitutes what used to be thought of as being,'[16] This glosses Hegel's 'being and non-being are abstractions devoid of truth . . . the first truth is to be found in becoming', though it is perhaps equally obscure. The rest of this paper will be an attempt to make this clearer.

If pure being is taken 'immediately' it is empty, and the same applies to nothing, yet what meaning each term has depends on the opposition to the other. In the *Lectures on the history of philosophy*, Hegel says:

> The real fact is that each particular tone is different from another — not abstractly so from any other, but from *its* other — and thus it can also be one. Each particular only is, in so far as its opposite is implicitly contained in its notion. Subjectivity is thus the 'other' of objectivity and not of a piece of paper, which would be meaningless; since each is the 'other' of the 'other' as its 'other', we have here their identity. This is Heraclitus' great principle; it may seem obscure, but it is speculative. And this to the understanding which maintains the independence of being and non-being, the subjective and the objective, the real and the ideal, is always difficult and dim.[17]

This could be glossed as the claim that no word can be understood in isolation, but each must be, at the very least, defined in terms of its opposite or 'other'. However, even if this Saussurean-sounding idea is accepted, it is not obvious that this implies that the two are identical, nor is it clear why their union or identity should be 'becoming'. If this is meant to apply to every word, then it would seem to be false, for not all words are definable in terms of an opposite; some are related to a cluster of other terms, e.g. colour-words. Indeed it could be argued that the majority of words are like this rather than simple opposites. It may be that Hegel, in this quotation, is trying to explain 'Heraclitus' great principle', not the whole of language, i.e. what he gives us is an analogy on which we can come to grasp the identity of being and nothing in becoming.

A passage from the *Science of logic* may help here (Hegel is talking of arising and passing away):

> Both are the same thing, namely becoming; and even when taken as different directions they penetrate and paralyze each other. One direction is a passing away: being passes over into nothing; but equally nothing is its own opposite, a transition to being, that is arising. This arising is the other direction: nothing passes over into being, but being equally cancels itself (*hebt sich auf*) and is rather a transition to nothing, a passing away — they do not cancel mutually, nor one the other externally; each cancels itself in itself, and in itself is its own opposite. (*SL* 118)

Being (or nothing) is the other of its other and in this sense the other of itself. To continue with the example of definition of words: it is not just that we have to define one in terms of the other, but the other is also to be defined in terms of the original, of its other. As we saw in the quotation on p. 65, unless care is taken, the result will itself be static, and hence will not perform the task required. It would seem that 'becoming' cannot be defined in terms of its opposite, for it is its own opposite, which is why it is harder to grasp than being or nothing.

Pure being is inadequate as a philosophic concept, both because it is empty and because it implies changelessness, indeed has normally been so taken. Hence all we can actually conceptualise are determinate beings; we only imagine we have a clear concept of being. But if we merely show the inadequacy of pure being and proceed, by a dialectical move, to determinate being, this too will be static and changeless. But no determinate beings are changeless. Therefore an extra move is required, to allow for the possibility of change and, in due course, of time. Hence becoming has to be introduced at this point. The transition from becoming to determinate being is itself problematic, but there is no space to discuss that here.

What we have in this opening chapter is the attempt to characterise the type of concepts which are required for philosophy, and this involves separating them from empirical ones. However, the claim of dialectic is that even everyday concepts are, when properly understood, similar, in that they do not denote static and timeless entities. This could be expressed by saying that our ordinary language is radically misleading, and, as far as traditional philosophy is concerned, this has been exemplified in a misunderstanding of the word 'being'. Philosophy has forgotten Heraclitus, who made moves which were correct in principle. Thus the argument of the *Science of logic* depends on the introduction of becoming at this early stage. However, as I said earlier, I am not here concerned to investigate the truth of the claim, only to show what Hegel argued and why it is impossible to ignore becoming in any treatment of his thought.

Notes

1. There is a problem in whether to use capital letters in the case of these three words. I have kept to lower case throughout my discussion, and have also altered all quotations from Johnston and Struthers to conform to my usage.
2. Page references are to Hegel's *The Science of logic,* (*SL*), trans. W.H. Johnston and L.G. Struthers (London 1929). I have occasionally modified their version.
3. G.W.F. Hegel *Lectures on the history of philosophy*, trans. E.S. Haldane (London, 1892), p. 17.
4. Ibid., p. 18.
5. J.M.E.M. McTaggart, *A commentary on Hegel's logic* (Cambridge, 1910), p. 20.
6. C. Taylor, *Hegel* (Cambridge, 1975), p. 232.
7. Ibid., p. 233.
8. Ibid., p. 233.
9. Ibid., p. 232.
10. M.J. Inwood, *Hegel* (London, 1983), p. 310.
11. Preface to *Phenomenology*, trans. W. Kaufman, in *Hegel* (London, 1965) p. 444.
12. Ibid., pp. 393–4.
13. This sentence is a literal translation of the German; I presume it should conclude with 'exists'.
14. Hegel *Lectures on the history of philosophy*, p. 279.
15. Ibid., pp. 286–7.
16. The sentence is adapted from G. Deleuze, *Nietzsche and Philosophy* (London, 1983), p. 48, though he is talking of Nietzsche's Eternal Return.
17. G.W.F. Hegel *Lectures on the history of philosophy*, p. 285.

4

Sense and Meaning in Hegel and Wittgenstein

David Lamb

The forming of the five senses is a labour of the entire history of the world down to the present. (K. Marx[1])

Hegel and Wittgenstein

For many years it was supposed that Ludwig Wittgenstein's contribution to philosophy was an unprecedented phenomenon, exploding into the Anglo-Saxon tradition with revolutionary ideas unparalleled in the history of Western thought. Of late, however, some scholars have attempted to show that, far from being unique, Wittgenstein's contribution belongs to a current of thought that can be traced back to Kant via Schopenhauer.[2] But the thesis that there is a close affinity between the later Wittgensteinianism and Hegel on meaning and sense-certainty has received surprisingly little attention.[3] For precisely because Wittgenstein was never a Hegelian, it would be an ironic note indeed if the philosophical revolution, through the later Wittgensteinianism, were to issue into and newly confirm the old Hegelian or neo-Hegelian tradition against which it originally defined itself. The considerable convergence of the later Wittgenstein, as commonly understood, and the Hegelian understanding of language thus deserves to be spelled out more fully. It is striking that the two philosophers argued very similarly against the sensory realist account of the relation between language and reality.

The following passage by Russell can be considered as typical of a theory of language which they repudiated:

The meaning of an object-word can only be learnt by

70

hearing it frequently pronounced in the presence of the object. The association between word and object is just like any other habitual association, e.g., between sight and touch. When the association has been established, the object suggests the word, and the word suggests the object.[4]

The underlying assumption here is that the meaning of a name must be identical with the bearer of that name, which Wittgenstein attributed to a tendency to 'sublime the logic of our language' connected with the conception of naming as an 'occult process', a '*queer* connection of a word with an object' caused by the philosopher's attempt to 'bring out the relation between name and thing by staring at an object in front of him and repeating a name or even the word "this" innumerable times' (*PI* 38). To free the philosopher from this picture he points out that certain things can happen to the bearer of a name which need not happen to the name itself. The bearer of the name 'NN' may die, but this does not imply that we cannot meaningfully use the name 'NN' again. Wittgenstein's point (*PI* 38–43) is that the meaning of a name is determined by the rules of usage, not by the thing it refers to. Having rejected the empiricist ontology, Wittgenstein anchored his inquiry to the concept of a 'form of life'. Hegel for his part rejected what the atomists have said about the foundation of language by showing how participation in the concrete universal (objective or intersubjective spirit) is epistemologically prior to the alleged immediate certainty of sensory particulars. 'This bare fact of certainty, however, is really and admittedly the abstractest and poorest kind of truth' (*PG* MM 82/M 149). Like Wittgenstein, Hegel draws attention to the fact that sense experience itself is dependent upon a wealth of institutionalised practices, culture and training, and to deny this is to engage in a most 'abstract' enterprise which illicitly ignores the system of relations in which a reference to sense immediacy is made. Hegel therefore opens the first chapter of *The phenomenology of spirit* with an examination of the empiricist account of language and knowledge.

The title of the first section, 'Sense-Certainty: The This and Meaning', draws attention to the kind of assumption that Wittgenstein detected in the logical atomism of Russell. This assumption, which can be called 'the proper name theory of language', is expressed by Russell as follows:

The only words that one does use as names in the logical

sense are words like 'this' or 'that'. One can use 'this' as a name to stand for a particular with which one is acquainted at the moment . . . It is an *ambiguous* proper name, but it is really a proper name all the same, and it is almost the only thing I can think of that is used properly and logically in the sense I was talking of for a proper name.[5]

What Hegel does, however, is different in certain respects from Wittgenstein, in that Hegel actually takes this view more seriously. To understand why he does this is to understand something very important about the nature of his phenomenological method. What he does is ask us to imagine that we really do come to learn about the world in the way that Russell's atomism would require. For example, the distinction between the 'I' that experiences and the datum of sense-immediacy experienced is presented strictly as it appears in the arguments of traditional empiricism.

It is not only we who make this distinction of essential truth and particular example, of essence and instance, immediacy and mediation; we *find* it in sense-certainty itself, and it has to be taken up in the form in which it is there, not as we have just determined it . . . We have thus to consider the object, whether as a matter of fact it does exist in sense certainty itself as such an essential reality as the certainty-claims; whether its essential concept corresponds to the way it is present in that certainty. We must not, for that purpose, reflect and ponder about it, but only deal with it as sense-certainty contains it. (*PG* MM 83–4/B 150–1)

It is in this way that we can understand Hegel's claim that when embraced consistently doctrines such as Hume's empiricism or logical atomism corroborate, with equal plausibility, their dialectical opponents. This is largely because opposing schools of philosophy, by virtue of the fact that they can enter into a discourse with each other, can be seen to stand in the same metaphysical ground. This point has been well expressed by M. Clark, who says:

It is a primary lesson of Hegel's dialectic that progress by opposition is always to a complementary abstraction that remains fundamentally at the same level of inadequacy. To deny 'categorically' an opponent's views is to affirm that one stands in the same metaphysical ground. Where the distance is too great the luxury of denial is no longer possible.[6]

Accordingly an epistemology which emphasises the object and denies the mind's contribution to the cognitive process, stands in the same metaphysical ground as the solipsism which places an equally one-sided emphasis upon the knowing mind.

Sensory realism

Hegel first considers the naïve realist standpoint according to which: 'The object . . . is the real truth . . . the essential reality, quite indifferent to whether it is known or not' (*PG* MM 84/B 151). A refutation of this position is not attempted; Hegel simply asks whether sense-certainty can fulfil its claim to provide an expression of foundational certainty. 'Sense certainty', he says, 'has thus to be asked: What is the This?' (*PG* MM 84/B 141). When Hegel asks: 'What is the This?' (*PG* MM 84/B 151), he is highlighting the problem of giving an account of language faced by those who ignore the historically conditioned social conventions built into the act of communication and concentrate solely upon ostensive definition. 'This', for Hegel, is analysed in terms of the moments 'Here' and 'Now'. Yet the expressions 'This', 'Here' and 'Now' do not refer to particular places and times but are, in fact, among the most universal of all expressions.

Hegel's approach consists in asking the following question: 'If it is in immediate experience that you find certainty, then tell me what it is that you know.' And if your reply is 'I know there is a table in front of me', you are bringing in other matters. You are making a classification, correctly applying terms in a highly complex system of language. The reply might be as follows: 'Well, language may be highly sophisticated, but what I know for certain is that object in front of me.' And so ultimately the reply is 'This', accompanied by a pointing gesture. Language may be misleading but the gesture is held to be correct since it is somehow in an immediate relationship to the object. This is supposed to be the case with words like 'Here' and 'Now', which are alleged to make an immediate and unique reference to place and time. If I say that this stapling machine is eight inches from

my nose at ten p.m. on 18 March 1987, I have brought in a refer-
ence to the whole history of mankind.[7] So we refine it down to a
'This' of unspecified form — the ultimate in particularity. But
Hegel shows in his dialectic of the 'Now', 'Here' and 'This', that
'This' connotes the ultimate in generality.

The 'Now'

Says Hegel:

> To the question what is the Now? we reply, for example,
> Now is night time. To test the truth of this certainty of sense
> a simple experiment is all we need: write the truth down. A
> truth cannot lose anything by being written down, and just
> as little by our preserving and keeping it. Yet if we look
> again at the truth we have written down, look at it *now*, and
> this *noon-time*, we shall have to say that it has turned stale
> and become out of date. (*PG* MM 84/B 151)

The position challenged by Hegel can be expressed as follows:
The word 'now' stands for a particular, namely the present
moment, but like pronouns it stands for an ambiguous particular
because the present is always changing. The sensory realist
claims to be experiencing an item of sense-certainty at a specific
moment in time, so Hegel says: 'Write it down now, a truth
cannot lose anything by being written down.' But the trouble is
that the content of the 'Now' has gone, it is now night-time.
Implicit in this request is recognition that the mere recording of a
datum of experience cannot serve as an adequate reference since
something, not given in sensory experience, is required. The
exponent of sense immediacy who writes the word 'Now' on a
piece of paper to designate the time of his experience must be
prepared to explain whether his 'Now' is 'determined through
and by means of the fact that something else, namely day and
night, is not' (*PG* MM 84/B 152). Hegel's point is that with time
we make a necessary reference to before or after, which is
impermissible from the standpoint of sense-certainty.

The 'Here'

Hegel's next move is to ask his protagonist to specify what he is referring to; first it is a tree, but when he turns around it is a house.

> The Here is e.g. the tree. I turn about and this truth has disappeared and has changed into its opposite: the Here is not a tree, but a house. The Here itself does not disappear; it *is* and remains in the disappearance of the house, tree, and so on, and is indifferently house, tree. The This is shown once again to be *mediated simplicity*, in other words, to be *universality*. (*PG* MM 85/B 152–3)

The picture is of someone on a roundabout trying to indicate a specific object, but precisely in the absence of a more sophisticated conceptual apparatus his gestures express an ultimate in generality.

Can we conclude that Hegel is denying the possibility of making any intelligible unique reference to particulars on the grounds that whatever we refer to with the words 'Here' and 'Now' and 'This' cannot be isolated because sensory particulars, although they are absolute realities, are in such a state of flux that they can *never* be arrested? This conclusion is, in fact, the other side of the realist coin and is still anchored to the Russellian assumption that language is essentially a process of naming — albeit an inadequate process. This interpretation is advanced by Loewenberg, who suggests that Hegel's argument is based on the Heraclitean thesis that one cannot step twice into the same river, since time and matter are never at rest. Says Loewenberg: 'an instant intuition simply does not endure long enough to permit its datum to be directly indicated: the datum indicated is but a datum of another intuition. How point to an intuited datum without freezing the intuition entertaining it?'[8] On this view it would follow that Hegel is saying that our ordinary concepts of 'Here' and 'Now' and 'This' are somehow inexact — a conclusion drawn by philosophical sceptics. But this is not Hegel's position at all. Like Wittgenstein he holds that language, as the form in which spirit exists, founds sense-certainty rather than being founded by it, and that 'language . . . is the more truthful' (*PG* MM 85/B 152).

To understand what Hegel is doing we must remember that he is thinking himself into the same frame of mind as the sensory realist who treats 'Here' as a proper name for a datum of sense and 'Now' as a proper name for a unit of time. If we take seriously the words 'Now' and 'Here' as proper names many oddities must follow. For example, what are we to make of: 'Do it now, boy!'

It is conceivable that one might point out that it is too late. But in a very queer sense it is always too late to comply with this order, since a portion of time has passed since the utterance of the command. Nevertheless, if one replied that it was already too late because 'Now' has passed, it would be treated as the sort of triviality one might expect from a 'smart Alec' schoolboy. 'Do it now, boy!' means 'get cracking', 'don't linger', and so on. No specific time is referred to. If the boy replied with 'which now?' his remark would be treated by his teacher as either trivially impudent or completely unintelligible.

But Hegel's point is that the question 'Which now?' or 'Which here?' has a very important philosophical significance when put to a philosopher who claims that space and time can be interpreted as a series of sensory 'Heres' and 'Nows'. It reveals that there is something odd about his conception of 'Here' and 'Now'. So while in ordinary usage 'Which Now?' or 'Which Here do you mean?' has no meaning at all, it does serve as a very important corrective to the postulates of an atomistic theory of knowledge.

The 'This'

A similar argument applies to Russell's 'This'. When a philosopher speaks of 'This' as a proper name, and maintains that pointing is logically prior to language, it is permissible, if he points to a pencil, to ask 'Which pencil?' — even if it is in immediate proximity to his finger. For if it is said that pointing and naming precede general grammatical rules and cultural conventions, the isolated act of pointing and naming should be sufficiently clear. We reveal the falsehood of the assumption by asking 'Which pencil?' feigning ignorance of all the conventions and grammatical rules involved. Hegel's argument here is echoed in Wittgenstein's attitude towards the commonsense realism of Moore.[9] Referring to Moore's claim to know that he has a body Wittgenstein says: 'If somebody says "I have a body", he can be asked "Who is speaking here with this mouth?"' (*OC* 244). This is exactly what Hegel has in mind when he says: 'it is reasonable that the person making this demand should say what "this thing" or *what "this I"*, he means: but to say this is quite impossible' (*PG* MM 87/B 154). And:

They 'mean' this bit of paper I am writing on, or rather, *have* written on: but they do not say what they mean. If they really wanted to say this bit of paper which they 'mean', and they wanted to say so, that is impossible, because the *This* of sense, which is 'meant', cannot be reached by language, which belongs to consciousness, i.e., to what is inherently universal. (*PG* MM 91/B 159)

Hegel's procedure consists of taking the sensory realist seriously showing how he cannot make a unique reference, cannot indicate what he means. Whatever he points to when he says 'This, here, now' we can always ask 'What, where, when?' This is because his words and gestures are incomplete outside of institutions which in turn presupposes a highly complex learning system. Hegel is very close here to Wittgenstein's view that words only have a meaning within the context of a system of general rules. But this is the very opposite of the claims of a consciousness to whom pointing and gestures are the grounds upon which the edifice of language is built, since it now appears that we cannot have the grounds without the language.

Having failed to find satisfaction in the objective account of the foundations of language, the inquiry now shifts to the subjective account. In this transition Hegel demonstrates how easily abstract philosophical doctrines pass into their opposites, how realism passes into subjective idealism and solipsism.

Solipsism

Hegel effects the transition from the object to the subject by means of the term '*meinen*', which has a more personal connotation than '*bedeuten*'. The object referred to is meant in the sense of 'my meaning'. The most accurate equivalent word would be the old English verb 'to opine'. Thus having failed to indicate a particular of sense-certainty Hegel's protagonist is portrayed in terms of a subjective appeal. We can imagine him saying 'Well, at least I know what I mean by this', pointing affirmatively. As Hegel says: 'the truth now rests in the object as my (*meinem*) object, or lies in what I mean (*meinen*); it is because I know it. Sense certainty is thus indeed banished from the object, but is not yet done away with; it is merely forced back into the I' (*PG* MM 86/B 153).

Realism and solipsism have traditionally been held to stand in strict antithesis to each other. But Hegel, like Wittgenstein, held that commonsense realism cannot provide an adequate refutation of solipsism. When Wittgenstein puts into the mouth of the solipsist the words, 'It is essential that the other should not be able to understand what I really mean' (*BB* 65), he is revealing that the solipsist is operating with a logical exclusion which the realist misunderstands as a lack of information. For Wittgenstein the refutation of solipsism must consist in showing that solipsism is unthinkable. Hegel's argument is similar to Wittgenstein's, and it is clear, from the way he depicts solipsism as a development of realism, that the refutation of solipsism must also entail a refutation of realism as well.

In what sense do solipsism and realism coincide? For the realist a solipsist is one who claims that another's experience is problematic. His response is to argue that no difficulty exists since we know, by analogy with our own experience, what another person experiences. It is a matter of common sense, he would say, that other people experience what I experience. But here the realist has failed to grasp that an appeal to one's own experience does not provide us with a criterion of the identity of experiences that make it possible to ascribe them to others. In order to provide an adequate refutation of solipsism the realist must get at the roots of the solipsist's assumptions, but in doing so discovers that he adheres to them as well as his protagonist. According to Hegel they both share the assumption that the only proper names are 'This', 'Here', 'Now' and 'I'. One might think that on the question of the 'I' they are furthest apart. For example:

a. There is no 'I' only a bundle of sensations! (Hume)
b. You cannot be certain of anything other than your own mind. (Descartes)

Yet for Hegel these are two variations on the same theme. One can either say the mind does not exist or the world does not exist. One is simply going backward and forward in the same dialectic. We have seen how the 'Here', 'Now' and 'This' of Hume or Russell either refer to nothing or everything; so it is also with the 'I' of the solipsistic idealists. Cartesians assume that the expression 'I' has a referent, but the kind of referent it has for the solipsist is very much the same as the 'This' for the realist. What,

78

for example, is this 'I' that is given independent of the world's existence? Suppose we admit the possibility of knowing only one's own existence; what description could anyone offer of such an experience? Hegel puts the following words into his protagonist's mouth: 'I am directly conscious, I intuit and nothing more, I am pure intuition; I am — seeing, looking' (*PG* MM 89/B 155). In this way we arrive at the assertion of pure immediacy. But a creature in this state cannot say anything; cannot classify, compare, or individuate, but would be in a state of pure solipsism, akin to what Santayana once described as 'solipsism of the moment'.[10] Such a creature would not even know what the 'I' was, since it would have no relevance.

It is interesting to compare the solipsism of the sensory realist with the tendency towards solipsism in Wittgenstein's *Notebooks*. In the *Notebooks* when Wittgenstein tells us that 'Things acquire "significance" only through their relation to my will' (*NB* 84), he is thinking of naming as an essentially *private* activity. In his later writings it is clear that Wittgenstein had detected, like Hegel, the common characteristics of solipsism and sensory realism. In the *Blue and Brown Books* Wittgenstein argues that both solipsism and realism are bound up with the phenomenon of *staring*; from a fixation with static objects: 'Thus we may be tempted to say "Only this is really seen" when we stare at unchanging surroundings, whereas we may not at all be tempted to say this when we look about us while we are walking' (*BB* 66). If we remember that the realist was snared into solipsism by trying to give a determinate account of referring, claiming that sensations were 'my own' (*meinen*) as he pointed affirmatively, we can see a connection between Hegel and Wittgenstein who both maintain that solipsism has its source in certain assumptions peculiar to the standpoint of sense-certainty, that one can 'bring out the relation between name and thing named by staring at the object in front of him and repeating a name or even the word "this" innumerable times' (*PI* 38).

Once we think of how tables, chairs, or stoves, look to oneself we are halfway towards thinking of a world that belongs to oneself alone. Once started on the search for the absolute determinacy of sense it is not long before one concludes with Russell that language is too vague to capture a precise reference, that only I know what I mean by 'This'. And so, like Hegel's protagonist, the early Wittgenstein adopted a psychological approach to the problem of correlating a name with its bearer, attempting to indicate what *he meant*, by pointing affirmatively and saying: '*Ich weiss, was ich meine; ich meine eben DAS*' (*NB* 70). With uncanny similarity to the sensory realist in Hegel's example with the piece of paper, Wittgenstein imagines himself telling someone that 'the watch is on the table'. But, given the vagueness of language, how can he make a unique reference to it?

> To anyone that sees clearly it is obvious that a proposition like 'This watch is lying on the table' contains a lot of indefiniteness, in spite of its form's being completely clear and simple in outward appearance. So we see that this simplicity is only constructed. (*NB* 69)
>
> It is then also clear to the *uncaptive* mind that the sense [*Sinn*] of the proposition 'The watch is lying on the table' is more complicated that the proposition itself. (*NB* 69)

Wittgenstein imagines telling someone 'The watch is lying on the table' (*NB* 70), but now his interlocutor asks him what he means by 'lying'. How can he fix the exact determination of this term? Only by saying '"I know what I mean; I mean just THIS." pointing to the appropriate complex with my finger' (*NB* 70).

The assumption of both solipsism and sensory realism is that what is sensed is in some way private to the perceiver. By challenging the solipsist to provide a content to his experience — namely his experience of himself — Hegel is challenging the very roots of solipsism, for in the absence of a public language the solipsist cannot specify 'what this "I" refers to' (*PG* MM 87/B 154). What Hegel is trying to say is illuminated by P.T. Geach who has argued that the use of the personal pronoun is a public activity. But what of those occasions when we use the term 'I' in soliloquy? When used in soliloquy it is not used in order to direct one's attention to oneself. When I say to myself 'I am in a muddle', I am not referring to myself; in such cases the term 'I' is superfluous. In soliloquy we can quite easily express our thoughts without use of the first person pronouns. As Geach puts it:

> The use of 'I' in such soliloquies is derivative from, parasitic upon, its use in talking to others; when there are not others, 'I' is redundant, and has no special reference. 'I am very puzzled at this problem' really says no more than 'This problem is puzzling' (*demonstratio ad intellectum* again).[11]

Unless we are familiar with general and interpersonal rules of linguistic use, with what Hegel calls the 'universal', we cannot make use of the first-person personal pronoun. The cogito held by Descartes as the foundation of knowledge and certainty, is parasitic upon a mastery of language and the possession of intersubjective knowledge. Remove language and we cannot arrive at the concept of an 'I' that thinks.

In so far as knowledge and language are held to be reducible to the contents of particular experiences indicated by the 'proper names' 'This', 'Here', 'Now' and 'I', there is little distinction between sensory realists and solipsists. Both remain in the same metaphysical ground merely emphasising different aspects of an assumption which Hegel depicts as common to both of them; namely that thought and language can be reduced to reference to and denomination of particulars given in immediacy. Hegel expresses this connection by saying that both 'the "object" and the "I" are universals' (*PG* MM 87/B 155). We cannot isolate the 'I' or the 'This' and present the act of referring to and naming either of them as the foundation of language and thought. It is necessary to bring in something else. How much else, however, is a matter that cannot be settled by abstract speculations. The very attempt to isolate and refer to an ultimate particular causes it to evaporate into everything.

The adequacy of language

Hegel's protagonist has one avenue left open to him: if he is to retain the cognitive primacy of individual sense-experience over 'the universal', that is, over general grammatical rules expressing a particular life-form, he must deny the adequacy of language. So the question arises, why not condemn speech rather than sense-immediacy? The objection is that looking at language is really an all too indirect way of looking at the world. Might it be the case that language can never depict the world correctly, that language may somehow distort what is given in experience? This is how the problem appears to Loewenberg, who objects to 'Hegel's cavalier treatment of the claims for sense-certainty' which demands the 'sacrifice of experienced intimacy to descriptive propriety'.[12] 'Why disparage sense experience?', asks Loewenberg,

Why not challenge instead the hegemony of thought? He who silently enjoys the sensible qualities of things cannot be charged with contradiction unless he stoops to argue. And if induced to argue, and to argue absurdly, he may refuse to graft upon his intuition the equivocations attending his words.[13]

But against Loewenberg it is important to note that the onus is on Hegel's protagonist to prove the inadequacy of language. He who does not argue forfeits his ability to convince. It is clear that language cannot be criticised in words, for:

Language is the more truthful; in it we ourselves refute directly and at once our own 'meaning'; and since universality is the real truth of sense-certainty, and language merely expresses *this* truth, it is not possible at all for us even to express in words any sensuous existence which we 'mean'. (*PG* MM 85/B 152)

Hegel does not accept, as Loewenberg does, the existence of a strict dichotomy between experience and speech. Instead he draws attention to the importance of language in the acquisition of even the most elementary knowledge, and he insists that language, being general or universal, precedes and orders the individual's sense-experience, a view which is matched in Wittgenstein's: 'It is only in a language that I can mean something' (*PI* p. 18 footnote). The limits of language are the limits of human knowledge or sense experience. There is nothing about sense impressions which can be known or even meant without being expressible in language. One cannot mean something that one knows independently of language, since 'language as the universal simply expresses the knowing activity of consciousness itself' (*PG* MM 91–92/B 159). Hegel's protagonist is not prevented from saying what he means because language is inadequate, but because his meaning, as unsayable, is inadequate as meaning. Any knowledge which language is inadequate to express is itself inadequate to qualify as knowledge. Raymond Plant takes up a position similar to Loewenberg's when he writes: 'Hegel's assertion of the harmony between thought and being, despite his dialectical virtuosity in an attempt to prove the contrary, remains a presupposition which is neither rationally checkable nor disprovable.'[14] Against this view James Ogilvy argues:

The very idea of a global 'check' that would compare our

logic against the real is superseded by the realization that every conceivable 'check' is and always has been *internal* to the self-developing process that links the history of knowledge with the equally historical development of what qualifies as an object of knowledge.[15]

In this way we find that the demand for a foundational 'check' on language falls into the logical circle of 'knowing before you know', which Hegel attributed to the Kantian critique of knowledge. For if it were true that a 'global check' were possible how could we substantiate this claim? What kind of language would do the job? Parallels can be drawn between Hegel's objection to Kant's critical method and Wittgenstein's later criticism of the *Tractatus*. In the *Tractatus* Wittgenstein had attempted to discover the 'general form of a proposition' but ostensibly failed to resolve the same logical circle which Hegel saw in the Kantian critique, namely, that one must use language (knowledge) in order to examine language (knowledge). The attempt to express the essence of language cannot be expressed in language. The reason why Wittgenstein eventually took it upon himself to describe the actual use of language is not unrelated to Hegel's decision, in the *Phenomenology*, to describe the actual experience of knowledge.

Another way of resolving the charge that language is inadequate is to ask whether there is an essential difference between finding out what a word means and finding out about the world. In an essay related to the present topic Stanley Cavell asks us to imagine a situation where

> you are in your armchair reading a book of reminiscences and come across the word 'umiak'. You reach for your dictionary and look it up. Now what did you do? Find out what 'umiak' means, or find out what a umiak is? But how could we have discovered something about the world by hunting in a dictionary? If this seems surprising, perhaps it is because we forget that we learn language and learn the world *together*, that they become elaborated and distorted together, and in the same places.[16]

Mastery of language and knowledge of the world are here one and the same activity. For this reason Hegel's argument is not faulted on an alleged contradiction between sense-certainty and speech. When Hegel says that 'language as the universal simply expresses the knowing activity of consciousness' he means that in the absence of language we could have no knowledge of our sense impressions. In this respect he shares with Wittgenstein the belief that sensations are linguistically rule-governed and are not ultimates upon which language is allegedly founded. Hegel goes to greatly exaggerated lengths to justify his conclusion that *sinnliche Gegenständen* are not the ultimate and absolute constituents of reality. In a rather bizarre example he first appeals to the classical wisdom of the Eleusian mysteries, of Ceres and Bacchus, and he concludes by invoking the behaviour of 'dumb animals, who fall upon and devour these objects,' to illustrate his claim that: 'all nature proclaims, as animals do, these open secrets, these mysteries revealed to all, which teach what the truths of the things of sense really are' (*PG* MM 91/B 159). Such examples, though seemingly ludicrous, testify to the seriousness with which Hegel combats the claim to ground the foundations of human knowledge in particular items of sense-experience.[17] His seriousness can be appreciated if we remember that he is combating a tendency towards scepticism which lurks within the sense-certainty. Referring to his contemporaries, Hegel says: 'Of a metaphysics prevalent today which maintains that we cannot know things because they are absolutely shut to us, it might be said that not even the animals are so stupid as these metaphysicians; for they go after things, seize and consume them' (*Enz.* 246).

Language games

There is a very close connection between Hegel's sensory realist and Wittgenstein's famous example of the builders in the *Investigations*. In both cases a faulty account of language and reality is exposed. Wittgenstein's imaginary builders in fact cannot be speaking a language, for a 'language' confined only to the occupational aspect of their total life is not really a language at all.[18] Wittgenstein's builders, his 'imaginary' languages consisting only of orders and so on, like Hegel's exposition of sense-certainty, are designed to show that the existence of language and society are necessary preconditions for any particular language-game. The words 'Slab', 'Block' and 'Beam' of Wittgenstein's builders and Hegel's 'Here', 'Now' and 'This' are not ultimates of language to which we add 'Please bring me a Slab, here now.' Instead, they depend upon an entire system of human language and culture.

To disregard human culture, as Hegel and Wittgenstein encourage their respective protagonists to do, is to commit oneself to solipsistic silence. For this reason a language game is given sense by virtue of the possible use of its expressions in other (albeit different) language games. This is essentially Wittgenstein's point when he says 'I want to say: it is essential to mathematics that its signs should also be used in civil life' (*RFM* IV.2). Unless the conclusions we draw in a piece of mathematical reasoning (or any other discipline) can have some bearing on other aspects of our lives, it cannot be called a meaningful piece of reasoning. That the component expressions can be used elsewhere gives them a point in mathematics. There is a parallel between the way in which mathematics depends upon an external use of its expressions and the way in which the language of the builders, or Hegel's exponent of sense-certainty, depends on an external use of their expressions; and sense-certainty's naming game of 'This', 'Here' and 'Now' cannot get started unless the expressions used within it already have meaning outside of it. For both Wittgenstein and Hegel there are no foundations for language and no foundational language games.

Their alternative to a reductionistic foundational approach is to describe the uses of language as it is employed within a given system of knowledge. This is what is done in Hegel's *Phenomenology* and in Wittgenstein's later writings: 'it is important to emphasize . . . that knowledge is only real and can only be set forth in the form of science, in the form of a system' (*PG* MM 27/B 885). But this bears comparison with the position Wittgenstein took when he gave up the foundational approach of the *Tractatus*. By *On Certainty* his position had converged with Hegel's own: 'When we first believe anything, what we believe is not a single proposition, it is a whole system of propositions. (Light dawns gradually over the whole)' (*OC* 141). And matching Hegel's 'the truth is only realized in the form of a system' (*PG* MM 28/B 85) is Wittgenstein's assertion that 'it is not the single axioms that strike me as obvious, it is the system in which the consequences and premises give one another *mutual* support', (*OC* 142. See also 143, 144, 410). An understanding of the truths expressed by language is not dependent upon there being a realm of foundational certainty, but upon a wealth of knowledge about human life-forms. Here Wittgenstein and Hegel are in agreement. But Hegel claimed to show that what Wittgenstein called 'life-forms' have histories and pre-histories. A *deeper* understanding of language may depend on a wealth of knowledge about human history.

Taking perception seriously

In the chapter on perception Hegel turns to a more sophisticated version of realism, which he characterises as 'Perception'. The title of this chapter signifies a typical Hegelian pun: *Warhnehmung*, which literally means 'to take truly', implies taking truly that which is given in sense experience. In an even deeper sense it reflects one of the guiding principles of Hegel's phenomenological method: to take truly, or seriously, the presuppositions which underpin philosophical standpoints — until they collapse under the weight of their inner contradictions.

Among the traditional problems about perception are the following: should we regard the Perceiver as playing a major or minor part in the activity of perception? Should we analyse perception in terms of the subject or the object of perception? Does the object's being depend on it being perceived? Or does it exist independently of a system of mediations? The tension Hegel uncovers, when he depicts perception as the 'taking truly of the sensuously given', is between perception-as-passive-reception and perception-as-an-act-of-knowledge.

From the standpoint of sense-certainty the choice was between self-contradiction and solipsistic silence but the domain of *Wahrnehmung* is a public one. Unlike sense data, percepts are describable in terms of perceivably determinate properties. Perceiving, herein depicted, is characterised in terms of a relationship between a subject that passively receives and an object that is perceived. From this standpoint the truth lies in the object; it matters little whether it is perceived, the act of perceiving being what Hegel depicts as a 'non-essential moment'.

So what, asks Hegel, is this object confronting the Perceiver? According to the assumptions of commonsense realism the Perceiver 'takes truly' what is perceived and passively receives what is given in experience. Hegel's approach consists in asking the Perceiver-philosopher to demonstrate the ability to passively record the given object — in this case a cube of salt — as a thing endowed with determinate properties since, according to the Perceiver, 'the object shows itself by so doing to be a *thing with many properties*' (*PG* MM 94/B 162). What is seen is sense-dependent, but what the senses reveal are universally recognisable properties.

> The sense element is in this way itself still present, but not in the form of some particular that is 'meant' — as had to be in the case of immediate certainty — but as a universal, as that which will have the character of a *property*. (*PG* MM 94/B 163)

But, asks Hegel, given that we perceive universal properties and not particular unrelated sense-impressions, are we any better off than the standpoint of sense-certainty? Unless we know something over and above these properties we could not understand which properties belong to the object and which do not; we would lack a principle of classification. These universal properties, then, being 'self-related, are indifferent to each other, each is by itself free from the rest . . . they interpenetrate without affecting one another' (*PG* MM 94–5/B 164). As such, the universal qualities perceived are themselves abstractions, which Hegel characterises as 'Thinghood' (*Dingheit*), and are 'nothing else than the Here and Now as This on analysis turned out to be, viz., a simple togetherness of many Heres and Nows' (*PG* MM 95/B 164).

Hegel's treatment of the perceiving standpoint is similar to his treatment of sense-certainty. He says to the Perceiver: 'Here is a piece of salt, but you cannot call it a piece of salt since, according to you, it is merely a collection of universal qualities which, as you say, "do not affect each other in their interpenetration". There before you are the properties of whiteness, tartness of taste, and cubical shape. But you, who recognise these universal properties, must tell me what principle you employ to unite these manifold distinct properties in one object. Moreover, if as you say, the "many determinate properties are utterly indifferent to each other, and are entirely related to themselves alone, they would not be determinate; for they are so, merely in so far as they are *distinguished* and related to others as opposites"' (*PG* MM 95/B 165). In other words, we cannot learn of properties in isolation from other items of knowledge. To recognise a property involves, amongst other things, knowing how to recognise what it is not. This is essentially the point that post-Wittgensteinian philosophers have made when they argue that knowing the concept 'red' is bound up with knowing what is not red; that there is not another realm of negative facts — as Russell and the naïve realists thought — which can be learnt in addition to the 'facts' standing in immediate relationship to the senses. As Geach says: 'Surely what I exercise in using the term '"not red" is simply the concept *red*; knowing what *is* red and knowing what *is not* red are inseparable — *eadem est scientia oppositiorum.*'[19]

If someone claims to have knowledge of an object by virtue of its properties something should be known about the properties it does not have. But these properties are not given in the immediacy of perception and are external to the simple consciousness depicted in the present phenomenal standpoint. Yet for a percept to possess determinate properties in its own right it must possess properties which are not given in passive perception, since only in the possession of them can it enjoy independence. This is the paradox of the Perceiver's standpoint. But Hegel, who takes seriously the standpoint of the Perceiver, must assume that knowledge of a thing and its properties is exactly as the Perceiver claims.

Given Hegel's method, what is the criterion for deciding whether the reported perceptions are correct? If the object, on this view, is 'true and universal' then might it not be the case that 'consciousness apprehends the object wrongly and deceives itself'? (*PG* MM 97/B 167) Hegel allows the Perceiver to be aware of this possibility, but points out that the only possible criterion could be 'self-sameness', and that as the data before him is diverse the procedure will consist of 'relating the diverse moments of his apprehension to one another' in a simple one to one correlation (*PG* MM 97/B 167). However, we should note that because this standpoint assumes the object to be true and independent of a system of mediations the responsibility for the failure to match two experiences together would lie with the Perceiver and not the object. It is in this way that the area of interest in Hegel's example falls upon the subject rather than the object of perception.

Hegel asks the Perceiver 'what sort of experience does consciousness form in the course of its actual perception?' (*PG* MM 97/B 167) What kind of experience is this passive reception of sensory qualities? 'The object, which is apprehended, presents itself as purely "one" and single', replies the Perceiver. 'Moreover I am aware of the "property" (*Eigenschaft*) in it, a property which is universal, thereby transcending the particularity of the object. The first form of being, in which the objective reality has the sense of a "one", and thus was not its true being; and since the *object* is the true fact here, the untruth falls on my side, and the apprehension was not correct. According to my account of the universality of the property I am therefore required to take the objective entity as a community (*Gemeinschaft*) of properties' (*PG* MM 97/B 167). This is the contradictory standpoint of the perceiving consciousness; the object is perceived as both one and many.

So the questions now put to the Perceiver are 'Is the object perceived one or many?' Is it to be considered as a community of properties or as one thing? What is the principle employed to unite these properties into one object? If these properties are universal and could belong to any object how do we know that they belong to this object — this cube of salt — before us? How do we know that the tartness of taste, cubical shape, and whiteness before us belong to one object and to nothing else? Normally of course, these questions would be irrelevant, but it does make sense to ask them of a philosopher who maintains that the activity of perception involves nothing more than the passive awareness of properties sensuously given. One might think that the One-Many argument that Hegel is employing is not a satisfactory refutation of the Perceiver's standpoint. It is obviously not, but then Hegel's method is to present the problems as they occur within the standpoint he is depicting. For this reason Hegel's employment of a sceptical argument of this nature is justified as a short-term measure. The Perceiver's dilemma is: whether to say the thing is one and deny the universality of its properties, holding that they can only belong to this cube of salt, or to assert the universality of its properties and deny that the thing is one? According to Hegel the Perceiver reacts to this dilemma by falling back on the claim that all we see are atomic properties; that the given object is experienced as a plurality of properties. But this position abandons the perceptual standpoint, for now the Perceiver cannot maintain his claim to perceive a concrete object before him, experiencing only a set of disconnected properties. The position forced on him is that of sense-certainty.

Critical realism

Should the Perceiver return to the standpoint of sense-certainty or revise the standpoint of Perception? A return to sense-certainty is ruled out since there is no point in maintaining a discussion with one who retreats to a position already refuted. On the strength of this dilemma the dialectic moves forward, although it should not be forgotten that we are still dealing with the basic assumptions of an object-receptor theory of knowledge.

Seeing the above-mentioned dilemma from the standpoint of the Perceiver, it appears that the latter is aware that he does perceive one object, but the 'evidence of his senses' supports the assertion that what is seen is a community of properties. He therefore resorts to a subjective appeal, a 'return back into consciousness', saying: 'I am aware of the thing as a one, but, if in the course of my perceiving something crops up contradicting that then I must take it to be due to my reflection' (*PG* MM 99/B 169). That is to say, perceiving the object as a many is due to the diversity of the sense-organs; this solitary cube of salt is in point of fact, 'merely white to our eyes, also tart to our tongue, and also cubical to our feeling, and so on' (*PG* MM 99/B 170). With this line of reasoning we can conclude that the object's diversity comes not from the thing, but from the sense organs. The distinctness of the sense organs entails that the perception of the object will be of its diverse properties. So whilst the Perceiver 'knows' the thing to be one, sense-experience is of its many properties. Hence: 'We are consequently, the universal medium where such elements get disassociated, and exist each by itself' (*PG* MM 99/B 170). On the other hand the one-ness of the object is determined by the unifying process of the mind: 'Putting these properties into a "one" belongs solely to consciousness', says the Perceiver (*PG* MM 101/B 171). It is the transference of the many properties of the thing to the unifying mind which re-establishes the thing's unity and 'self-sameness'. The unifying mind supersedes the disparate sensory properties. What is wrong with this account? In the first place it is held that the salt is objective because its qualities are objective, but the activity of the mind in the uniting of these qualities into a single entity is subjective. There is no criterion for determining whether the object is one; all that has been argued so far is that consciousness holds the properties together. But given that the mind unites them, why should the salt, in itself, be a unity any more than a plurality? Which is more important? And what is the criterion according to which the mind determines the unity or plurality of phenomena? The mind can either unite or separate them with equal plausibility. By what principle does the mind unite the qualities of whiteness, tartness, etc., into a single cube of salt?

Now being of equal plausibility these two alternatives entail a third possibility; if the operation of the mind can reveal divergent results the thing must be capable of adapting itself to antithetical categories. For instance: 'Now I see it as a many, now I see it as a one', just as we can say with duck-rabbit pictures, 'Now I see it as a duck, now a rabbit'. From the standpoint of *Wahrnehmung* if the senses reveal antithetical categories then the object must possess antithetical properties and is capable of changing from a one to a many. Apparently the object exhibits two contradictory modes of being. Otherwise an explanation of how the thing appears independently of actual perception would be required and that would supersede the standpoint of perception. The position which the Perceiver is obliged to accept is that: 'Consciousness thus finds through this comparison that not only *its* way of taking the truth contains the diverse moments of apprehension and return upon itself, but that the truth itself, the thing, manifests itself in this twofold moment' (*PG* MM 101/B 172). If the object is given in this twofold manner the Perceiver must abandon the idea that the mind is the source of the object's unity or plurality. In this way the experiment with critical realism returns once more to the naïve realism of sense-certainty.

The claim to alternate between seeing the object as one or a many has certain affinities with the point expressed in Wittgenstein's example of the duck-rabbit in the *Investigations* II.xi. When considering the report 'Now it is a duck, now it is a rabbit' it is possible to draw two conclusions. We may (i) think that we are interpreting the same data differently, or (ii) think that the object must be changing. But Wittgenstein argues 'seeing as' involves (i) no difference of interpretation, and (ii) no change in the properties of the object, but merely seeing under a different aspect. This, of course, involves a more active consciousness than the perceiving consciousness. The same argument can be applied to the Perceiver's account of the object's plurality and singularity.

Figure 4.1

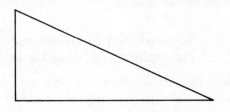

'Now I see it as a one, now I see it as a many' does not involve any change in the object or the perceptual apparatus.

Wittgenstein's point is that seeing implies a grammar and a considerable exercise of the imagination. For example to see the triangle as an object that has fallen over, says Wittgenstein, 'demands imagination' (*PG* II.xi). Similarly he asks, 'Doesn't it take imagination to hear something as a variation on a particular theme? And yet one is perceiving something in so hearing it' (*PI* II.xi). Wittgenstein's argument here can shed light upon Hegel's treatment of the perceiving consciousness. Both Hegel and Wittgenstein stress the internal link between seeing and thinking. Says Wittgenstein: 'Is it a question of both seeing *and* thinking? or an amalgam of the two, as I should almost like to say?' (*PI* II.xi). And 'It is almost as if "seeing the sign in this context" were an echo of thought. "The echo of a thought in sight" — one would like to say' (*PI* II.xi). The point is that there is more to perception than the exercise of the relevant sense organs. Wittgenstein, like Hegel, draws attention to the internal relation between the present, the past and other objects with the object of perception. For example: 'I meet someone whom I have not seen for years; I see him clearly, but fail to know him. Suddenly I know him, I see the old face in the altered one' (*PI* II.xi). In this example the 'dawning of an aspect' does not involve any change in the visual data; instead a connection is made between the present experience and previous ones. This is why Wittgenstein says that 'what I perceive in the dawning of an aspect is . . . an internal relation between it (the object) and other objects' (*PI* II.xi). But according to the Perceiver there is no employment or contribution of knowledge to the act of perception. The Perceiver claims to receive sense-impressions which are assembled into a plurality or a singularity without any contribution other than the senses and the unifying operation of the mind. For that reason, when faced with contradictory accounts of an experience, or changing aspects, he must assert that either the structure of the object is changeable or the senses are deceptive. It is clear that a more sophisticated version of the perceiving standpoint is required.

Sophisticated commonsense: the sophistry of 'in so far as'

This new position attempts to have it both ways; to maintain the advantages of naïve realism from one point of view and the advantages of critical realism from another. In Hegel's terms, the object of this consciousness 'is now the entire process which was previously shared between the object and consciousness' (*PG* MM 101/B 172). The Perceiver, however, becomes a prey for sophistry, betraying himself with a reliance upon the qualifying expression 'in so far as'. The thing is held to be one 'in so far as it is for itself' and not 'for another'. The object is whatever it becomes by virtue of its various relations. For example, 'in so far as it is influenced by this . . . it will exhibit qualities differing from those when it is taken by itself'. Crucial here is the fatuous qualification 'It all depends on . . . ' A thing is held to have no fixed status; what is perceived is relative to different points of view. The cube of salt would have one set of qualities in so far as it is seen from this aspect, and another set of qualities in so far as it is seen from another aspect.

The standpoint of 'Sophisticated Commonsense' might be expressed thus: unity and diversity belong to the thing perceived, but in no absolute fashion. A thing is one in so far as I focus my attention on it, but in so far as I shift my gaze to its many properties I alter my perspective and view it as a medium of disparate universals. The sophistry of 'in so far as' seeks, in this way, to render the contradiction between the one and the many innocuous. For example:

> The thing is, thus, doubtless as it stands (*an und für sich*) selfsame, but this unity with itself is disturbed by other things. In this way the unity of the thing is preserved, and, at the same time, the otherness is preserved outside the thing as well as outside consciousness. (*PG* MM 102/B 173)

Of course this position does express a certain truth, but grasping what is true involves considerable knowledge and informed discrimination, not the sensation-based opinion of the Perceiver. To see something as either a duck or a rabbit or a fallen triangle in a drawing requires a little knowledge and imagination, but the question Hegel raises is not swept aside with references to the imagination's ability to see something *as* something. One might, with the aid of the imagination, see the duck-rabbit as either a duck or a rabbit, but this is not similar to seeing a cube of salt as either a solitary cube or a manifold of unrelated properties. We do not, for example, speak of seeing something as either a cube of salt (with the possible exception of a discussion about artistic representation) or a manifold of unrelated properties. Seeing a cube of salt is not a mere exercise of the imagination on a par with the ability to see either a duck or a rabbit in a picture. This indicates the limitations on Wittgenstein's model of 'seeing as', which is why it should only be employed as an initial step towards breaking the hold of the theory-observation distinction. For if someone speaks of seeing something as something it is always possible to ask 'What is it that is seen as something?' To see something *as* something actually presupposes a neutral fact, the 'thing' independently of how we see it. The duck-rabbit sketch, is such a neutral thing; it is a standard example in psychology, a drawing intended to be seen this way or that according to one's *gestalt*. Similarly the example of the fallen triangle is a drawing on a page which can be seen this way or that. There is something objective on the page to which we can switch our *gestalts*. But these types of *gestalt* switches do not take place with regard to real objects. If we are confronted with a fallen tree across the road we do not see it *as* a fallen tree, we *see* a fallen tree. What else could we see it as? Drawing attention to *gestalt* switches is only helpful in making an inroad into the theory-observation distinction. Kuhn, for example, recognises both the limitations and the value of *gestalt* switch models. Speaking of 'paradigm' switches he remarks how:

> Others who have noted this aspect of scientific advance have emphasised its similarity to a change in visual gestalt: the marks on paper that were first seen as a bird are now seen as an antelope and vice-versa. That parallel can be misleading. Scientists do not see something *as* something else; instead they simply see it . . . Nevertheless, the switch of gestalt, in particular because it is today so familiar, is a useful elementary prototype for what occurs in full-scale paradigm shift.[20]

Whilst an exchange of conceptual frameworks, or in Hegel's terms a transition from one shape (*gestalt*) of consciousness to another, resembles the prototype of 'seeing as', in neither science nor everyday life is it possible to switch backwards and forwards from one to another. No scientist would conceive of switching backwards and forwards from phlogiston theory to oxygen theory. Similarly with the conceptual switch accompanying the Copernican revolution. Says Kuhn:

Looking at the moon, the convert to Copernicanism does not say, 'I used to see a planet, but now I see a satellite'. That locution would imply a sense in which the Ptolemaic system had once been correct. Instead, a convert to the new astronomy says, 'I once took the moon to be (or saw the moon as) a planet, but I was mistaken'. That sort of statement does recur in the aftermath of scientific revolutions.[21]

A change of paradigms involves a commitment to a different conceptual framework which is hard to reverse.

Lavoisier . . . saw oxygen where Priestley had seen dephlogisticated air and where others had seen nothing at all. In learning to see oxygen, however, Lavoisier also had to change his view on many other more familiar substances . . . as a result of discovering oxygen, Lavoisier saw nature differently . . . after discovering oxygen Lavoisier worked in a different world.[22]

Having made the switch it is not possible to return to the previous position without rejecting that very commitment to the new paradigm that made the initial switch possible.

Returning to Hegel's example of the cube of salt, it is now apparent why we cannot switch from seeing it as a cube to seeing it as a manifold of properties. In order to see a manifold of properties it would be necessary to belong to a different way of life, to live, as Kuhn suggests, in a different world. Such a world would then exist in which different visual experiences would present themselves to someone confronted with what in our world is a cube of salt. This world would be radically different from the present and the adoption of its practices would not be a reversible choice: it would be a commitment to a set of practices radically different to those known at present. To be able to alternate between seeing something as a cube of salt and seeing it as a manifold of properties, one would need to live in a world where this difference was relatively unimportant. Only under such circumstances could we speak of *seeing it as* a cube of salt, since the possibility of conflicting accounts would make sense. But in the present world the claim to see it as a cube of salt must be countered with the question 'What else could it possibly be?' What is the point of classifying it as something else? Such a new set of conventions for classifying the world cannot be adopted without committing ourselves to a full-scale rejection of existing practices.

However, the perceiving consciousness has no concern with paradigms, *gestalts*, or conceptual frameworks; he is simply trying to describe the properties before him in so far as he chooses to see this or that aspect. In accord with Hegel's advice we (the phenomenological observers) must make no contribution and, refraining from all talk of paradigms and conceptual frameworks, immerse ourselves in the standpoint of the Perceiver. Hegel therefore asks: if it is merely a question of how one chooses to see the cube of salt then suppose we decide to see it as a unity and therefore ignore its manifold relationships, what then? Suppose one isolates, for exclusive notice, a single object disregarding its relationships; how can one speak of its perceived unity? A thing can enjoy distinction only when it is differentiated from other things. But things cannot be differentiated apart from their properties, and since properties are universal, the lack of a criterion for their unification reappears to plague the assumption of a perceived unity. The Perceiver must therefore introduce a qualification into the account. Hegel depicts him introducing a distinction between 'essential and inessential properties'. The recognition of the former, it is claimed, serves as a criterion for the perception of the object's unity. In this way the 'determinate characteristic, which constitutes the essential character of the thing and distinguishes it from all others, is now so defined that thereby the thing stands in opposition to others, but must therein preserve itself for itself (*für sich*)' (*PG* MM 103/B 174).

This qualification, however, exposes further anomalies in the Perceiver's standpoint. If we attempt to focus attention upon the object's essential property, ignoring all others, how do we then decide what this essential property is? Does this activity render all other properties inessential? Consider the Perceiver's position. He has attempted to isolate a thing by virtue of its essential nature, but the very act of picking out the essential property implicitly reveals that attention has been focused upon other properties outside the immediate field of sensory experience. For example, if the salt's whiteness is singled out it would invoke a grammar of colour concepts. But these are excluded. The attempt to perceive the true nature of a thing by focusing on the perception of its essential nature is ultimately doomed for the very reason that a thing can be essentially itself only if it can be explicitly distinguished from other things.

But what if singularity itself appears to be the essentially determinate property? Hegel is prepared for this objection since he has already argued that exclusiveness is entirely dependent upon otherness. There can be no perception of a thing in its absolute independence:

> It is, however, a thing, a self-existent 'one', only so far as it does not stand in relation to others. For in this relation, the connection with another is rather the point emphasised, and connection with another means giving up self-existence, means ceasing to have a being on its own account. It is precisely through the absolute character and its opposition that the thing relates itself to others, and is essentially this process of relation, and only this. The relation, however, is the negation of its independence, and the thing collapses through its own essential property. (*PG* MM 102/B 174)

For Hegel logical relations have priority over sensory perception. We can bring this out with reference to Wittgenstein's remarks on logical relations. 'If I know an object, I also know all its possible occurrences in states of affairs. (Every one of these possibilities must be part of the nature of the object.) A new possibility cannot be discovered later' (*TLP* 2.0123). To know the nature of an object is to know its internal properties, those properties which an object must possess, and which it is unthinkable that it should not possess. Says Wittgenstein: 'A property is internal if it is unthinkable that its object should not possess it' (*TLP* 4.123). 'If I am to know an object, though I need not know its external properties, I must know all its internal properties' (*TLP* 2.01231). An internal property of a pencil would be its dimension, whereas an external property of a pencil would be its specific colour. If we did not know its internal properties we could not be said to know the object in any sense, whereas a knowledge of its external properties is inessential. Knowledge of an object's internal properties is a conceptual matter. There are properties, for example, that one cannot conceive of a pencil possessing, such as honesty, kindness, intelligence, and so on. Both Hegel and Wittgenstein would find themselves in agreement with the view that unless some conceptual knowledge precedes experience we cannot make a primary identification of the object, since we would lack a knowledge of the relevant properties that one identifies it with. A knowledge of an object's internal (conceptual) properties is necessary for any meaningful perceptual experience. One may acquire a knowledge of its external properties, such as colour, by looking, but a knowledge of the internal properties is logically prior to sense-experience. One does not look at a pencil to see whether it has a size or a colour, as one does to determine the exactitude of its size or colour.

From the epistemological standpoint of the Perceiver there is no conceptual difference between internal and external properties, since the former are assumed to be more properties of the same kind. Like Wittgenstein, Hegel maintains this distinction and recognises that the perceiving consciousness does not. This is why the latter cannot meet Hegel's challenge to individuate a cube of salt from a multiplicity of perceptual sensations. Hegel stresses that there is more to seeing than mere looking, than the mere exercise of the senses, when he says that: 'sensible singleness thus disappears in the dialectical process of immediate certainty and becomes universality', but merely sensuous universality, since the role of the intelligence in the act of perception has not yet been introduced (*PG* MM 104/B 176).

Hegel concludes the dialogue with the Perceiver with a timely polemic against the appeal to commonsense, which was responsible for the tension between unity and plurality which bedevilled the Perceiver's standpoint. In order to avoid the contradictions built into the assumption of perception-as-reception the Perceiver sought refuge behind a cloak of sophistry. The object was held to be one in so far as it was seen as one, but many in so far as it was seen as many. When this failed to provide an adequate account of the object an equally fatuous attempt was made to identify the object in terms of its essential property. But the ultimate irony Hegel sees in the standpoint of commonsense is that on examination the objects of sense are as equally vacuous as the alleged abstract objects of thought which are held to occupy the philosopher's mind in moments of speculative excursion. How, for instance, do we consider the objects of sense without some recourse to conceptual activity? This is the challenge commonsense has failed to answer. Hence:

These empty abstractions of 'singleness' and its antithetic 'universality' and also of 'essence', that is attended with a 'non-essential' element which is all the same 'necessary', are powers the interplay of which constitutes perceptual understanding, often called 'sound commonsense' (*Menschen-*

verstand) which takes itself to be the solid substantial type of conscious life, is, in its process of perception, merely the sport of these abstractions; it is always poorest where it means to be richest. In that it is tossed about by these unreal entities, bandied from one to the other, and by its sophistry endeavours to affirm and hold fast alternatively now one, then the exact opposite, it sets itself against the truth, and imagines philosophy has merely to do with 'things of the intellect' (*Gedankendinge*), merely manipulates 'ideas'. (*PG* MM 105–6/B 176–7)

The appeal to commonsense, far from being the antidote to the abstractions of philosophy, actually involves an even deeper commitment to metaphysical abstractions. Commonsense is no refuge from philosophy; it is only bad philosophy. The main difference between the two camps, says Hegel, is that the philosopher is at least aware that he is dealing with *Gedankendingen* and is therefore 'master of them' (*PG* MM 106/B 177). But the commonsense realist, says Hegel, 'takes them for the real truth, and is led by them from one mistake to another' (*PG* MM 106/B 177). In this way Hegel draws attention to the language employed by those philosophers who appeal to commonsense in order to debunk metaphysics. For in the texts of those who assert the primacy of commonsense one finds a surprising dependence upon philosophical terminology.

Referring to the abstract language of commonsense, Hegel asks us to consider what experience is being described by the expressions 'universality and singleness', and what is this 'essentiality' which is necessarily connected with 'inessentiality'? For in this jargon, says Hegel, lurks a tendency to deceive us about the very nature of experience.

When understanding tries to give them truth by at one time taking the untruth upon itself, while at another it calls their deceptiveness a mere appearance due to the uncertainty and unreliability of things, and separates the essential from an element which is necessary to them, and yet is to be inessential, holding the former to their truth against the latter: when understanding takes this line, it does not secure them *their* truth, but convicts itself of untruth. (*PG* MM 107/B 178)

Because there is more to the activity of perception than the exercise of the senses, the appeal to *Sinnliche Gegenstanden* belongs to the same ghostly realm as their allegedly antithetical *Gedankendingen*.

Notes

1. K. Marx, *Economic and philosophical manuscripts of 1844* (Moscow, Progress, 1959), p. 108. References to Hegel's texts are to *Werke* volumes I–XX edited by E. Moldenhauer and K.M. Michel (Frankfurt am Main, Suhrkamp, 1970), hereafter indicated by the initials MM. As an additional guide each reference to the German text of the *Phenomenology* will be accompanied with a reference to the standard English text and the translator's initial. Abbreviations are as follows: *PG, Phenomenology of mind*, the English text being the J. Baillie edition (London, 1942); *Enz., The encyclopaedia of the sciences*. References to Wittgenstein's texts will be to paragraph numbers unless otherwise stated. They are abbreviated as follows: *PI, Philosophical investigations; BB, Blue and Brown books; TLP Tractatus logico philosophicus; NB, Notebooks 1916; OC, On certainty; RFM, Remarks on the foundations of mathematics*.

2. See A. Janik and S. Toulmin, *Wittgenstein's Vienna*, (London, 1973).

3. Charles Taylor, '*The opening arguments of the* Phenomenology', in *Hegel*, ed. Alasdair MacIntyre (New York, Doubleday, 1972).

4. B. Russell, *An inquiry into meaning and truth*, (London, Allen and Unwin, 1940), p. 64.

5. B. Russell, *Logic and knowledge 1901–1950*, ed. R.C. Marsh (London, Allen and Unwin, 1956), p. 201.

6. M. Clark, *Logic and system*, (The Hague, Martinus Nijhoff, 1971), p. 35.

7. In this respect Marx's criticism of Feuerbach reveals a striking affinity with Hegel's account of sense-certainty: 'He [Feuerbach] does not see how the sensuous world around him is not a thing given direct from all eternity, remaining ever the same, but the product of industry and of the state of society; and, indeed, in the sense that it is a historical product, the result of the activity of the whole succession of generations, each standing on the shoulders of the preceding one, developing its industry and its intercourse, modifying its social system according to changed needs. Even the objects of the simplest "sensuous certainty" are only given him through social development, industry and commercial intercourse. The cherry tree, like almost all fruit trees, was, as is well known, only a few centuries ago transplanted by commerce into our zone, and therefore only by the actions of a definite society in a definite age it has become "sensuous certainty" for Feuerbach.' (*German ideology* (London, Lawrence and Wishart, 1971), p. 61.

8. Jacob Loewenberg, *Hegel's phenomenology: dialogues on the life of mind*, (Illinois, Open Court, 1965), p. 35.

9. See also Wittgenstein's case of a pupil whose reactions to the teaching of arithmetic differ from our own, which he compares with a person who naturally reacts to the gesture of pointing with the finger outstretched by looking in the direction of a line from the finger tip to the

wrist (*PI* 185). For a more definite account of the social nature of gestures one should turn to G.H. Mead, who argues that 'every gesture comes within a given social group or community to stand for a particular act or response, namely the act or response which it calls forth explicitly in the individual to whom it is addressed, and implicitly in the individual who makes it; and this particular act or response for which it stands is its meaning as a significant symbol'. *Mind, self and society* (Chicago, 1963), p. 47.

10. G. Santayana, *Scepticism and animal faith*, (London, Constable, 1923), p. 15.

11. P.T. Geach, *Mental acts* (London, Routledge, 1957), p. 120.

12. Loewenberg, *Hegel's phenomenology*, p. 39.

13. Ibid.

14. R. Plant, *Hegel*, (London, Allen and Unwin, 1973), p. 105.

15. James A. Ogilvy, 'Reflections on the absolute', *Review of Metaphysics*, *vol. xxviii*, no. 3 (March 1975), p. 521.

16. S. Cavell, *Must we mean what we say?* (New York, Scribner, 1969), pp. 19–20.

17. Hegel's example may not appear so bizarre if we consider that many twentieth-century biologists also reject the primacy of sense-certainty in animals. For example: 'One should hesitate, although some do not, to apply such words as "consciousness" or "perception" to an amoeba, for instance, but it is perfectly obvious from the reaction of the amoeba that something in its organization performs acts of generalisation, it does not react to each bit of food, say, as a unique object, but in some way, in some sense of the word, it *classifies* innumerable different objects all within the class of foodstuffs. Such generalisation, such classification in that sense, is an absolute minimal requirement of being or staying alive' (G.G. Simpson, *Principles of animal taxonomy* (New York, Columbia University, 1961), p. 3.

18. Unless we interpret the builders analogy as an attempt to show the impossibility of foundational language games it is difficult to see what light this sheds on the nature of language. Imagine a group of builders only having the expressions 'slab', 'beam' and so on. What sort of building site is this? It is an interesting but scarcely observed fact that on a real building site in the United Kingdom expressions like 'Bricks', 'Sand', 'Mortar', when uttered in isolation, signify moments of tension. They are uttered to make public the fact that someone has failed to maintain a supply of materials. They signify a convention for revealing that someone is not 'up to the job', an informal means of telling the management to dismiss him. It is clear that far from being elementary expressions, in actual usage, 'Bricks', 'Mortar', etc., are permeated with economic and political concepts.

19. Geach, *Mental acts*, p. 25.

20. T.S. Kuhn, *The structure of scientific revolutions*, (Chicago, University of Chicago, 1971), p. 85.

21. Ibid., p. 115.

22. Ibid., p. 118.

5

Hegel on Political Economy

Christopher J. Arthur

In Hegel's main work of political theory, his *Philosophy of right* of 1821, the achievements of the political economists are mentioned with approval. Smith, Say and Ricardo, are cited in this connection. As a matter of fact, Hegel's interest in the subject goes back a long way. We know that, early on, he wrote a manuscript on Steuart, since lost. In the case of Smith we have a passage in a manuscript known as Hegel's *First philosophy of spirit*, of 1803/4, in which he makes reference to Smith's discussion of the division of labour in a pin factory. This is referred to the Basle edition of the English text of *The wealth of nations*, published in 1791. We know that Hegel had such a copy in his library, presumably acquired while he was a tutor in Berne from 1793–97.[1]

It is noticeable that in Hegel's early works the system of needs and labour is given some ontological weight in the foundation of spirit; whereas in the *Philosophy of right* the emphasis is on free-will as socially constitutive, beginning with the positing of property. Another difference is that in the *First philosophy of spirit* we get a terrifying picture of market movements as 'a self-propelling life of the dead',[2] but in the *Philosophy of right* the market appears as a fundamentally rational structure, albeit prey to problems that cannot be solved within it. However, I shall not enter here on a discussion of Hegel's development.[3] I shall be concerned largely with the role of political economy in his mature system, especially in the *Philosophy of right* (cited as *PR* with paragraph numbers).

I

Hegel's political philosophy presents an account of the necessary articulation of the system of right in its developed form. The modern state is to realise this idea in its fullness.

While Hegel understood the appeal of the ancient *polis* in which all the activities of citizens were bound up with the whole ethical life of the state, he recognises equally that there is no going back to this immediate unity of the individual with the political community. History has moved on (*PR* § 185). The right of the individual to be himself as such, and to pursue his own interests, must be respected, even if this moment appears immediately as a negation of the unity of the whole. Hegel calls this sphere of *particularity* the realm of 'civil society' (as distinct from the state proper). He claims that 'the principle of the modern state has prodigious strength and depth because it allows the principle of subjectivity to progress to its culmination in the extreme of self-subsistent personal particularity, and yet at the same time brings it back to the substantive unity' of the whole (*PR* § 260).

The sphere of civil society is, in dialectical terms, the moment of 'difference', while in the exercise of political sovereignty the state achieves its 'identity'.

In the modern world it is within the sphere of civil society that provision for the needs of the people is made. The structure of civil society is primarily economic. Hegel says that political economy 'is one of the sciences which have arisen out of the conditions of the modern world' (*PR* § 189), because only in the modern world has 'the system of needs and labour' differentiated itself from family provision on the one hand, and political relationships and processes, on the other. Needs are met largely through the network of relationships established by private persons holding various goods as private property and contracting with one another to exchange them. As Hegel points out, the bulk of these goods require human labour to produce them (*PR* § 196).

Hegel remarks that in the sphere of civil society as a whole we are dealing with *bourgeois* relations (using the French term itself); but when we deal more specifically with the system of needs the presupposition is simply that of human beings as such, he adds (*PR* § 190).[4]

It is in the context of the discussion of 'the system of needs' that Hegel remarks on the achievements of political economy. He says: 'Political economy is the science which starts from this view of needs and labour but then has the task of explaining mass-relationships and mass-movements in their complexity and their qualitative and quantitative character.' This science is interesting because it extracts from the endless mass of detail 'the simple principles of the thing' (*PR* § 189).

In order to grasp the achievements (and limitations) of the science of political economy as understood by Hegel, we must attend to the nature of its object and its relation to it. We must see if *its* logic is the logic proper to the *object*.

It is germane here to notice that Hegel says of political economy that it shows 'the Understanding effective in the thing and directing it' (*PR* § 189). The standpoint of Understanding is not the standpoint of philosophical Reason; it is the faculty of analysis rather than synthesis; it works with an explanatory framework constituted in terms of binary oppositions rather than dialectical identities. As Hegel is always at pains to stress, real results are obtainable with this approach, e.g. Newtonian science, and all further progress is built upon it. But for him it is only an aspect of the full power of thought, and the full realisation of Reason in the world.

As Knox points out,[5] the explanatory categories of the doctrine of essence in Hegel's *Logic* are those relevant to it, notably those of appearance and essence. In civil society there is precisely a situation in which the appearance of things presents a domain of particularity obscuring any underlying essence. Universal and particular, form and content, fall apart in this sphere. The effort of Understanding is to bring them back into connection, to demonstrate that the universal is at work even in the contingencies of individual transactions guided only by the perception of private interest on the part of those concerned. As Hegel puts it in his lectures: 'to discover this necessary element here is the object of political economy, a science which is a credit to thought because it finds laws for a mass of accidents'. As he comments, it is remarkable that there are such laws 'because at first sight everything seems to be given over to the arbitrariness of the individual'. Significantly, as we shall see, he also observes a parallel in natural science: the solar system 'displays to the eye only irregular movements, though its laws may none the less be ascertained'.[6]

So political economy is a credit to thought because it shows how apparently arbitrary events in its domain are linked together systematically. None the less, there are limits to this totalisation. This is not only because the Understanding is inherently a dualistic form of thought, distinguishing and relating things in terms of the categories of essence, but not synthesising them in a self-identical whole through philosophical conceptualisation. It is also because civil society *itself*, the object of study, forms only 'a relative totality' as Hegel puts it in an illuminating paragraph. Civil society is characterised as the stage of *division* in the articulation of the ethical order: 'to particularity it gives the right to develop and launch forth in all directions; and to universality the right to prove itself not only the ground and necessary form of particularity but also the power standing over it . . . ' Here the unity of the ethical order 'is present only as a relative totality and as the inner necessity behind this outward appearance' of opposed extremes (*PR* § 184).

In his *Encyclopaedia* Hegel actually *defines* civil society in this way — as 'the relative totality of the ties relating independent persons to one another in a formal universality'[7] (*Enz.* § 517). In a relative totality the moments of the whole, e.g. form and content, are merely *related* to one another, not *integrated* in an organic unity.

That Hegel can compare this social structure with that of the solar system shows that the nature of the object itself has a merely mechanical order of regulation — not a self-determining one. Indeed, Hegel in his *Encyclopaedia* calls civil society an 'atomistic' system (*Enz.* § 523). He had already mentioned there that, 'the atomic theory' in political science considers 'the will of the individuals as such is the creative principle of the state' because it believes 'the attractive force is the special wants and inclinations of individuals'. Here the universality of the state is reduced to the relatedness of a social contract (*Enz.* § 98).

In trying to grasp Hegel's attitude to 'the atomic theory' in political science, we have to remember that, though we are not dealing here with atoms but with political animals whose very individuatedness has socio-historical determinants, it is nevertheless the case that in their dealings with one another *in civil society* they *take themselves* to be self-subsistent units, and their relations with others as external to their essence.

In commenting on 'the atomic theory' in political science Marx will later note that 'the egoistic individual in civil society may inflate himself into an *atom*', but nevertheless need directs these egoistic individuals into material intercourse with one another.[8]

Both Hegel and Marx grasp very well that the deficiency of 'the atomic theory' is that it absolutises the standpoint of the individual in civil society without grasping the fact that it is the *social* relations that create such forms of individuality rather than the other way round. A Stock Exchange speculator may be a paradigm of egoism but he is 'a rational man' only according to the standards of a social order that makes the fulfilment of need dependent on such mediations as a Stock Market.

The difficult point philosophically in evaluating the logic proper to the system is to do justice both to the 'objective validity' (Marx) of the categories of political economy, and to its conditionality as the system's own self-presentation.

When Hegel says obscurely that 'the Understanding is effective in the object' he might mean that the categories of political economy are logically continuous with those of the agents themselves. But, while human self-understandings must of course be explained by social theory, the explanations offered may require a different order of knowledge. In truth, Hegel knows this very well. In contrast to the unexamined concept of need, or preference, used by political economy, Hegel refers it to the development of the social formation itself, in other words a dialectical evolution. (*PR* 190–5)

The problem in understanding Hegel's dialectical development of the polity is this: if the achievements of political economy are limited to its appropriation in thought through the tools of the Understanding of the moments of the system of needs, and if, therefore, it can give no adequate account of the normative foundation of the economic order in property right, never mind those aspects of the ethico-political order beyond its purview, then in pushing the dialectic to a higher stage which, to put it simply, takes account of explicitly ethical aspects of social integration, as well as individual need and private interest, are we, in this movement of transcendence of the standpoint of political economy presenting it as a stage to be negated in the philosophical appropriation of the object, or are we presenting it as the logic of a *real sphere* of social life whose objective contradictions are to be shown as mediated in further institutional arrangements standing over it?

The logic of the Understanding seeks to explain phenomena by rendering them determinate through identifying them with fixed categories and definitions. It arrives at these through a two-fold process of abstraction, first by separating a given domain of inquiry from other domains and second by grouping items with many differences into abstract commonalities whose identity is established by perhaps only a single parameter.

But is political economy not in the right in employing this

logic? For is it not *really* the case that the economy in modern times operates independently of any substantive normative regulation worth talking about, requiring only an administration of justice to enforce contracts and fair dealing?

It is true that civil society is not a *bellum omnia contra omnes* because it functions on the basis of right, and alienation occurs not through forcible expropriation but through free transfer of entitlement.

None the less, these structures are purely formal, actualising abstract universals; the concrete content of these rights and prohibitions is simply that of egoistic interest and private purposes; the predominant moment is particularity. Furthermore, in commodity exchange the individuals establish a domain of market value abstracted from the material differences in the objects concerned.

Is there not then a space for political economy and an object appropriable by it? Certainly Hegel seems to think so. Hence his praise of political economy. He does not, therefore, criticise political economy for abstracting from the determinations of the ethical order as a whole, because the system of needs and labour *is*, really, partly thus abstracted. Marx will later defend Ricardo against those who charged him with abstracting from ethics, by saying that Ricardo allows political economy to speak its own language, and, if it does not speak ethically, this is not Ricardo's fault, but is a consequence of the real estrangement of these domains.[9]

A more telling case than that of Ricardo would be Adam Smith, because Smith actually wrote a book of moral philosophy whose principal figure was 'sympathy': yet his *Wealth of nations* starts from the proposition that 'it is not from the benevolence of the butcher, the brewer or the baker that we expect our dinner, but from their regard to their own interest'.[10] In other words, Smith finds himself compelled to abstract from his own ethics!

In spite of its 'atomistic' character, civil society forms a unity, but it is not consciously organised as such, it arises from the relatedness of individuals within a formal universality. Because of this, Hegel says, 'unity is present here not as freedom but as necessity, since it is by compulsion that the particular rises to the form of universality, and . . . gains stability in that form' (*PR* 186). But there are no resources within dull economic compulsion to enable the individuals concerned to recognise one another as more than individual centres of rights. No genuine community of citizenship is present here. The state enforcing right appears in civil society as 'the external state, the state based on need, the state as the Understanding envisages it' (*PR* § 183).

It has been argued, notably by Marx, that Hegel's solutions to the problems of civil society are useless, and indeed that the modern state itself is powerless to produce any genuine community of citizenship. However, as far as political economy is concerned, the problem is not its abstractedness in itself, for that models a reality, but that it is uncritical of its object and inclined to absolutise its methodological orientations.

Raymond Plant puts it this way: 'Throughout his description of the system of needs as the object of political economy, Hegel presupposed two things. First, that the phenomena so constituted, the system of needs, is an abstraction. Secondly, that the explanation of this from the standpoint of political economy is itself abstract and capable of transcendence.'[11]

Although political economy correlates masses of data within the forms of the system of needs it does not adequately ground these relations in the *social* formation. Rather, it more or less covertly appeals to *naturalistic* presuppositions about the givenness of need and interest. It is at home with quantitative questions such as the magnitude of exchange values but does not investigate the conditions of possibility of the form of value itself. Hegel understands these limits very well. Thus his praise of political economy cannot stretch to the derivation from it of an ethical theory (utilitarianism) or a political theory (liberalism). For Hegel, the spheres of family relations and of the state, stand outside civil society and the system of needs, representing other essential moments of the social system.

To round off this half of the paper I would like to mention briefly a striking interpretation of Hegel's views put forward by R.D. Winfield.[12] Winfield says that there are two common accounts of economic relationships firmly rejected by Hegel. One considers economic activity on the model of a natural function. The object of study is taken to be the metabolism between man and nature. This is an immutable condition, giving rise to a sphere of necessity lying outside all normative considerations. The second he characterises as 'monological', because it determines economic relations through some function of the self, a self which takes itself to be dealing with external objects, even if these include other economic agents, thus again excluding questions of social justice.

Winfield then defines the object of economic science as a sphere of normative social relations. This he believes to be Hegel's approach, and this sounds not unreasonable. However, there follows a non-sequitur. Having objected to the exclusion of the social he then proposes *to exclude the natural and the monological*. But the whole interest of the subject lies in the *interplay* between the realm of necessity and the realm of freedom, and in the contradictory way the rationality of the system of needs and labour constructs the individual of civil society as a monological subject who at the same time is supposed to play fair by his fellows and respect their rights.

II

In the second half of this paper, I want to raise a question about Hegel's theory of value. Given Hegel's unqualified praise for the achievements of political economy, and his specific mention of Smith and Ricardo in this context, one might have expected him to adhere to the labour theory of value. But we find nothing of the kind.[13] Why not? — one wonders.

In truth there is a gesture in this direction in a very early text. In a manuscript of around 1802/3 called *System of ethical life* there is the following striking passage:

> The universality of labour or the indifference of all labour is posited as a middle term with which all labour is compared and into which each single piece of labour can be directly converted; this middle term, posited as something real, is *money*.[14]

This remarkable analysis (anticipating Marx's category of 'abstract labour' rather than recalling Smith's 'labour commanded') is not taken up later on, unfortunately.

It is worth noting in passing also another passage from the young Hegel — this time from the *First philosophy of spirit* (1803/4). In this Hegel mentions the importance of the tool as universal mediator of desires and objects, and he notes that in the 'common work' of society labour 'becomes here a universal' because, although carried on by an individual, in its content it is 'a universal labour for the needs of all, so as to be appropriate for the satisfaction of all his needs; in other words it has a value'.[15] At first it seems this is a good thing as knowledge of discoveries and skills spreads. But then, in some unexplained way, with the *machine*, nature 'takes its revenge upon him' and 'the more he subdues it, the lower he sinks himself'; indeed 'the labouring that remains to man becomes itself more machine-like'; labour diminishes 'only for the whole, not for the single' labourer; 'for him it is increased rather; for the more machine-like labour becomes, the less it is worth, and the more one must work in that mode.'[16]

All this occurs because, through the division of labour, man subjects nature to himself but in a 'formal, and false, way' such that 'the individual only increases his dependence on it'. Moreover, 'the labour becomes that much deader, it becomes machine work, the skill of the labourer is infinitely limited, and the consciousness of the factory labourer is impoverished to the last degree of dullness'.[17] This passage remarkably anticipates Marx's description of alienated labour[18] — but the *Philosophy of right* is much less critical. In the treatment there of civil society, a couple of cursory references to value in exchange occur. However, Hegel's thematisation of value is not carried out in that section at all, but much earlier, in the treatment of private property and contract. This, it seems, is because the system of needs and labour is presupposed to be structured through exchange, and the juridical categories give this its *form*. Let us take note in advance, then, of the interesting fact that Hegel chooses to thematise value within the *forms presupposed* in commodity exchange rather than on the ground of the *content regulated* by exchange.

Let us now rehearse Hegel's argument. Hegel introduces the notion of value in the course of his discussion of the uses of property (*PR* § 63). He starts by saying that useful things have a certain quality, different in each case, which relates to specific needs, and at the same time they come in definite amounts: thus, a dozen eggs, a pair of shoes, a litre of wine.[19] Hegel's argument is that in so far as the useful articles satisfy various needs they can be compared as instances of a universal determinable, and hence, he says, commensurable. Although Hegel does not give this universal a special name, distinguishing it from the utility the objects have as they meet certain needs, what he is addressing is exchange value, the equivalent exchangeability of two commodities. For there would be no point in developing this idea of consciousness comparing and commensurating them if this does not lead to the possibility of exchange; certainly that is the context of most subsequent discussion of value in the *Philosophy of right*.[20]

Because consciousness imposes this concept of universal value on the things, by *abstracting* from the specific qualities of the things, it is a purely quantitative relation. In his lectures he gives a mathematical analogy to illustrate his point. A circle, an ellipse, and a parabola are very different curves, but, in spite of this, the distinction between each of them can be erased in their algebraic expressions, in so far as it reduces to a question of the magnitudes of coefficients.[21]

In the *Encyclopaedia* much the same definition appears: value refers to the quantitative terms in which heterogeneous things are made comparable when commodities are treated as abstract general equivalents. (*Enz.* § 494) While value is a pure quantity abstracted from quality, Hegel points out that in order to serve as a *measure* of the different things value needs a *quantum*, and, in so far as the use-values themselves provide this, their qualitative aspect is preserved, as well as superseded, in value.[22] We do not only need to say shoes and sealing wax are both valuable but that they become commensurable quantities when their relationship is determined such that, for instance, one pair of shoes is worth a hundred kilos of wax.

In his marginal notes to this paragraph in his own copy of his *Philosophy of right* Hegel anticipates Marx by explaining that what makes up the value of the one commodity is a determinate amount of *another*; thus that value when expressed in money terms is thereby presented 'for itself' as he puts it; and, conversely, money cannot be of utility *immediately* but must therefore first be transformed into specific use-values.[23] (Incidentally, if use-values are thus able to provide value with a *quantum* because they themselves have a quantitative dimension, this is not perfectly so. Thus certain shops will sell you half a loaf, but they will not accept half a tie in exchange. It is an important feature of the money commodity that 'small change' be possible.)

Money, therefore, expresses the value of things in the *abstract*. Hegel is perfectly clear that the specific quality of the money commodity, whether gold or paper, is thus unimportant because, as he puts it, money is a symbol. Considered as a value a thing counts not as itself but as what it is worth, he says. Money has the specific function of symbolising the measure of this value.[24] Money is thus not a *particular* type of wealth but the *type itself*, the universal given an external embodiment so that it can be taken as an object of the will and a vehicle of social action (*PR* § 299). All this recalls Marx's treatment of the value forms in *Capital*, as does Hegel's distinction between contracts involving the simple exchange of a *specific* use-value for another (different) one,[25] and contracts involving exchange of a specific thing for one 'characterized as universal, one which counts as value alone and which lacks the other specific determination, utility — i.e. for money' (*PR* § 80).

Hegel insists that, in contrast to the specificity of use-value, value as such is a universal (*PR* § 63,77). It is now time to ask some hard questions about the *reality* of this universal. For example, because Aristotle could not see a substance of value inherent in the goods themselves and thus providing a common measure, he assumed that money price does not express a real universal but is merely a makeshift for practical purposes.[26] Hegel takes a contrary position. He claims that it is precisely in value that the genuine substantiality of the thing 'becomes determinate and an object of consciousness' (*PR* § 63). Knox glosses this extraordinary claim by explaining that this is because value is a concept existing for thought not sensation, and rightly tying this to Hegel's idealism.[27]

It can now be understood why in this discussion of value there is no reference to a labour theory of value of the kind advanced by Smith and Ricardo. There is a clear sense that value could not express such a content because it is a form *imposed by the activity of consciousness* on the things concerned when they are made the subjects of contracts. In this, consciousness does not reflect some attribute of the things themselves, such as the labour embodied in them; nor is it heteronomously determined in its activity by psychological determinants such as utility maximisation. When it creates value as an abstract universal it freely posits this form without such determinations imposing themselves on it. Things are not exchangeable because they have the property of value as single items. They have value because they are posited by their owners as equivalents of one another. Value is a pure form which does not express any pre-existing substance of the things themselves. Marx distinguishes the external measure (money) of value and its immanent measure (socially necessary labour time).[28] For Hegel money is the *only* measure of value.

But, given that Hegel clearly omits any reference to labour, the question still arises whether or not he adheres to a utility theory of the substance of value. After all, he develops the category in the section on the uses of property. Is there not some kind of subsumption, however weak, of particular needs under a general category of utility that would serve as a content and even a measure of the value posited in the form of exchange? This question is hard to settle definitively but I think the answer is in the negative. It is true that exchange is only of use-values but Hegel stresses the heterogeneity of these goods and the need to abstract from their specific useful qualities if they are to be treated as identical in value. It is surely significant that, although Hegel speaks of need in general, he makes no attempt to derive a *measure* of value from utility. Nor does he speak of any necessity for value in exchange to be determined by it. Rather, when he says use-values are comparable as such he simply means that only use-values are exchangeable; he does not derive any rules of proportionality from this characteristic. The crucial problem is the precise sense to be attached to the process of *abstraction* that Hegel marks out as the key feature in the positing of value. Just as it is helpful to think of the structure of civil society in terms of the logic of Hegel's doctrine of essence, so it is helpful to look at the more abstract opening section, on private property, in terms of the categories of the doctrine of being, notably those of quantity and quality. Hegel accomplishes the transition from quality to quantity by arguing that being considered as 'being for itself' distinguishes itself from other such beings as indifferently other than them, as a One. But the negative attitude of the many Ones to one another is just as essentially 'a connective reference of them to each other' (*Enz.* § 98). This reference actualises itself as Quantity. The important thing about Quantity is that Hegel defines it as no longer immediately identical with Being, but posited as indifferent and external to it (*Enz.* § 99). (We may remark also in passing that in his lectures Hegel explicitly assails the influence of the mathematical category of magnitude in social science. There is a real danger, he says, in uncritically exaggerating the range of validity of such a category, and in considering as exact sciences only those the objects of which can be submitted to mathematical calculation.[29])

Returning to the main point on Quantity, it seems clear that Hegel has established a *pure* category, in Quantity the specificity of Being is superseded. Unfortunately the matter becomes slightly clouded when he endeavours to shed further light on the question of the relative priority of Quality here by saying:

We observe things, first of all, with an eye to their quality —
which we take to be the character identical with the being of
the thing. If we proceed to consider their quantity, we get
the conception of an indifferent and external character or
mode, of such a kind that a thing remains what it is, though
its quantity is altered, and the thing becomes greater or
less.[30]

To give an example: the shapes of squares or similar triangles
remain the same whatever size they are, and it is the shape that
defines them.[31] Or, to mention Hegel's own mundane example,
by an increase in size a house does not necessarily cease to be a
house (*Enz.* § 99).

The point to which I wish to draw attention is that it is one
thing to specify a quantitative relation completely indifferent to
quality *as such*, and another enterprise simply to talk about the
same quality varying in magnitude. The relevance of this
distinction to our present problem may be grasped when we look
at Eugen von Boehm-Bawerk's defence of the marginal utility
theory of value against Marx. In his search for the substance of
value Marx dismisses utility because in an exchange we are
dealing with qualitatively different use-values and hence in
making them equivalents we must be abstracting from these use-
values. Boehm-Bawerk complains that we must not confuse
abstraction from the genus altogether with abstraction from the
specific forms in which the genus manifests itself.[32] Thus, if we
have to disregard the special forms under which the value in use
of commodities may appear, whether they serve for food, shelter,
clothing, etc., we certainly cannot disregard utility in general.
After all, if the goods did not have some use to somebody they
would not be exchangeable and hence be of no value. So the
value-substance, according to Boehm-Bawerk, is utility. Of
course, there remains the problem of determining its magnitude;
and here the theory has to take a subjectivist turn, get into
marginalism, personal preference schedules and so forth. This
does not concern us here.

What I do want to say is that Hegel does not get into such a
discussion. In my view his procedure has something in common
with the original derivation of Quantity in the *Logic*, namely that
value is *indifferent* to the utility of the objects rather than a
measure of their *general* utility. (In this respect Hegel's example of
the reduction of curves to algebraic variables is instructively more

radical than comparison of the sizes of similar triangles.) I am arguing that in his derivation of value Hegel undertakes the more radical abstraction. That is, Hegel does not have an alternative theory of value to the labour theory of value, he simply does not see it as the form of a pre-given substance at all. The form is an abstract universal arising from the activity of social subjects. There is no suggestion that this abstract universal, although it necessarily has a measure, actually represents a predetermined quantity of something. Rather the thing counts as an instantiation of the value posited by consciousness, and imposed on the qualitatively different use-values as 'indifferent and external to them' (to use the words of the *Logic*). This prioritisation of form over content, and inversion of the abstractly universal and concretely particular, is typical of idealism of course. Given this, it is not strange that Hegel does not adhere to a labour theory of value of the traditional kind, but it *is* strange that he failed to criticise this theory as it appears in Smith and Ricardo.

Returning once again to Richard Winfield's provocative paper, he argues that Hegel recognises that value is 'neither instrinsic to the natural qualities of the exchanged commodities, nor rooted in a psychological estimation of them, nor determined by anything preceding the mutually agreed exchange act setting them in their actual relation of equivalence'.[33] From the purity of this form he concludes that there is no material determination of the rates of exchange arrived at. Rather, values are established from the free choices of the agents themselves, unconstrained by any external factors, such as socially necessary labour times, nor conforming to any stipulated model of economic rationality.

To postulate such total contingency seems to be an exaggeration. It is not clear that Hegel held this position, because, at the same time as he stresses the apparently arbitrary *form* of the choices made, he refers, in his discussion of the system of needs and labour, to the '*compulsion*' exercised on the particular by the system standing over against him (*PR* § 184, 186). In this way the needs of society are met: in other words he adheres to the same kind of dialectic as Adam Smith's analysis of 'the hidden hand'[34] (*PR* § 199).

At all events, however freedom and necessity are supposed to interpenetrate, I would like to observe that, even if the economic agents impose this social form on the contents of need and labour, this does not preclude the possibility that the content regulated by this form none the less impresses itself somehow on the value magnitudes in law-like fashion. Marx's own labour theory of value may still be re-interpreted in such a light. In this enterprise it would be important to distinguish (as Marx does but Winfield does not) between the oscillations of market price and real underlying values. Finally, we must observe that Hegel's intentions are manifestly apologetic. In spite of his awareness of the grave problems arising from the structure of civil society and market phenomena, he endorses these forms as moments in the realisation of the idea of freedom. When Marx covered the same ground he approached it in more critical fashion.

In one of his first notebooks, on James Mill, he says that 'value is an alientated designation of the product itself, different from its immediate existence, external to its specific nature, a merely *relative* mode of existence of this'.[35] The terms used here, especially the idea of a 'merely relative mode' recall Hegel's discussion, but what Hegel endorses as the emergence of a higher universal, even if it is abstractly opposed to the particular, Marx condemns as estranging.[36] In *Capital* Marx has a section on commodity fetishism analysing the peculiar way in which this universal value is taken to be inherent in the body of the commodity itself, as if it were one of its naturally given properties, which then expresses itself in exchange ratios rather as the furriness of a coat expresses itself in keeping us warm. Hegel understands very well that value is not a natural property of the object but a social form acquired by it; but then he declares this social form *itself* to be the substantial actuality of the thing, thus fetishising the commodity-*form*, if not the commodity-*body*.

At the same time, it should be recognised that the peculiarities of the form of value find their way into Hegel from *reality*. This means that he picks up the question of *form* in a way the political economists had not. It is, indeed, surprising, in view of his anti-naturalistic tendencies, that he praises political economy without explicitly dissenting from its labour theory of value.

In conclusion, it may be said that Hegel's emphasis on social forms makes his discussion of continuing interest today to those trying to develop economics as a *social* science.

Notes

1. It has been proved that Hegel cites the English text, not the German translation. Hegel learnt his English in Berne, and bought most

of his English books then, according to Norbert Waszek: 'The origins of Hegel's knowledge of English' (with a list of English books in Hegel's library extracted from the auction catalogue), *Bulletin of the Hegel Society of Great Britain*, 7, 1983.

2. Jena Systementwürfe I, *Gesammelte Werke* 6 (Hamburg, 1975), p. 324.

3. For Hegel's development see Georg Lukács *The young Hegel: studies in the relation between dialectics and economics*, trans. R. Livingstone (London, 1975); Manfred Riedel *Between tradition and revolution*, trans. W. Wright (Cambridge, 1984). Also see Raymond Plant 'Hegel and political economy' *New Left Review*, *103–4*, 1977, for remarks on Smith and Stewart.

4. Marx supplies this reference to support his claim that in civil society 'a general or a banker plays a great part but man as such plays a very mean part' *Capital* vol. I (Harmondsworth, 1976), p. 135. (Unfortunately the editor, in supplying the quotation itself, garbles it.)

5. Hegel's *Philosophy of right*, trans. T.M. Knox (Oxford, 1952), p. 353.

6. Ibid., § 189 Addition, p. 268.

7. *Enzyklopädie der philosophischen Wissenschaften (1830)*, Hamburg, 1969. Paragraphs from this are given in the text with their numbers distinguished from the *Philosophy of right* references by the prefix *Enz*.

8. Marx-Engels *Collected works* vol. 4 (London, 1975), p. 120.

9. Marx-Engels *Collected works* vol. 3 (London, 1975), p. 310–11.

10. Adam Smith, *The wealth of nations* (Chicago, 1976), p. 18.

11. *New Left Review*, *103*, p. 91. Compare A.S. Walton 'Economy, utility and community in Hegel's theory of civil society', in *The state and society* ed. Z.A. Pelczynski (Cambridge, 1984).

12. R.D. Winfield, 'Hegel's challenge to the modern economy' in *History and system: Hegel's philosophy of history*, ed. R.L. Perkins, (Albany, 1984).

13. When Hegel discusses labour in the civil society section, he mentions that it 'confers value' on things 'and gives them their utility, and hence man in what he consumes is mainly concerned with the products of men' (*PR* 196). But it is perfectly clear that this passage refers to value in use, not value in exchange, although, of course, the latter presupposes the former.

14. *System of ethical life and first philosophy of spirit*, trans. H.S. Harris and T.M. Knox (Albany, 1979) p. 154.

15. Ibid., pp. 230, 242–7.

16. Ibid., p. 247.

17. Ibid., p. 248.

18. K. Marx, 'Economic and philosophical manuscripts of 1844', *Collected works vol. 3*, pp. 270–82. Marx himself did not know of these Hegel manuscripts, of course.

19. Marx's *Capital* begins by making the same point, p. 125–6.

20. But see *PR* 214 in the section on the administration of justice, in which application of the law to a single case is said to enter into the 'sphere of the quantitative as such, of the quantitative as that which determines the relative value in exchange of *qualia*'. In trying to fix

quantitatively the punishment merited by a particular offence 'vacilla-tion' occurs. 'This vacillation must be terminated, however, in the interest of getting something done . . . ' observes Hegel.

21. *Philosophy of Right*, Addition to § 63, trans. Knox, p. 240.

22. Ibid.

23. *Grundlinien der Philosophie des Rechts, mit Hegels eigenhändigen Rand-bemerkungen* ed. J. Hoffmeister (Hamburg, 1955), p. 344.

24. *PR*, Addition to § 63, trans. Knox p. 240.

25. Knox (and Hegel) is a bit awkward here: 'exchange of one *specific* thing for another of the same kind' — Hegel's stress — he does not mean two things of the same species, but two things that are both *specific* (but different) use-values.

26. *Nicomachean Ethics* 1133.

27. *PR*, trans. Knox, p. 325–6.

28. *Theories of surplus value*, Part Three (London, 1972), p. 163.

29. *Hegel's Logic (being Part One of the 'Encyclopaedia of the Philosophical Sciences'* 1830), § 99 *Zusatz*, trans. W. Wallace (Oxford, 1975), p. 146.

30. Ibid., § 98 *Zusatz*.

31. This is the case in Euclidean geometry. In other (more dialectical?) geometries size and shape are functionally related.

32. *Karl Marx and the close of his system*, ed. P.M. Sweezy, (London, 1975), p. 74.

33. Winfield, 'Hegel's Challenge to the Modern Economy', p. 233.

34. However, the peculiar emptiness of his category of value makes this aspect of his theory reminiscent more of Austria than Chicago.

35. *Collected works* vol. 3, p. 219.

36. For more on the Hegel-Marx relationship see C.J. Arthur *Dialectics of labour* (Oxford, 1986). Also G. Hunt 'Hegel and Economic Science' (a reply to Winfield) in *Hegel today*, ed. B. Cullen, (Gower Press, forthcoming).

6

Marx's Hegelianism: An Exposition

Michael George

The relationship between Marx and Hegel is one of the as yet unresolved problems in Marxist scholarship. It is the purpose of this paper to examine the relationship between the two afresh. Unfortunately the subject is too extensive to be fully treated in an article of this length and so I shall restrict myself to a consideration of the question from the point of view of key ideas alone. I shall make only such reference to the writings of Marx and Hegel as are required to justify my assertions. A closer textual analysis of Marx's writings, with its much needed reinterpretation and retranslation, must be left to a future time.

It will be my contention that Marx was, in essence, an Hegelian and that his (Marx's) distinctive philosophical position should be seen not as a rejection of Hegelianism but rather as inherently dependent upon Hegel's philosophy for its foundation. I shall attempt to demonstrate that Marxism, for all its seeming radical shift of emphasis, is nothing more than a continuation and logical extension of Hegel's ideas. But I shall also argue that though Marx's 'extension' of Hegelianism was constructed upon a foundation that had already been laid by Hegel it was a foundation whose radical implications were never fully understood or developed by Hegel himself.

It has been fashionable in certain Marxist circles to play down, or even to discount altogether, the influence of Hegel's philosophical system upon Marx. Henri Lefèbvre's short work *Le Matérialisme dialectique*, published in the late 1930s, set the tone for much of the subsequent, and continuing, attempt by continental Marxists to rewrite Marxism without reference to its Hegelian heritage. But though Lefèbvre ultimately rejects the Hegelianism of Marx his attempt to found Marxism upon 'materialistic' premisses is suggestive, paradoxical as it may appear, of the way in which Hegelianism was, in its turn, *aufgehoben* by Marx and thus preserved, in a transposed form, at the very core of Marx's own world view. Lefèbvre states:

> The Hegelian universe therefore is nothing more than the world of the metaphysician Hegel, the creature of his own speculative ambition. It is not the world of men, in all its dynamic reality.[1]

And again:

> The form to which thought raises the content must be seen as fluid and capable of improvement. Thought must accept the contradictions and conflicts in the content, it must determine their transcending and their solution in accordance with the movement of that content, and not impose *a priori* and systematic forms upon it.[2]

I shall seek to demonstrate that these quotes from Lefèbvre are substantially correct and contain precisely the reason why no Marxist scholar can afford to *ignore* the influence upon Marx of that old sage of Berlin, Hegel.

Aufheben and the transcendence of the material world

The term *aufheben* is central to Hegel's philosophical system for it is the operative term of the dialectic as such. Its rendering into English has remained problematical but it is worth noting at this juncture that Edward Aveling's rendering of *aufheben* in his translations of Marx is wholly incorrect. Aveling's less than sensitive translation of Marx may indeed be the primary cause of the distorted way in which Marx's thinking has been received in the Anglo-Saxon world. Aveling habitually translates *aufheben* as 'abolition' or as 'overcoming'. The latter term is always to be preferred to the former but neither will really do. Aveling failed to appreciate that though *aufheben* does mean, in common German parlance, 'abolition' or 'doing away with something', or even 'leaving something aside for future use', Hegel's and Marx's use of the term is very much more technical and precise. The English words 'sublation' and 'redintegration', though archaic, connote something of the philosophical significance of *aufheben*. 'Sublation' means to resolve into a higher unity and 'redintegration' has the meaning of bringing again into a wholeness that which is fragmentary. However, the only real advantage to the use of either term in translations is that they alert the reader to the place where *aufheben* is employed by Hegel and Marx in the original German texts. The more cumbersome compound 'to transcend-and-preserve' is perhaps nearer an adequate rendering of the meaning of *aufheben*, but even this has too mechanical a connotation to convey the subtler aspects of the German. I shall consider further the meaning of *aufheben* below but before doing so it is necessary to make clear certain presuppositions of Hegel's idea of logic.

Hegel's philosophy adopted and extended the distinction common in German thinking of the eighteenth century, and also manifested in Kantianism, between what was termed the *Understanding*, whose function it was to establish the abstract identity of concepts or ideas, and the realm of *Reason*, which sought to connect or unify that which the 'Understanding' had divided. For the 'Understanding' each thing, concept or idea is possessed of an individual identity which must be analytically determined and, moreover, is something which is capable of being determined analytically, in isolation from all other such concepts and ideas. 'Reason', on the other hand, holds fast to the fact that the attempts of the 'Understanding' to define 'in isolation' constitutes only and solely a process of *abstraction*: that is to say a process of 'drawing out from a given context'. The function of 'Reason' is thus to make manifest the *concrete* relation in which an idea, concept or thing subsists. 'Concrete' is here to be understood in its literal meaning of a 'throwing together' and thus refers to the implicative contextual connectedness in which concepts, ideas and even objects subsist. Kant believed that the capacity of 'Reason' to perform such a task was limited. Hegel, however, regarded 'Reason' as the indispensable corrective to the deficiencies of the 'Understanding'. It was Hegel's purpose in his philosophical system to demonstrate both the method by which, and the extent to which, 'Reason', understood dialectically, could be just such a corrective. To demonstrate how Hegel achieves this task we must first consider more closely the role of *abstraction* and *concretion* in Hegel's system.

As has been stated 'Abstraction' removes a concept or idea from its context in order that it might examine it in isolation and thereby establish the *distinctive* attribute pertaining to it. The word has the literal meaning 'to draw away from', and this 'drawing away' can be observed in the two functions of 'Abstraction'. On the one hand it draws an object or idea away from its context in order for it to be considered 'in itself', i.e. as what it is as distinct from other concepts. At the same time, and by the same process, 'Abstraction' draws out one common feature from different objects in order to create universals. Indeed in the creation of universal concepts or ideas we make use of both aspects of 'Abstraction'. It is by fixing our attention upon *one* distinct quality that is shared by a series of particular objects that we are able to remove, or 'draw out' the common element within each instance from the 'context' in which it is bound in our perception. We may then attend only to that quality in itself as possessive of a distinct attribute. The concept, for example, of a 'family' is just such a universal idea. It entails the 'Abstraction' of one quality from a series of different individuals: namely the social relationships in which they stand one to another. The concept 'family' thus treats of a group of individuals as if they manifested one attribute and one attribute only: their relationship to one another. It ignores all other attributes which may, with equal justification, be predicated of these same individuals. Conversely, in order to ascribe an identity to someone or something it is necessary to reverse the process and to limit a subject to a simple identity with the predicate that is being predicated of it. Thus the statement 'the cat is black' postulates an identity relation between the subject 'cat' and the predicate 'black'. In this relation there is admitted no other aspect or quality of either 'cat' or 'black' and for this reason it is not possible, Hegel argues, to deal with the full meaning and significance of the 'catness' and 'blackness' within such restrictive predication.

It is, however, the purpose of 'Reason' to go beyond such restrictive limitations. For the dialectic, as Hegel states in the *Science of logic*, it is the 'non-identity' between a subject and a predicate that is of concern.[3] The concepts 'family' and 'black' are, within the dialectic, treated not as isolated concepts but rather as standing in an intimate and dependent relation with other like concepts. In the case of the 'family' it is concepts such as Citizenship, the State and Civil Society that form the conceptual contextual background. In the case of 'black' it is the entire colour spectrum, and for the 'cat' it is the animal kingdom. Thus, for Hegel, related concepts form a nexus of ideas that reciprocally 'limit', and thus define, one another. It is this intimate connectedness between concepts and ideas that forms what Hegel terms the *concrete* nature of thought. Whereas analytical abstractive thinking restricts itself to a consideration of concepts etc. in isolation, concrete reasoning must make clear the means by which, and the reasons for which, such concepts do in fact form a nexus of mutual interdependency. The definition of any concept, so far as Hegel is concerned, therefore entails a 'positive moment', which is the explication of what that idea is 'in-itself' and also a 'negative moment' in which, *at one and the same time*, each concept or idea is connected with others and is *delineated* by just this relation. For Hegel this process of delineation is the process of inscribing a logical 'boundary' or 'horizon' or 'limit' around a concept. It is this 'limit', formed from the relationship of ideas one to another, that must be 'passed beyond' in thought and that forms the basis of the Hegelian dialectic.

As has been already stated, the verb *aufheben* is the central idea of the dialectic. It may be seen as manifesting three distinct logical moments. First it has the moment of 'transcendence', in which it goes beyond a 'limit' or 'boundary'; secondly it is the 'negation' of this first negation, this 'limit', in which it is, 'overcome' or removed; and thirdly it is the moment of 'preservation', in which what has been 'gone beyond' or transcended is brought again into a new relation. But though these 'moments' of *aufheben* may be regarded as distinct from the point of view of *abstract* exposition they should not be thought of as a mechanical process taking place in time. Rather they form a unitary process of logic which is differentiated into its various components only for the purposes of aiding an 'understanding' of the process itself. The very process by which an idea 'passes beyond itself' and points to another idea to which it is intimately related is, at one and the same logical moment, the process by which it 'transcends' its limited abstract self-identity, 'negates' that solipsistical identity and emerges into a connected unity or nexus; in which context it is preserved as an intrinsic part of some greater whole.

An example of this process may serve to engender greater clarity on the part of the reader than an extended exposition. The relationship between correlative pairs of concepts, such as Whole and Part, manifests the workings of the dialectic. Indeed the reason that correlatives are correlatives is, so far as Hegel is concerned, because they are founded upon a dialectical relation. A Whole, Hegel would argue, is only a Whole in so far as it is a

Whole of Parts and so the idea of a Whole cannot be fully comprehended in isolation from its implied correlative term Part. The dialectical relation can also be reversed. In the same way the idea of a Part entails that of a Whole precisely because the idea of a Part 'points beyond itself' and implies a Whole of which it is a part. The concept Whole is thus the logical implicative of Part and Part the logical implicative of Whole. The two ideas stand in an *inseparable* connection in which each finds its completion in the other. The dialectical process of *aufheben* is thus the way in which a concept, seen from the perspective of 'Abstraction' must transcend its limited analytical and isolated definition and become embedded in a wider nexus of concepts.

The triadic relation 'thesis', 'antithesis', 'synthesis', which is of Fichtean origin, is not the form of the dialectic to which either Hegel or Marx subscribed. The Fichtean and the Hegelian dialectics are effectively opposites. The Fichtean triadic view of the dialectic requires the idea of a necessary and direct opposition between two *distinct, pre-existing* and *complete* concepts with each reciprocally 'negating' or 'limiting' the other and also requires the subsequent creation of a third concept, the 'synthesis', whose function it is to 'unify' these pre-existing, independent, and self-defining, opposites. But as Hegel demonstrates the logical distinction between correlative concepts is merely a matter of 'Abstraction' from a given and pre-existent 'unity' or, what is a better term, a pre-existent 'inseparability'. It is not that we, qua Fichte, start out with two ideas such as Whole and Part and then attempt to produce some third unifying term but rather that we separate, by a process of 'Abstraction', what are intrinsically conjoined ideas or concepts into their distinctive components. In the *Science of logic* Hegel explicitly rejects the process of *synthesis* as the basis of his dialectic.[4] The word 'synthesis' means literally 'a together placing' and implies thereby a setting together of what was originally separate. It is for this same reason that the two terms 'sublation' and 'redintegration' will not serve to render *aufheben* into English — for they imply an original state of separatedness followed by a conjoining *in thought*. But, according to Hegel, what we find on closer examination is that we have separated into distinct component concepts that which cannot stand in isolation. It is this 'concrete' aspect of such ideas that is the real basis of our understanding. It is the purpose of dialectical reason to make this clear. For Hegel therefore what he terms the 'Being' of the concept, or what it is in-itself, must always be supplemented by what it is 'Not' but in which it stands, nevertheless, in an intimate implicative order. Whereas the traditional interpretations of the dialectic have entailed a placing together, in some newly created third synthetic concept, two antagonistic, opposed original concepts, Hegel's dialectic in fact requires that we commence with a 'synthesis', which is the original unity of our ideas and concepts, and 'abstract' them from this 'concrete' unity into two distinct and supposedly independent concepts.

On this model the Whole/Part relation can be thought of in the following way: in thinking about the concept Whole, the concept Part would remain as an implied 'background' concept and vice versa in the case of Whole — which would always entail its complementary concept Part to complete it as an idea. To employ the language of Phenomenology, one of this binary pair of concepts would form the 'foreground', the other the 'background' and between them there would subsist an 'horizon'. Whilst of course such visual imagery and allusion is of use in conceptualising Hegel's meaning it should always be remembered that the dialectic is first and foremost a 'logical' relation. Thus, for Hegel, the consideration, in abstraction, of any one concept implies a correlation not only with the immediate correlative concept but also with all the other concepts of the Logic; for the whole forms, via the various dialectical relations that are established, an entire implicative web or nexus wherein each concept finds its place in relation one with another.

Lenin, in a letter to Berthold Aürbach, presents his own view of the dialectic: a view which I would argue is radically in error. He says:

> The identity of opposites (more accurately, perhaps, their 'unity', although the difference between the expressions 'identity' and 'unity' is not very essential here. In a certain sense both are correct) is the recognition (discovery) of the *mutually exclusive* and opposed tendencies in all the phenomena and processes of nature (including spirit and society).[5]

Lenin's assertion that the difference between the expressions 'identity' and 'unity' is not an essential one implies that the dialectic is concerned with 'identity' relations between pre-existent opposites. His assertion that the dialectic is concerned with '*mutually exclusive*' opposites is further evidence for this. In fact, as was noted above, Hegel's dialectic is concerned with *'mutually inclusive'* opposites; if by 'inclusion' we understand 'a closing in' of two concepts into one inseparable unity and by 'exclusion' we understand 'a shutting out' of two concepts into a merely antagonistic opposition. If we begin with the idea of 'identity' then we can see more clearly why this is the case. The word 'identity' has the literal meaning of 'a state of being the same' and entails thereby the idea of two concepts or ideas being possessed of the same attributes. But if we admit of the dialectic that it is founded upon such a concept then nothing follows from the assertion. The mere identity of two things or ideas gives rise to no third thing, for it is simply a matter of stasis that two things X and Y are identical. Nor can it be argued that the dialectical transitions within Hegel's *Logic* between 'identical' concepts, for in such a case the term 'transition' would be meaningless. Hegel in fact explicitly equates such a 'system of identity' with the pantheism of Schelling.[6]

Lenin is therefore quite correct if he wishes to claim that the essence of the dialectic lies in the fact that what, hitherto, have been regarded as distinct and separate ideas are, if correctly examined and understood, interdependent and interconnected. But if he wishes to hold that two ideas are 'opposites', and also that they 'mutually exclude' each other, then we are left either with a sheer tension of opposition or else are obliged to seek some third 'synthesis' by which to overcome or remove such opposition in order to produce a real union of these distinct and independent ideas. The dialectic understood in this manner seems to suggest that the relationship which obtains between paired concepts is merely one of 'exclusion' or 'incompatibility'. But, as we have seen, the whole thrust of the dialectic is towards the recognition that the relationship which actually obtains between concepts is not one of 'exclusion' but is rather one of intimate dependency or 'inclusion'. Thus the ideas of Whole and Part stand in a relation which may be characterised, in a loose sense, as one of 'opposition' but it is an 'opposition' which must be understood in the strict latinate sense of the term, i.e. as an *ob postumum*, or a 'setting against', and not as necessarily implying contradiction. The German term *Gegensatz* also has the same connotation, meaning literally as it does 'an against positing' and it, not contradiction (*Widerspruch*), is the basis of Hegel's dialectic.

It may seem strange to philosophers brought up in the English tradition to think of correlative terms as manifesting dialectical logic — for indeed correlative pairs of terms have long been accepted in Anglo-Saxon thought — but it is precisely the reason why correlatives are correlative that concerned Hegel and this is in fact the essence of the dialectic. Hegel, however, wishes to claim that it is not only the correlatives with which we are familiar that demonstrate this inseparability and mutual dependency but that, in a very strong sense, *all* our logical concepts form a chain or nexus of just such a correlation, and for Hegel this inseparable unity of all our concepts is itself ultimately derived from the very nature of the Ego. Lenin, I suggest, has fully recognised what may be termed the 'unity' thesis of opposites in Hegel but has failed to recognise that it is precisely *because* concepts such as Whole and Part and Essence and Appearance form paired correlates that these ideas form a series of mutually *inclusive*, rather than *exclusive*, terms.

If, therefore, we understand Hegel's *Logic* as a gradual explication and development of the 'connectedness' or 'linkedness' of the categories of thought, with each category taking its place in an implicative order, then the dialectic is to be understood as the explication of a series of logical relations pertaining between such categories or concepts. But such a 'dialectical nexus' of ideas and concepts is not itself sufficient to account for our knowledge of the world. It must confront a world which is given. That is to say it must have a relation to the objective world of matter into which man daily finds himself thrown. Hegel recognised this and states, at the end of his *Geschichtsphilosophie*, in a passage noted by Marx, that he (Hegel) 'has considered the progress of the *concept* only'.[7] Hegel well recognises that the reintegration of man and his world that he (Hegel) has made possible through his *Logic* is a reintegration at the level of ideas alone and is thus, in Marx's sense of the term, an idealistic reintegration.

It is in the *Phenomenology of mind* that Hegel first outlines the three means by which the external material world may be *aufgehoben* by man or, what is the same thing, can be removed from its given state as something 'other' to man and made into something which exists 'for' him as a world in which he can find and make his home. The three means that Hegel postulates by which man dialectically transcends the alien externality of the world are Will, Thought and Activity, or, to translate these terms into Marx's language, Will and Mental and Physical Labour.

For Hegel, as for Marx, man is obliged to go out beyond himself and lay hold of, or seize upon, a world that at first confronts him as something distinct from himself and without any purpose or significance for him. Man is *forced* to do so, for his condition of existence in this world leaves him no choice but to relate to the world as it is and make use of its various parts to satisfy his innate needs. And, whether he wishes it or not, man must first make use of his Will in this enforced confrontation with the material world. In so doing he 'grasps' a part of that world and utilises it to service some need. Thus, for example, a hungry man plucks an apple from a tree and eats it. In so doing he has 'overcome' the world, but in a way which preserves its own nature. In grasping the apple he has made it something 'for him', something which has a significance and which is now to be distinguished from all other objects in the world, for this object, this apple, is 'his'. Yet he in no way destroys the materiality of the apple; indeed it is precisely the material element of it which will eventually satisfy his hunger. In this elemental action of grasping something, man has transformed the external world from what Hegel understands by the category *Gegenstand* into the category *Objekt*. The merely material and unincorporated external world is at first a mere *Gegenstand*, in the literal meaning of the German word, an 'against standing' or that which stands opposed to us, and to which Hegel ascribes the term the 'other'. In so far as man's action, be it through his Will, Thought or Activity, 'transcends' this externality then the world ceases to be an 'other' and becomes an Object for us the Subject. It still embodies and manifests its original materiality but it is now a materiality that has come to embody something derived from a Subject. This relation can be diagrammatically represented as in Figure 6.1.

Figure 6.1

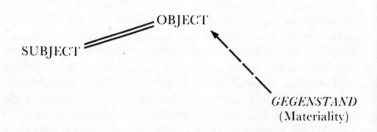

The Subject and Object form a correlative pair whereas

Materiality is something unincorporated and not yet something for the Subject. In order for the material world therefore to become correlated to a Subject it is necessary for man to perform a Mental or a Physical act in respect of the given thing, or make an expression of Will. Thus I may make a judgement about what it is that I am presented with via my senses and thereby make this thing into something with mental as well as physical properties. Or I may perform some labour upon it and transform it by doing so into a tool or implement for me etc. Or I may exercise my Will and establish a *property* claim to this part of the world as something now intimately connected with me.

To consider the exercise of Will first. In its most primitive form, for example in the life of early man, this 'staking a claim' via an expression of Will might be nothing more than the occupation of a cave for shelter. But in so far as this early man comes to regard this cave as 'his' cave, that is to say in so far as he ceases to be nomadic and settles in one place for a period of time, the cave becomes endowed with a special significance for him. The cave is no longer regarded as a mere geological feature of a landscape dissociated from man's needs and desires, it becomes now an 'Object' for a 'Subject' and stands distinct from all other caves.

In the same way as the exercise of the Will makes something that was originally merely external now something of significance for man, so too does the exercise of his mental and physical capacities 'overcome' the world as a something detached from man himself. Through the use of Thought, or Reason, man comes to understand, classify and name his world.

In his practical Activity, man literally *forms* the base matter of the world to suit his purposes and needs.

The Object becomes the carrier of something *from* a Subject but yet also retains its original material component. In making of this given material world an Objective reality man thus makes it something for himself as *Subject*. The material world no longer stands opposed to the human subject but becomes something to which the subject has an intimate connection or relatedness and which will be the basis for any development of the Subject as an individual and social entity. As we have already noted, Marx adopts this Hegelian threefold dialectical 'transcendence' of the external alien world. But though he took his cue directly from Hegel's *Phenomenology of mind* Marx was to draw radically different conclusions from it than those of Hegel.

Master and Servant

In the *Phenomenology of mind* Hegel postulates that man first seeks to *aufgehoben* the material world through the exercise of his Will. Until the Will has become active the subject must remain passive before the objective world. In the Master/Slave dialectic Hegel demonstrates what are the social consequences for mankind of his attempt to construct his own sense of Self, his need for recognition by another human being, upon the basis of an exercise of his Will. There is an immediate conflict of Wills with each party attempting to exact from the other an enforced 'recognition'. This conflict is only resolved when one of the parties, under the threat of death from the other, yields his Will and grants a forced recognition of the other. In this moment one becomes the dominant party the other subservient and there is created the realm of the Master and Servant, the classic Robinson Crusoe, Man Friday situation. But as a result of the conflict of Wills there is also created something more than this mere domination of one man by another. As Hegel appreciates that the resolution of this conflict has produced, on the one hand, an enforced recognition and, on the other, a sense of unease. The Servant only acknowledges the Master because he is obliged to do so. The Master can never know that the Servant would have so recognised him out of the exercise of his, the Servant's, own free Will. The recognition that the Master receives is but his own Will reflected back to him via the Will of his Servant, which Will is now exercised only at the dictate of the Master. The Will of the Servant is nothing more than the Will of the Master and therefore the Master in effect merely recognises himself, which is no recognition at all.

The Servant on the other hand, having been granted no recognition, has been forcibly obliged to exercise what remains of his own Will upon the physical material world. He thereby begins the task of 'overcoming' the otherness of the material world through his labour and the development of the skills entailed therein. Hegel understands that the outcome of the struggle between Wills for recognition is the creation of an unstable situation, a Master who is not confirmed in his mastery and a Servant who labours for another without the recognition of himself as a Self. It is precisely at this point that Marx begins his transformation, or rather logical extension, of Hegelianism. Marx sees that the outcome of the Master/Servant dialectic is the creation of two separate realms in which the other means of worldly *aufheben* are to come about. The Master becomes the exerciser of Mental Labour and the Servant the bearer of Physical Labour, and, as Marx rightly notes, the distinction between Mental and Physical Labour is the first Division of Labour.[8] Not surprisingly Marx sees this first division of labour as the condition of the two antagonistic classes of Bourgeoisie and Proletariat, the former commanding the world and having a mentalistic approach to it, inhabiting as it does the realm of ideas, and the latter developing a practical and active transformative relationship with the world but with no understanding of why it labours or to what end.

As Marx states in *The German ideology*, '[the] division of labour only becomes truly such from the moment when a division of material and mental labour appears'. And further, 'because the *division of labour* implies the possibility, nay the fact that intellectual and material activity . . . devolve in different individuals, . . . the only possibility of their not coming into contradiction lies in the negation in its turn of the division of labour'.[9] The relationship between Will, and Mental and Physical labour can for Marx be represented as in Figure 6.2.

Figure 6.2

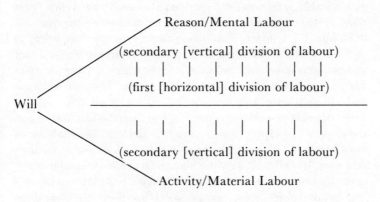

This division between the mental and the physical means of transcendence of the world's materiality results in a divorce between the conceptual and the actual. It is this divorce which is at the foundation of ideology. As Marx states, again in *The German ideology*:

> From this moment onwards consciousness can really flatter itself that it is something other than consciousness of existing practice, that it really represents something without representing something real; from now on consciousness is in a position to emancipate itself from the world and proceed to the formation of 'pure' theory, theology, ethics etc.[10]

And it is this point that Lefèbvre expresses so well in the first quotation from *Le Matérialisme dialectique* above. Hegel has confused the logical and the actual, the conceptual relations for the real, immediate ones established by human interaction and sociality.

It is this fact that is the most central and important advance made by Marx over Hegel for its implications are fundamental. Marx recognises that beneath the mediated dialectical relations that Hegel establishes between social concepts there lie real or immediate material relations. Hegel is quite correct to argue that in respect of Logic and those areas of knowledge about the world which man has as an external and detached being — for example the hard sciences — the establishing of conceptual relations at the level of concepts is vitally necessary. In the case of Logic it is only possible to interconnect such concepts according to an innate dialectical logic as was demonstrated above with the Whole/Part relation. However, when it comes to interconnecting the concepts of Family, Civil Society and State, this must be done according to the real dialectic of immediate human relationships and not according to some Aristotelian syllogistic scheme. Hegel in effect has ignored the fact that through the Master/Slave dialectic his dialectical scheme has become something more than logical. What Marx is postulating is nothing less than the fact that within the dialectic of Hegel there is another dialectic, the dialectic of head and hand, mind and body, mediate relations and immediate relations. It is after all only the Slave who achieves a real mastery over the world. It is he who must exercise both immediate skill and mental judgement as he seeks to form the world to humanity's needs.

Reification of the world and fetishism of commodities

Marx's critique of Hegelianism thus revolves around the fact that, for Marx, Hegel has remained at a bourgeois 'mentalistic' level in the way in which he has related social concepts one to another. For Marx, Hegel therefore makes the Civil Service the Universal or the major premise, Civil Society the Particular or minor premise and the social individual or citizen the conclusion of these two logical moments. Real human relationships have thus been determined *a priori* according to Aristotelian logic. Marx on the other hand states that social concepts must be understood as having their own *real* content, a content that is to be derived from the real social relations which subsist between individuals and classes in society.

It was the purpose of Marx's PhD thesis on the atomism of Democritus and Epicurus to establish what he means by such a 'material' content. In his PhD Marx provides a clear account of what that content is and how it is to be understood. He states: 'when I relate myself to myself as something which is directly an other, then my relationship is a material one'.[11]

Marx's meaning is, I think, clear. When I relate myself to the world via Reason I do so in a mediated manner, that is to say via concepts and ideas. If I understand myself as a rational animal and relate myself to myself via my capacity to understand what reason and intellect are, then my relationship to myself is an ideal or intellectual one. On the other hand when I relate to the world as to a mere material entity, as a *gegenstand*, then my relationship is an 'immediate' one. In the same way I can relate to myself on a material basis as a being with passions, instinct, drives and bodily needs. Thus when I relate myself to myself as towards an immediate other my relationship to myself is as a being with innate needs and desires. I relate therefore to what Kant would term my 'lower appetites'. It is the satisfaction of these 'lower appetites' that for Marx is the primary condition and the first motivational force for men in the world. In so far as I recognise myself as a being with material needs and immediate drives and wants I stand in a 'material' relationship with myself and similarly with my relationship to other men where that relationship is concerned with the satisfaction, either individually or mutually, of the most basic human bodily requirements.

This however, is not to deny the need for a realm of ideas. Many misunderstandings of Marx have been engendered by the failure to recognise that for Marx the realm of Thought, of ideas, is an independent realm with its own intrinsic value and purpose. As Marx notes, again in his PhD, it is the purpose of Thought or

Logic to create the universal categories, ideas and concepts which provide the forms under which we may subsume the content of the various particularities of the perceptual material world. Marx declares:

> abstract individuality can make its concept, its form-determination, the pure being-for-self, the independence from immediate being, the transcendence and preservation of all relativity, effective only by *abstracting from the being that confronts it*; for in order truly to overcome it, abstract individuality had to idealise it, a thing only universality can accomplish.[12]

Marx's passage in *The German ideology* where he states, 'The hazy [or confused] constructs (*Nebelbildungen*) formed in the human brain are also, necessarily, sublimates of their (men's) material life-process . . . '[13] should also be understood in a similar vein. Marx is not arguing for some Skinnerian ontologically materialist thesis of ideas or human reasoning. Rather Marx means that it is the most immediate conditions of men, the satisfaction of their material wants and needs, that forms the basis for their intellectual constructs. Thus when we consider the ideas and concepts that men use to describe their situation we should recognise that these are but the manifestation, transposed into a higher and distinct form, of both those needs themselves and the means by which men seek to satisfy them.

But the failure to return again to the physical world having once accomplished this task of abstraction in order to formulate universal ideas leads to pure idealism, the dwelling only in the realm of abstract ideas which are then taken to have an independent subsistent validity of their own. Hegel's failure, so far as Marx is concerned, is that having achieved the formulation in thought of the ideas and concepts necessary to describe reality Hegel fails to descend once again from the heavens and interconnect these concepts according to their manifested *real* content, as opposed to their logically *ideal* one. He who remains at the level of abstract ideas alone can never use those ideas as the basis for an understanding or transformation of the world. Thought thus becomes divorced from Activity and the latter is left directionless. It is upon this problem that Marx was to found two other of his notable ideas, that of Reification and the Fetishism of commodities. Because the bourgeois does not test his ideas in the world he is condemned to transpose for the real world the world of his ideas. He thus achieves a mentalist approach to reality which ideas he regards as reflective of the world but which in reality, because of their detached nature, become the source of self-delusion, of ideology. On the other hand the proletarian is obliged to labour in the material world but has no knowledge of why he labours, nor even does he understand the full process of which his labour is but a part. Neither the bourgeois in his mental isolation nor the proletarian in his daily confrontation with the brute matter of the world, can appreciate the purpose for which they labour in their different ways. What the worker produces becomes for the bourgeois a 'commodity' i.e. something abstract which can only be understood in terms of the most abstract idea of economics, the idea of money value. The 'commodities' which the capitalist therefore possesses at the end of a day's production become for him merely so many artifacts of indifferent utility which only have the significance that they can, at a future time, be transformed again into money. The proletarian on the other hand comes to see his labour process as something which does not belong to him, and his product as something which remains a *gegenstand*, i.e. as something standing over against him and opposed to him. What he produces he can only reappropriate as a consumer, a buyer of commodities. Yet even when he has 'reappropriated' the world as a consumer his 'appropriation' of that world remains defective. It is a reappropriation that remains at the level of the Will only; it is a grasping of something which remains exterior in its intrinsic nature and use from the grasper. Because, therefore, neither the bourgeois nor the proletarian stand in a *human* relationship one with another, but are merely Master and Servant, that which they produce with capital and labour is not understood in its true significance by either of them.

Alienation, heaven and earth and the standing of Hegel on his head

Upon the same base that he constructed his theory of Reification and Fetishism Marx also constructed his so-called idea of Alienation. His theory in fact makes use of three distinct ideas or terms, those of *Entfremdung*, (Estrangement), *Entäußerung*, (Externalisation) and *Veräußerung*, (Commercial Relations).

As we have seen it is the condition of man in this world that he must 'go out beyond himself' to confront a given material reality. But that 'reality' is one which requires an integrated form of 'transcendence' that makes use of all man's powers, his Will, his Reason and his Labour. But the need for man to 'externalise' himself and make of the *Gegenstand* a world for himself is precisely the process that is frustrated by the division of society into two classes and the concomitant division of man's labour into the dissociated realms of the Mental and Physical. For Marx mankind can never, under the conditions prevailing within capitalist society, make of this material world his own social and human world. The proletarian is condemned to exercise his practical skills without knowing what he is making, nor for whose benefit he is making it, nor what purpose it serves. What he produces at the end of a day's labour remains a thing that still stands 'over against him' as an unincorporated materiality, as a fetish in the literal sense of something which he regards with an *irrational* reverence. It is a 'commodity' which belongs to another, the capitalist, and which he (the labourer) can only reappropriate via a Commercial Relation as a consumer. Yet even at this level, as we have noted, he acts towards the world of material things as a fragmented individual, for it is his Will alone which is the means of this 'reappropriation'. Because of this both the bourgeois and the proletarian are equally precluded from achieving, either individually or collectively, that wholistic and integrated 'transcendence' of the 'otherness' of the world which alone can transform the brute otherness of material reality into something *for* man. Both classes are condemned to remain 'estranged' from material reality and from each other. It is precisely the 'collective' effort required to produce a human world that is inhibited by the social relationships that lie at the base of capitalist society. Hegel was unable to see this because he still made use of the old classification of society into Estates and Guilds. In the Guild the Master, or Mental realm, and the Servant, or Physical realm, were united in the task of production. Though head and hand were not united in each individual neither were they as totally divorced, on the immediate and the human level, as they were to become in the factory system. In capitalism Marx saw around him the process of industrial manufacture rending apart what remained of this unity in the old Guild system. Marx's own adoption of the idea of classes enabled him to recognise that the divorce between head and hand was becoming more pronounced. Whereas Hegel's theory of Estates and Guilds preserved some vertical interconnection between Master and Servant, the new capitalist era was divided horizontally into two antagonistic classes whose relationships to the world were totally separated.

Because man fails to produce a truly human world he remains estranged in one other important aspect for Marx; he remains estranged from his own 'species-essence'. Man's human 'essence' remains to him as something that is external and unincorporated into his daily life. It, his essence, is preserved in that final relationship that it is the duty and destiny of man, for Marx, to 'transcend', that is, man's relationship to God. In perhaps Marx's most famous passage upon religion we can detect the cry of the oppressed.

> The suffering of religion is at once the expression of actual suffering and at once the protestation against that actual suffering. Religion is the sigh of the afflicted creature, the heart of a heartless world, as it is the soul of a souless condition. It is the Opium of the people.[14]

Religion remains the sole source of succour for those afflicted by the inhumanity of the new industrial era. The idea of man, qua Feuerbach, subsists still, but in an abstract form divorced from the real lives of men. Projected into heaven it becomes the image of God and man's relationship to his own essence becomes then a matter for religion and not his actual social life. It is for this reason that Marx's reaction to religion is ambiguous. On the one hand religion is the manifestation of the gap between human potentiality and human actuality and on the other hand, in its imagery and message of hope, it is the only form of relief from the misery of the world. The atheism of Marx is thus social rather than metaphysical and his demand for the overcoming of religion is the demand of those religious humanists such as Lessing, Kant and Hegel, for the creation of heaven upon earth. Only when man himself becomes a fully integrated and harmonious individual will the need to hold man's essences as something external to him be ended. Heaven and earth will be united. It is this hope which is expressed in another famous and oft-quoted sentence from Marx's *Economic and philosophical manuscripts*: 'The transcendence of religion as the illusory happiness of the people is the demand for their actual happiness.'[15] That is to say that it is not the mere abolition of religion which is being called for but rather its earthly realisation. Religion is a constant reminder of the gap between human earthly social reality and the potential essence of mankind. As such the concept of God presents to man, albeit in an ideal and heavenly form, that very goal of humanity towards which mankind must strive.

Conclusion

I have attempted in this paper to give an indication of the relationship between Marx and Hegel and to demonstrate how the philosophical predisposition of Marx is built upon the foundations already laid by Hegel. If a short account of this relationship was to be given it would be as follows. The dialectic, for Marx as well as for Hegel, is based upon the relationship between ideas, between, that is to say, those essential concepts which man must use in order to be able to come to 'know' the world and to achieve that transcendence over it which is the special characteristic or essence of the human species. To begin this process man must first create himself as something distinct from that world, he must raise himself to the level of rationality, to the level at which he is an abstracted individuality no longer bound to or governed by the mere immediate and instinctual relationship that he has to the world as a mere animal. This abstraction of man from the world entails, of necessity, an abstraction, or a drawing away from, the immediate in the human condition, the passionate and instinctive side of man. It was upon this process that Kant founded his theoretical view of human nature, distinguishing between the realm of the 'higher appetites' and the realm of the 'lower appetites', between mind as intellective and rational or mind as 'emotive' and 'instinctual'. Man becomes free for Kant only when he raises his will from the lower to the higher realm, that is to say when he allows his will to be governed only by the dictates of reason. But this essential and unavoidable first step has the undesirable consequence that man becomes dissociated from the immediate material word in which he has, also of necessity, to find his home and to satisfy his biological needs as a material entity amongst material entities. Whereas Kant limited enquiry into the *a priori* conditions of the human intellect and to the establishment of those categories and concepts needed to present to human consciousness a stable perceptual manifold of experience, Hegel, with his conception of Reason and dialectic, sought to provide an explication of *all* of the category required by man to make sense of the whole world of his experience and not merely its perceptual element. Hegel thus employs his dialectical method to demonstrate that the discrete concepts and categories of Kant's Logic actually form a unified nexus of interdependent ideas. Having provided an elucidation of this schema in his Logic, Hegel goes on to demonstrate how his logic is applied in our understanding of the world, but he does so from the side of logic itself. The entire thrust of Hegel's philosophy and view of man's transcendence of the material world is thus from a position that Marx comes to term the idealistic, or intellectualist. It is because Hegel remains at the level of ideas and the mental that, in seeking to integrate his concepts solely according to an innate logic of those ideas, he is driven to connect them at a logical level only. Hegel thus falls into the error of thinking that whatever relationship he is able to establish between concepts in the realm of ideas is also established in the realm of material reality. Marx, on the other hand, recognises that this human condition requires that man confront a given world, and once having confronted it needs to produce from it a social and political world in which he will have his being. The means by which man seeks to satisfy the most basic requirements for his continued existence in the world are not neutral in their import for the social and political life which he subsequently establishes. Indeed in the very processes by which man seeks to transcend the immediate material realm and to produce those material goods necessary to sustain him, man, though he does not realise it, also produces the social and political relations which become the form of his social and political existence.

Hegel postulates that the condition of man's coming to be at home in the world is dependent upon his innate powers and capacities; that he is endowed with a free will, with intellect and with physical capacity and learned skills. In making of the externally given world of matter a world which is his, man must make use of these powers. In so doing man transforms brute matter and thus comes both to know and understand as well as to make his world. The world becomes Objective for him and its immediacy is incorporated into the mediate world of his social life. But Hegel restricts himself in his account of how man comes to be at home in the world to the level of intellect or Reason. In so doing Hegel explains, he transcends the world at the level of the rational Ego. But to so do is to make of *aufheben* a mentalistic or idealistic endeavour only. Man must first abstract himself from the world as given in order to be able, from a detached perspective, to know it in a mediated, rational manner. In taking no heed of the needs of man as a bodily animal it ignores the immediate transcendence which is so fundamental for Marx. Indeed because the Master/Slave relation is the first condition of human existence the forms of transcendence, mental and physical, become the domain and preserves of different classes. It is the ruling class that establishes the ruling ideas of the age precisely because it is this class alone that is privileged to inhabit the realm of ideas. It is in this sense that Marx's assertion that 'it is not the consciousness of men that determine their existence, but their existence that determines their consciousness'[16] should be read. Marx means the German term for 'consciousness' to be understood in its fully German etymology. *Bewusstseins* has the literal meaning of 'an awareness of being'. Because of the outcome of the Master/Slave dialectic, each class finds itself with a different relation to and awareness of the being of the world. The bourgeois adopts a mentalistic, idealistic and detached awareness and the Proletarian becomes aware of the brute 'otherness', the immediate materiality, of the world.

The consequence of this for Marx is that the intellect in Hegelianism is left to confront the world in the same manner as it is in Kantianism, as something detached from the body in which it resides. But man confronts the material world not merely in the form of the 'other', the given stuff of existence, but also in the form of his own 'lower' self, or instincts, needs and drives. If man is to be a whole individual he must reconcile himself with the world as body as well as mind, as 'lower' as well as 'higher' mind. Marx's advance upon Hegel was to recognise that beneath the mediated, mentalistic relation that man has to the world and to himself there is an immediate and material relation also. And it is this immediate relationship to himself as body and passion that Marx realises holds the key to the way in which man creates for himself a social and political world. It is only in so far as man enters into a relationship of mutual recognition with his fellow man, and enjoins upon himself the respect for others that this entails, that man is able to achieve both a mediated and an immediate *aufheben* of the world.

In so far as I come to satisfy the most immediate needs and desires of myself and others through my labour I am reinforced not merely in their respect but also in their love. That rational respect for others that is enjoined upon us by the Moral Law is supplemented by an immediate love and concern for our fellow man. Reason and emotion thus stand in unison. It is for this reason that Marx believes that Hegel's rationalistic, or idealist reconciliation of man with his world is only a partial reconciliation. In the manner of Schiller, Marx believes that it is necessary to bring about a harmony of the rational and passionate in man, and in so doing create, for the first time, a truly human being. This desire of Marx leads to what may be described as his most 'utopian' aspect: namely his belief that such a harmonisation of the human being will produce a transformation of man's innate disposition to the world and towards his fellow man. Under the reign of such a transformed humanity the Kingdom of Ends, which is a rational construct, will be complemented by such a reconstruction of man's passions that each will be confirmed in their love for others at the most immediate level. It is for this same reason that Marx has no need of a State, for the State, at its best, is the guardian of the universal interest. That interest has now become inseparable from the particular interests of each, their being no difference between the good of one and the good of the all. For this reason Hegel's divorce between the Universal Will and the Particular Will is transcended and the two aspects of the Will are made one inseparable unity. This radical belief in the capacity of man to make of himself what he will as both a rational and as an emotive being is the foundation of the greatest danger in Marxism: for that which makes of Marxism so profound and sublime a humanism can also make of it the foundation for the most cruel totalitarianism.

Notes

1. *Dialectical materialism*, Henri Lefèbvre, trans. John Sturrock (Jonathan Cape, London, 1968), p. 58.
2. Ibid., p. 59.
3. *Hegel's science of logic*, trans. A.V. Miller (Allen and Unwin, London, 1969), p. 91.
4. Ibid., p. 95.
5. Letter to Berthold Aürbach, 2 Sept., 1841, M. Hess, *Briefwechsel*, E. Silberner (ed.) (Gravenhage, 1959).
6. *Logic*, p. 84.
7. *The German ideology*, Student Edn, C.J. Arthur (ed.) (Lawrence and Wishart, London, 1985), pp. 51–2.
8. Ibid., p. 51.

9. Ibid., pp. 51–2.

10. Ibid., p. 52.

11. *MEGA* vol. 1, 1, p. 39.

12. The German ideology, pp. 51–2.

13. Ibid., p. 51.

14. Introduction to the 'Critique of Hegel's *Philosophy of Right*' in *Karl Marx Early Writings*, Introd., Lucio Colletti, trans. R, Livingstone and G. Benton, (Penguin, London, 1975), p. 244.

15. Ibid., p. 244.

16. Preface to *A contribution to the critique of political economy* (Lawrence and Wishart, London, 1971), pp. 20–1.

7

The Actual and the Rational

Sean Sayers

What is rational is actual and what is actual is rational. On this conviction the plain man like the philosopher takes his stand, and from it philosophy starts its study of the universe of mind as well as the universe of nature.

(Hegel, *Philosophy of right*, p. 10)

I

These words, from the Preface to Hegel's *Philosophy of right*, are among his most notorious and controversial. Ever since their first publication, they have been attacked, ridiculed and dismissed as implying an extravagant idealism and an uncritical sanctification of the *status quo*. Hegel himself was surprised by the outraged response to what he calls 'these simple statements' (*Logic* § 6, p. 9), which he took to be stating views shared by 'the plain man' and 'the philosopher'. For the most part, he thought the opposition to be based upon simple confusions and misunderstandings of his meaning; and sympathetic commentators have, by and large, agreed. Thus Hegel is at pains to insist that he distinguishes mere 'existence' from what is 'actual', and that he is not justifying all that *exists* as rational. Nor is his philosophy to be equated with any simple sort of subjective idealism. With these points many commentators have also rested content.[1]

There has been a tendency, then, to greet Hegel's doctrine either with uncomprehending outrage or with uncritical sympathy. Neither response, I shall argue, is adequate. The reactions of outrage are not without their basis; for Hegel's words most certainly have conservative implications, which he welcomed and emphasised; and they also express the extreme idealism of his philosophy. Equally, however, there are profound and important ideas involved in these assertions, which are still of great relevance. It is these upon which I will be focusing. My concern is not primarily with Hegelian scholarship, but with the issues that his philosophy raises. I will be approaching this in the critical fashion that is necessary to all those who are prepared to 'avow themselves the pupils of that mighty thinker', and seeking to discern and distinguish the 'rational kernel' from the 'mystical shell' of Hegel's thought.[2]

II

When Hegel talks of the rationality of the actual, his first and most general purpose is to specify what he takes to be the scientific attitude, and this is a basic and important element of the rational kernel of his thought. Hegel is saying that actuality — which, for the moment I shall take to refer to the world in all its aspects — is orderly in its forms and law-like in its behaviour. It is rational in the sense of being regular, coherent and comprehensible — explicable in rational and scientific terms.

Hegel is a strong defender of the realism implicit in the scientific approach. He rejects the Kantian idea that order and necessity are merely our 'way of seeing things', mere subjective forms, which we impose on the world through our use of the 'categories'. On the contrary, Hegel argues, species and kinds, laws and necessities, are objective features of reality which science seeks to discover and to understand.[3]

Hegel's philosophy is so widely regarded as an extreme form of speculative, *a priori* — even mystical — metaphysics, that it may come as a surprise to find it praised for being scientific and realistic. Of course, there are strong speculative and unscientific aspects to Hegel's thought; but scientific and realistic themes are equally present, though less often perceived or appreciated. In particular, philosophy, Hegel insists, should study actuality. The content of Hegel's work is thoroughly realistic: to a remarkable and unique degree for a modern philosopher. It covers a truly encyclopedic range of topics, treated in a thoroughly concrete and empirically detailed manner.

Moreover, Hegel extends this realistic and scientific approach to the study of society; and his work contains a notable defence of the idea of a social science. He rejects entirely the Kantian idea that the social world cannot be grasped in scientific terms, but must rather be approached morally and 'critically'. Philosophy, he insists:

> must be poles apart from an attempt to construct a state as it ought to be . . . it can only show how the state, the ethical universe, is to be understood . . . To comprehend what is, this is the task of philosophy. (*PR*, p. 11)

By the time Hegel was writing, the scientific attitude had largely prevailed in the study of the natural world; but there was, he observed, a great resistance to regarding the social world in this manner. Despite the immense growth of the social sciences since then, this is still true today. The social and the natural realms, it is argued, are fundamentally distinct and different. The laws of nature are objective, they operate independently of us; and, for this reason, they must be accepted as they are and viewed in a scientific and objective manner. Social laws, by contrast, have a subjective aspect: they are *our* product, the creations of human consciousness, will and reason. To look upon the human world in purely objective terms, it is argued, is, therefore, inappropriate and wrong: it is to be passive and acquiescent when an active and *critical* approach is required. For reason, in relation to the human world, has not only a theoretical but also a practical role. It can guide action and show us what ought and ought not to be.

Hegel takes direct issue with these Kantian views. It is true, of course, that the human world differs from the natural world, and that in it consciousness, will and reason can play a constitutive role. Hegel does not deny this (and nor does Marx, for that matter). However, Hegel rejects the idea that reason is a transcendent and absolute quality which distinguishes mankind from the rest of nature. He rejects the idea of an absolute gulf and divide between these two realms.

When Hegel talks of the unity of the actual and the rational, however, it is also vital to see that he is not merely reducing the actual to the rational or vice versa. The relation between these opposites is conceived as a concrete and dialectical one. And, at least in the more rational parts of his work, Hegel is aware of the conflict as well as of the harmony of these opposites. It was Hegel's great achievement to see human consciousness, will and reason in concrete and dialectical, social, historical and developmental terms. Practical — moral and political — ideals, he insists, are not the product of transcendent reason operating *a priori*, nor are they purely subjective. On the contrary, they are historical products and arise out of and reflect 'the ethical world' (that is to say, social institutions and relations). He rejects the dualism which is presupposed by the Kantian philosophy. 'Reason is in the world', says Hegel, it is a social product, and does not need to be brought from outside by the 'critical' philosopher.

This is not to say that the scientific approach is necessarily 'uncritical'. However, there is a clear sense in which the scientific attitude involves a measure of acquiescence to reality or, in Hegel's words, 'reconciliation' with it. For being scientific implies that we accept objective conditions and adjust our ideas to them, so that our views correctly reflect these conditions, rather than imposing our ideas and ideals upon the world. This is the inherent nature of the theoretical and scientific attitude. However, it does not at all imply a passive or acquiescent attitude to the world when it comes to practice. On the contrary. A scientific and true understanding of the world and of its necessities is the essential basis for effective action upon it. To be sure, will and commitment are also necessary for action, but alone they are not sufficient to ensure success. For this the will must be guided by thought, by reason. We must understand the situation in which we act, and what is and is not really possible within it. Conversely, ignorance is the recipe for idle dreaming and for the construction of sterile utopias. The less a person knows, as Hegel says, 'the greater is his tendency to launch out into all sorts of empty possibilities' (*Logic* § 143z, p. 204).

Hegel is not denying that utopian and critical ideas have played a valuable and important role in social and political thought. He does insist, however, that if such ideas are to be more than mere wishful dreams, they must reflect and be disciplined by reality. For example, Hegel argues that Plato's *Republic* — the greatest of utopian works — is misunderstood if it is regarded simply as an ideal vision of how society ought to be organised. The *Republic* is rather Plato's attempt to understand the conditions, the developments and the problems of the society of his day. It is the attempt to grasp actuality in rational terms; for:

Philosophy is ... the apprehension of the present and

actual, not the erection of a beyond ... Even Plato's *Republic*, which passes proverbially as an empty ideal, is in essence nothing but an interpretation of the nature of Greek ethical life. (*PR*, p. 10)

III

Hegel, then, like Marx, advocates a realistic and scientific approach, and his account of society is historically concrete and dialectical. He rejects the utopian and merely 'critical' attitude as a basis for political thought and action. These are important elements of the rational kernel of his notorious principle. And yet Hegel's philosophy taken as a whole is far from being scientific or realistic. Its detailed contents are set within a philosophical system which purports not merely to understand and explain the world in a scientific fashion, but to rationalise and justify it. It is this which constitutes the mystical shell and which gives rise to the accusations of mysticism and conservatism.

These accusations are fully justified. Hegel is quite explicit — at times almost brutally so — about the conservative and idealising implications of his philosophy.[4] The recognition of reason in the world, he says, 'is the rational insight which reconciles us to the actual, the reconciliation which philosophy affords' (*PR*, p. 12). Philosophy gives not criticism but 'consolation' (*Logic* § 147z, p. 209f); it teaches us to give up the restless desire to condemn and repudiate the existing order.

Thus when Hegel talks of philosophy 'reconciling' us to the world, he means not only that we should approach the world scientifically and discipline our ideas to reality. He means that we should regard the world as rational in the sense of 'ideal'. The world, Hegel insists, is as it ought to be. The desire to criticise and to change it is the error of 'youth' which imagines 'that the world is utterly sunk in wickedness and that the first thing needful is a thorough transformation' (*Logic* § 234z, p. 291). The maturer and wiser view — the view, needless to say, embodied in Hegel's philosophy — is that 'actuality is not so bad and irrational, as purblind or wrong-headed and muddle-brained would-be reformers imagine' (*Logic* § 142z, p. 201). 'The Good is radically and really achieved' (*Logic* § 235, p. 291), and our discontents are groundless: 'all unsatisfied endeavour ceases, when we recognise that the final purpose of the world is

accomplished no less than ever accomplishing itself' (*Logic*
§ 234z, p. 291).

For Hegel, then, not only is actuality rational, but rationality is
actual, in the sense that it is actualising itself in the world.

> The actual world is as it ought to be . . . the truly good, the
> universal divine Reason is the power capable of actualising
> itself . . . God governs the world. The actual working out of
> His government, the carrying out of His plan is the history
> of the world. (*Reason in history*, p. 47)

World history is governed by Divine Providence — it is the
realisation of God's will on earth. The study of history and
politics must take the form of a justification of God, of a 'theodicy'
(*Reason in history*, p. 18). There is no place here for criticism — no
need for it. For evil, from this perspective, is a mere subordinate
and vanishing moment, and our reconciliation with it is achieved
'through the recognition of the positive elements in which that
negative element disappears as something subordinate and
vanquished . . . The true ultimate [rational and divine] purpose
has been actualised in the world and . . . evil cannot ultimately
prevail beside it' (*Reason in history*, p. 18).

Here is the 'mystical shell' of Hegel's philosophy in full
measure: that aspect of it which seeks, in Marx's words, to
'transfigure and glorify the existing state of things' (*Capital*, vol. I,
p. 20). It leads to the grotesquely idealised and unrecognisable
account of social life which Hegel gives in his political philosophy.
The state is pictured as 'inherently rational' and as the
'realisation of freedom', marriage as a harmonious union based
on love, etc. It is tempting to try to disregard these themes as
loose exaggeration and rhetoric on Hegel's part.[5] Unfortunately,
this is not possible. These views are, on the contrary, an essential
ingredient of his philosophy and of his idealism, constantly
reiterated as the ultimate and deepest significance of his thought.
As such, they have been taken up and repeated ever since by 'old'
and conservatively-minded Hegelians, who have wanted to
legitimate and rationalise the *status quo*.[6]

IV

It is a common view that the conservative and idealising aspect of

Hegel's thought is an inevitable and inescapable outcome of his identification of the actual and the rational. But this is not so. As Hegel himself insisted, and as the Young Hegelians were quick to point out, the unity of actuality and reason is a *dialectical* one, which includes within it conflict as well as harmony. Although Hegel often tends to take the side of conservatism and reconciliation in his later writings, his philosophy is more complex, more confused and contradictory — and also more profound and interesting — in its practical implications than this suggests. In the *Encyclopaedia Logic* (3rd edn, 1830), indeed, Hegel repudiated the accusation that he was seeking merely to justify the existing order and to rule out any criticism of it. 'Who is not acute enough', he asks, 'to see a great deal in his own surroundings which is really far from being as it ought to be?' (*Logic* § 6, p. 10)

The claim that the 'actual is rational' does not, he insists, mean that whatever *exists* is rational. 'Actuality' and 'existence' are both technical terms in his logical system. Of the two, existence is the lower grade of being. There are things which exist and yet which lack 'actuality' in Hegel's sense, for actuality is 'the unity of essence and existence, inward and outward' (*Logic*, § 142, p. 200). An existing thing is actual only when its existence is in harmony with its essence; when its existence corresponds with its proper notion, function or idea. On the other hand, 'when this unity is not present, a thing is not actual even though it may have acquired existence. A bad state is one which merely exists; a sick body exists too, but it has no genuine reality' (*PR*, p. 283).

Hegel's idea of actuality is closely associated with his account of truth, and usefully understood in relation to it. Truth is commonly regarded as a quality of propositions or ideas, which they possess when they correspond to their objects. For Hegel, however, this is merely the concept of 'correctness', and he distinguishes from it a deeper, 'philosophical' sense of truth, which refers to the correspondence of an object with its 'Notion', 'Concept' or 'Idea'.[7]

> Truth in the deeper sense consists in the identity between objectivity and the notion. It is in this deeper sense of truth that we speak of a true state, or a true work of art. These objects are true if they are as they ought to be; i.e. if their reality corresponds to their notion. When thus viewed, the untrue is much the same as to be bad. A bad man is an untrue man. (*Logic* § 213z, p. 276)

This may sound strange and unfamiliar, but, as Hegel points out, there are examples of this usage in ordinary language: 'thus we speak of a true friend: by which we mean a friend whose manner of conduct accords with the notion of friendship' (*Logic* § 24z, p. 41).

To be rational, actual and true, the objectivity of a thing must, thus, correspond with its notion, its existence with its essence: it must be a harmonious whole, not infected with contradiction. To be untrue, not fully actual, not fully rational, on the other hand, means 'to be bad, self-discordant' (*Logic* § 24z, p. 41). But the bad, to repeat the crucial point, although it lacks actuality, may none the less exist.

This distinction between actuality and existence puts the Hegelian view that the actual is rational in an entirely new light. Indeed, if 'actuality' is taken to refer only to fully rational existence, then Hegel's principle becomes true by definition. This is, no doubt, part of the reason why Hegel and his followers have tended to brush aside objections to this principle. Once we grasp what Hegel means by 'actuality', we cannot but agree that the actual is rational, for this is simply a tautology.

The problem, however, has only been shifted elsewhere. Although the actual may be rational, by no means all that *exists* is rational and actual. The question remains of how far this tautological notion of rational actuality is applicable to the existent world around us. On this crucial issue Hegel is ambiguous and unclear.

In his political and historical writings, as we have seen, Hegel often tends to suggest that the state and society, as they have developed and as they in fact exist, are rational and actual. This is the basis of Hegel's conservatism, and it is in these terms that he attacks would-be critics of society:

> Reason is not so impotent as to bring about only the ideal, the ought, which supposedly exists in some unknown region beyond reality (or, as is more likely, only as a particular idea in the heads of a few individuals)[8] (*Reason in history*, p. 11).

In more metaphysical and logical contexts, however, we are told that nothing finite is fully actual or rational. Indeed, Hegel says that

God alone is the thorough harmony of notion and reality.

> All finite things involve an untruth: they have a notion and an existence, but their existence does not meet the requirements of the notion. For this reason they must perish. (*Logic* § 24z, p. 41)

All 'finite' things, therefore, are contradictory and to that extent irrational. They can be criticised for their 'untruth'. Indeed, because of their contradictoriness — their irrationality and untruth — all finite things are destined to 'criticise' themselves in a practical fashion. They are ultimately doomed to change and to pass away. 'Finite things are changeable and transient . . ., existence is associated with them for a season only . . . the association is neither eternal nor inseparable' (*Logic* § 193, p. 259).

This is the dialectical side of Hegel's thought. It was seized upon by the Young Hegelians, who saw in it the seeds of a radical and critical philosophy. For, if nothing but God is fully actual, fully rational — if everything finite is animated by contradiction and in the process of change — then what in fact exists is *never* ideal. One must equally say 'what is actual is *ir*rational'. And so, for the Young Hegelians, the realisation of reason is not an established fact, but rather a goal and a task. The world as it is, the existing state of things, must be criticised and transformed: reason must be *realised*, it must be *made* actual.

Engels, in his excellent discussion of these issues, credits Heine with being among the first to appreciate the critical and revolutionary significance of Hegel's philosophy.[9] Heine expresses this charmingly in an imaginary dialogue between himself and Hegel, who goes under the title of 'the King of Philosophy'.

> Once when I was put out by the saying: 'all that exists is rational' he smiled in a peculiar way and observed: 'it could also mean: all that is rational *must* exist.' He looked around hastily but soon calmed down, for only Heinrich Beer heard what he said.[10]

I do not know who Heinrich Beer is, but it is clear that Heine's meaning is that Hegel was himself aware of the ambiguity and of the possibly revolutionary significance of his philosophy, but that he was afraid to speak it. I doubt that this is a correct account of Hegel's intentions; but whether it is so or not is unimportant here. For what is undoubted is that Hegel's philosophy contains strands and themes which, whether he intended them so or not, have a critical and revolutionary significance. It is these that were emphasised and developed by the Young Hegelians and by the young Marx.

Indeed, one of the clearest statements of this 'critical' interpretation of the Hegelian philosophy is given by Marx, in a letter to Ruge of September, 1843.

> Reason has always existed, but not always in a rational form. The critic can therefore start out from any form of theoretical and practical consciousness and from the forms *peculiar* to existing reality develop the true reality as its obligation and its final goal. As far as real life is concerned it is precisely the *political state* . . . which, even where it is not yet consciously imbued with socialist demands, contains the demands of reason. And the political state does not stop there. Everywhere it assumes that reason has been realised. But precisely because of that it everywhere becomes involved in the contradiction between its ideal function and its real prerequisites. (*Collected works*, vol. 3, p. 143)

This is pure Young Hegelianism. In the existing political state, Marx is saying, we can discern a contradiction between its 'ideal function' and its existing form: there is a discrepancy between its notion and its objective existence. To that extent, the state is irrational and untrue, and may be criticised as such.

Moreover, such criticism, the Young Hegelians insisted, does not involve bringing either Kantian *a priori* or merely subjective ideals and values to bear on reality from outside. The ideals according to which the existing state is to be criticised, on the contrary, are supposed, in Hegelian fashion, to be the *notion* of the state: something which is intrinsic to the state — its very essence.[11] Again Marx puts it memorably: 'We do not confront the world in a doctrinaire fashion with a new principle: Here is the truth, kneel down before it! We develop new principles for the world out of the world's own principles' (*Collected works*, vol. 3, p. 144).

V

This is the Young Hegelian, critical, approach. Like Old

Hegelian conservatism, it derives from themes which are central and essential to Hegel's philosophy; and initially, at least, it seems to offer an attractive alternative. Ultimately, however, it, too, conflicts with the rational — the scientific and realistic — side of Hegel's thought, and cannot provide a satisfactory basis for the study of politics or society. Indeed, this critical approach represents precisely the sort of utopian and subjective wishful thinking against which Hegel directs his polemics. The existing order is regarded as the imperfect and partial embodiment of the Notion or Ideal, which is its real essence, truth and ultimate destiny. The established order is measured against this Ideal and found wanting. The scientific attitude of studying what is, is abandoned, and the world is judged and criticised in the light of how it ought to be.

I will illustrate these points with some recent examples; for the Young Hegelian approach has not been confined to Hegel's disciples of the 1840s. It has had an enduring influence, and appears in some unexpected places. For example, in the Marxist tradition, and even amongst the hardest of hard-liners, who would be horrified by the thought that they had much in common with the early Marx, let alone with Hegel! It is particularly evident in the discussion of what Bahro has so usefully called 'actually existing' socialist societies, like those of Eastern Europe, the Soviet Union, Cuba and China.[12] How often have we heard the refrain that these societies are not 'genuinely' socialist, that they are not 'true' workers states. Of course, they exist in fact; but, in true Hegelian terms, what is being said is that they are not as they ought to be, they do not embody the concept, the notion — the ideal — of socialism: they lack 'actuality' and 'rationality'.

The un-ideal character of 'actually existing' socialist states is one of the major problems for contemporary socialist thought. An all too common response on the left has been to try to evade this problem by discounting these societies as 'exceptions' in the ways described. But this is clearly not a satisfactory response. It involves abandoning altogether the scientific approach to history and adopting instead a purely moral one. There can, of course, be exceptions in history; but when history comes to be entirely composed of them they cease to be exceptions and become the stuff and actuality of history. The ideal is then revealed as unreal, utopian and subjective.

Not that this style of thought is any monopoly of the left. One of the stranger products of the American far right is a writer called Ayn Rand, who propounds an extreme and simplistic brand of *laissez-faire* individualism. Among her works is a book with the arresting title, *Capitalism: the unknown ideal*. However, the title is designed not simply to capture attention; it accurately reflects the theme of the book. The ideal of capitalism is 'unknown', she believes, because it has not yet been tried! The essence and the ideal of capitalism is the free market. Capitalism, as it has existed for all these centuries — 'actually existing' capitalism — has never realised this ideal. *Laissez-faire* and the free market have always been restricted and compromised, she thinks, by excessive state interference under the influence of muddled and weak humanitarian do-gooders, etc. The destructive features of capitalism — the exploitation, stagnation, alienation, oppression and misery associated with it — are all the mere aberrant and monstrous products of the mixed economy. Pure capitalism, the 'unknown ideal', would not be like this.

To write history in this way is, of course, absurd. Socialists, however, are in danger of precisely similar absurdities when they reject actually existing socialist societies as 'exceptions', and persist in thinking of socialism as an 'unknown ideal'.

It is not the job of history or of the social sciences to criticise or condemn societies according to ideal standards: rather, they should seek to understand and explain the real world as it has in fact developed. The social sciences, that is to say, must reconcile themselves to the world, and avoid what Carr calls the 'might have been school of thought'.[13] Socialists, in particular, must confront the real world of socialism and come to terms with it, rather than dismissing it as an aberration. In saying this, I must stress, I am not suggesting that they should abandon all criticism, and simply endorse everything that has gone under the name of socialism. In the remainder of this paper, I shall try to show how Marx distinguishes what is rational from what is mystical in Hegel's principle and, on that basis, provides a method which is both scientific and critical.

VI

Old Hegelianism seeks to legitimise the existing order, whereas Young Hegelianism is dedicated to criticising it. At first sight they seem absolute opposites; but, as I have shown, they share in common the fact that they both adopt a moral rather than a scientific approach to the world. The basis for this moral approach, moreover, lies in the idealism which both share and which is a central feature of Hegel's metaphysics.

As we have seen, Hegel's philosophy involves an extravagant form of idealism. The actual is rational, he thought, because Reason, the Idea, the Ideal, is an active principle, expressing and realising itself in the world. 'Reason', says Hegel, 'is the soul of the world it inhabits, its immanent principle, its most proper and inward nature, its universal' (*Logic* § 24z, p. 37). Moreover, all this is given a theological interpretation, so that the objective world becomes God's creation and history a 'theodicy'. It is this idealism which gives rise to that paradoxically 'inverted' order so characteristic of Hegel's philosophy. For Hegel, it is reason, the idea, the ideal that comes first, and which then specifies, concretises and realises itself in its particulars. As Seth says, 'Hegel's language would justify us in believing that categories take flesh and blood and walk into the air ... that logical abstractions can *thicken* so to speak into real existence' (*Heglianism and personality*, p. 125).

Hegel's principle that the actual is rational is often identified as the locus and source of his idealism; and, as such, rejected in favour of the dualist alternative. (For example, this is what Seth goes on to do.) It is certainly true that Hegel expresses his idealism through this principle; but we must proceed carefully at this point if we are to disentangle what is scientific and rational from what is mystical and idealistic in it.

In particular, it is vital to see that materialism also involves the idea of the unity of actuality and reason. Human reason is nothing transcendent — it is a product of natural and social evolution. For this reason, Marx does not reject or discard Hegel's principle. Rather, as he says, he turns it 'on its feet'.

> For Hegel, the life-process of the human brain, i.e., the process of thinking, which, under the name of 'the Idea', he even transforms into an independent subject, is the *demiurgos* [creator] of the real world, and the real world is only the external, phenomenal form of 'the Idea'. With me, on the contrary, the idea is nothing else than the material world reflected by the human brain, and transformed into forms of thought. (*Capital*, vol. I, p. 19)

For Marx, that is to say, nature and society are not, as with

Hegel, the products of reason; on the contrary, reason — ideas and ideals — are the outcome and creations of natural and historical development. 'The phantoms formed in the human brain are . . . sublimates of their material life process . . . Morality, religion, metaphysics, all the rest of ideology and their corresponding forms of consciousness, thus no longer retain the semblance of independence' (*German ideology*, p. 47). Ideas and ideals have no autonomy from social life. They are the subjective aspect of actual and existing objective social relations: they are social through and through.

Marx's materialism does not, then, involve any denial of the unity of actuality and reason; but it does, as Marx says, 'invert' the Hegelian and idealist interpretation of it. Instead of starting with ideas and ideals, and either criticising or justifying reality in terms of them, Marx begins with social reality and explains ideas and ideals on this basis.

> In direct contrast to German philosophy, which descends from heaven to earth, here we ascend from earth to heaven . . . We set out from real, active men, and on the basis of their real life-process we demonstrate the development of the ideological reflexes and echoes of this life process. (*German ideology*, p. 47)

This sort of outlook has been enormously attractive and fruitful as a basis for social theory. However, it may well seem that such a straightforward kind of materialism is a reductive and crude philosophy which leaves unresolved many of the problems of the relation of reason to reality that I have been raising. In particular, it is often argued that such a philosophy is unable to do justice to the *critical* nature of thought. If reason were nothing but a product and a reflection of the established order, then, it seems, it could neither oppose existing conditions nor be critical of them. In order to acknowledge the critical power of reason, it is argued, reason must be viewed in a dualistic fashion as a force separate and distinct from the world.

Marx's materialism, however, is not reductive. On the contrary, it is a *dialectical* form of materialism which is not vulnerable to this argument. For a crucial aspect of the rational kernel that Marx retains from Hegel's philosophy is the dialectic. To the question: where do critical ideas come from? — Marx's response is clear and unmistakable. *All* ideas are social and historical products. All ideas are, in this sense, ideological. Critical ideas — just like uncritical ones — arise from and reflect social reality. In saying this, Marx does not deny that reason can oppose and criticise the established order. He does, however, insist that when it does so, that is a reflection of the fact that *existing conditions are themselves contradictory*. 'If theory, theology, philosophy, ethics, etc., comes into contradiction with existing relations, this can only occur because existing social relations have come into contradiction with existing forces of production' (*German ideology*, p. 52).

Criticism is not the prerogative of thought alone. Opposition, negation and contradiction are *in the world*: they are features of what is. For nothing concrete and determinate merely *is*. Nothing is simply and solely positive. Negation and opposition are essentially involved in all things. This is the first lesson of Hegel's logic, and the most vital principle of dialectic in all its forms. Mere being is an abstract and empty category. All concrete things are a unity of being and nothing, of positive and negative aspects; and these opposites are synthesised in the process of movement and becoming. Everything concrete is contradictory. 'We are aware that everything finite, instead of being stable and ultimate is rather changeable and transient' (*Logic* § 81z, p. 150).

Marxism is a dialectical philosophy. As such, it rejects the abstract, merely positivistic conception of actuality, according to which what is, merely is.

> To materialised conception existence stands in the character of something solely positive, and quietly abiding within its own limits . . . But the fact is, mutability lies in the notion of existence, and change is only the manifestation of what it implicitly is. (*Logic* § 92z, p. 174)

Thus negation, opposition and criticism do not need to be brought to the world by the thinking subject from the outside. The social world already contains negative, critical and contradictory forces within it. Nor is this criticism embodied merely in ideas or ideals. It exists first of all in *fact*. Only later is it apprehended by consciousness and reflected in thought. Thus Marx insists that 'Communism is for us not a *state of affairs* which is to be established, an *ideal* to which reality will have to adjust itself. We call communism the *real* movement which abolishes the present state of things' (*German ideology*, pp. 56–7).

Marx, then, essentially agrees with Hegel's view that

> dialectic is not an activity of subjective thinking applied to
> some matter externally, but is rather the matter's own soul
> putting forth its branches and fruit organically. This
> development of the Idea is the proper activity of its
> rationality, and thinking, as something subjective, merely
> looks on at it without for its part adding to it any ingredient
> of its own. To consider a thing rationally means not to bring
> reason to bear on the object from the outside and so to
> tamper with it, but to find that the object is rational on its
> own account. (*PR*, § 31, pp. 34–5)

What Hegel is describing here, albeit in the alien and
metaphysical language which is so much his own, is nothing
other than the scientific method. This approach undoubtedly
involves a measure of 'reconciliation' to reality, as we have seen.
It involves, as Hegel says, not 'tampering' with the world, not
imposing value and ideals upon it, but rather observing and
understanding it as it is. However, in Marx's hands at least, this
method by no means entails a conservative attitude or the
abrogation of criticism. For Marx does not set out to judge
capitalism against any pre-established moral values, nor to posit
an ideal socialist state of the future. Rather, he attempts to
understand and explain in scientific terms the working of existing
capitalist society. As Engels says, Marx 'never based his
communist demands upon this [moral principle] but upon the
inevitable collapse of the capitalist mode of production, which is
daily taking place before our eyes to an ever greater degree'
(Preface to Marx, *Poverty of philosophy*, p. 9).

In this way — by exposing, articulating and analysing the
critical and revolutionary tendencies and forces already at work
in the world — Marx provides the most powerful and effective
critique of capitalism: a *scientific* critique.[14]

Notes

1. See, e.g., S. Avineri, *Hegel's theory of the modern state*, pp. 115–31;
and W. Kaufman, *Hegel: a reinterpretation*, ch. 6.
2. These phrases are, of course, from K. Marx, *Capital*, vol. I, pp. 19–
20.

3. I am here condensing an account of Hegel's critique of Kant's theory of knowledge given more fully in *Reality and Reason*, chs 2–3.

4. See, e.g., the bitter attack on Fries in Hegel's Preface to *Philosophy of right*.

5. See, e.g., W. Kaufman, *Hegel: a reinterpretation*, ch. 6.

6. For a secular version of such Hegelian conservatism, see F.H. Bradley, 'My Station and its Duties', *Ethical studies*, ch. 5; and, more recently, R. Scruton, *The meaning of conservatism*.

7. The German term that Hegel uses is '*Begriff*', which is translated by Wallace as 'Notion' and by Knox as 'Concept'.

8. I have amended Hartman's translation in line with the version given by Nisbet in Hegel, *Lectures on the philosophy of world history: introduction*, p. 27.

9. F. Engels, *Ludwig Feuerbach and the end of classical German philosophy*, ch. 1.

10. From Heine's letter *On Germany*, quoted by Plekhanov in his *Notes* to the Russian edition (1892) of Engels, *Ludwig Feuerbach*, p. 104.

11. See H. Marcuse, *Reason and revolution* for an excellent account of the 'critical', Young Hegelian, reading of Hegel, which brings out this point particularly clearly.

12. R. Bahro, *The alternative in Eastern Europe*.

13. E.H. Carr, *What is history?*: p. 96. This work contains a useful and illuminating discussion of the role of reason in history.

14. I am grateful for comments and criticisms to Chris Arthur, Susan Easton, David Lamb, Joe McCarney and Gülnur Savran.

References

Avineri, S., (1972) *Hegel's theory of the modern state*, Cambridge University Press, Cambridge.

Bahro, R., (1978) *The alternative in Eastern Europe*, New Left Books, London.

Bradley, F.H., (1927) *Ethical studies*, (2nd edn) Oxford University Press, London.

Carr, E.H., (1964) *What is history?*, Penguin Books, Harmondsworth, Middlesex.

Engels, F., (1976) *Ludwig Feuerbach and the end of classical German philosophy*, Foreign Languages Press, Peking.

Hegel, G.W.F., (1952) *Philosophy of right*, trans. T.M. Knox, The Clarendon Press, Oxford.

—— (1953) *Reason in history*, trans. R.S. Hartman, Bobbs-Merrill, Indianapolis and New York.

—— (1975) *Lectures on the philosophy of world history: introduction*, trans. H.B. Nisbet, Cambridge University Press, Cambridge.

—— (1975) *Logic (Encyclopaedia of the philosophical sciences, part I)* (3rd edn) trans. W. Wallace, The Clarendon Press, Oxford.

Kaufman, W., (1964) *Hegel: a reinterpretation*, Anchor Books, Garden City, N.Y.

Marcuse, H., (1955) *Reason and revolution. Hegel and the rise of social theory*, Routledge and Kegan Paul, London.

Marx, K., (1961) *Capital*, vol. I, Foreign Languages Publishing House, Moscow.

—— (1975) 'Letter to Ruge (September, 1843)', in *Collected works*, vol. 3, Lawrence and Wishart, London.

—— (1955) *The Poverty of philosophy*, Progress Publishers, Moscow.

—— and F. Engels (1970) *The German ideology*, Part I, ed. C.J. Arthur, International Publishers, New York.

Rand, A., (1966) *Capitalism: the unknown ideal*, New American Library, New York.

Sayers, S., (1985) *Reality and reason: dialectic and the theory of knowledge*, Basil Blackwell, Oxford.

Scruton, R., (1980) *The meaning of conservatism*, Penguin Books, Harmondsworth, Middlesex.

Seth, A., (1887) *Hegelianism and personality*, William Blackwood and Sons, Edinburgh.

8

Hegel, Marx and Dialectic

Joseph McCarney

This paper is an attempt to establish the significance of dialectic for social scientific inquiry. Its topic is the idea of a dialectical social science, and the question it seeks to answer is the question of how such a science is possible. Its understanding of what dialectic is comes from Hegel. This is scarcely surprising, since his writings are the source of the modern debate and treat the basic theoretical issues with unparalleled richness. A convenient starting point in them is offered by a passage from the *Philosophy of right*:

> The concept's moving principle, which alike engenders and dissolves the particularizations of the universal, I call 'dialectic' . . . The . . . dialectic of the concept consists not simply in producing the determination as a contrary and a restriction, but in producing and seizing upon the positive content and outcome of the determination, because it is this which makes it solely a development and an immanent progress. Moreover, this dialectic is not an activity of subjective thinking applied to some matter externally, but is rather the matter's very soul putting forth its branches and fruit organically. This development of the Idea is the proper activity of its rationality, and thinking, as something subjective, merely looks on at it without for its part adding to it any ingredient of its own. To consider a thing rationally means not to bring reason to bear on the object from the outside and so to tamper with it, but to find that the object is rational on its own account; here it is mind in its freedom, the culmination of self-conscious reason, which gives itself actuality and engenders itself as an existing world.[1]

It is, of course, unwise to focus too hard on a single passage, but the risks are reduced in this case by the representative nature of the themes being addressed. Above all, the passage is representative of Hegel's dealings with dialectic through its placing of the category of reason at the centre of things. Much of the difficulty of the present inquiry consists in showing how this emphasis is to be conceived and justified in the context of dialectical social science. It is already clear that such a science will not qualify as rational just in virtue of employing a rational methodology: it has also to do justice to the rationality of its object. Even this will not suffice, if it is intelligible as merely 'an activity of subjective thinking applied to some matter externally'. To have a dialectical character, the science must somehow, it appears, participate in the activity of rationality it uncovers. For what is dialectical has to constitute an immanent progress, an organic development. These are demanding requirements, and likely to prove significantly more demanding for us than they were for Hegel.

If one asks how he met them, the answer suggested by the passage is, in general terms, clear enough: it is that one has to invoke his ontology. The matter in question is rational on its own account because it is the medium of existence for what is, under one aspect, identified as itself 'self-conscious reason', and under others as 'the Idea' and as 'mind' (*Geist*). A solution along these lines, however, poses a special difficulty for our project. In the usual litanies, from Croce onwards, of what is living and what is dead in Hegel, it is his ontological vision that is most readily assigned to the philosophical graveyard. The task of explaining why this is so is bound to be complex, and, fortunately, lies outside our scope. What seems undeniable is that the claims of self-conscious reason as matter and subject arouse few answering chords in the contemporary world, even among 'Hegelians'. The level of embarrassment is likely to be highest in philosophy of science, at least in so far as it is sensitive to contemporary scientific practice. The secular and reductive spirit of that practice is markedly unsympathetic to whatever it can construe as metaphysical excess. For anyone concerned for Hegel's thought as a living force, it may be instructive to accept this verdict, at least for the sake of the argument, and to explore the consequences. This would be to ask whether the dialectical character of science may be preserved without the original ontology. Is there a way other than the one Hegel took in which science may both reveal and contribute to the rationality of its object?

If recent theory of science is agreed on anything, it is agreed that the philosophy and the history should not be kept in watertight compartments. Philosophy of science, in particular, runs a risk of sterility unless it stays in contact with some concrete practice of science. To say this is to restate what was well understood by Hegel. His excursions into the subject are marked by scorn of 'mere formalism', with its imaginary examples and lifeless schemas, and by extensive reference to the details of the science of his time.[2] If one tries to follow this lead here, a certain body of work forces itself on one's attention. Marx consistently claimed that his science was dialectical and that the author of its dialectic was Hegel. As a social scientific achievement under such auspices, it has no serious rival in terms of scale of conception, thoroughness of execution and historical influence. There is a more specific consideration which commends it to us. Marx is a Hegelian for our time, at least in the negative sense that what he is crucially unable to accept is the ontology. From early to late, the burden of his complaint is always the treatment of the Idea as subject.[3] If one considers the details of this critique, it may well have to be admitted that it gives the ontology a somewhat simplistic reading, tending all too readily to take its subject as a transcendent being in relation to whose activity events in the ordinary world are epiphenomenal. Such a reading, it may be thought, fails to do justice to the central Hegelian claim to have rendered *aufgehoben* the traditional opposition of immanence and transcendence by virtue of a subject which is neither simply external to the finite nor wholly exhausted in it. For present purposes, however, it may suffice to work with fairly coarse-grained categories here: the radical character of Marx's break with his philosophical upbringing will be more significant than the element of caricature through which it was mediated. It is enough that he shares with our contemporaries an inability to accept the dialectic of society as a process through which reason engenders itself as an existing world, however that engendering is precisely to be conceived. In spite of this, he was to carry through a programme of social inquiry claiming the inspiration of Hegel's dialectic. Such an achievement must have considerable significance for our discussion. Hence, we may provisionally replace the original question with the more manageable one of how this claim is to be understood. In what does the dialectical status of Marx's science consist?

163

I

It should be said at once that rejecting the ontology is not like cutting away an excrescence that allows everything else to flourish as before. There is within Marxism a tradition, derived ultimately from Engels, of seeing the relationship with Hegel in just such facile terms. It is, on this view, a question of keeping the radical 'method' while dropping the conservative 'system'. Such a formula fails to register the way in which method and system are bound together in Hegel's thought. The point is easy to illustrate from within the range of present concerns. It is generally assumed that contradiction is a key dialectical category. Yet it is noteworthy that many commentators have failed to detect at various points in Hegel's dialectic the inner complexity which that category needs to take root.[4] Instead, they have seen a linear sequence in which every stage follows directly from the one before without the mediation of conflict within the stages. They have concluded that contradiction is not, after all, essential to dialectical movement. What is essential to it is the striving of incomplete and finite categories towards their completion in the infinite. The heart of the matter is taken to be, not the contradictions in things which generate their restlessness but, the 'absolute unrest' which typically, though not inevitably, finds expression in contradictions. It is not necessary to decide the merits of this interpretation here. But one should at least note that it focuses on a significant feature of Hegel's presentation, and one should note also the chief response available to the friends of contradiction. It is a response that enlists the ontology directly by making its subject the bearer of one side of the oppositions. Thus, it may be granted that in some stretches of dialectic the moment of internal conflict is lacking, while insisting that there remains, at every stage short of the last, the contrast between the existing state of things and what they will become in the fulfilment of reason. The mainspring of the movement through these stretches is the tension between the way the contents are at any particular point and the way they are potentially, in their concept and in truth. Momentum is sustained not through contradictions in the real, but through contradictions between the real and the rational. Clearly, the rational cannot, for Marx, have the existential status required for a solution of this kind. The break with Hegel now appears as a break with 'method' as well as 'system', since here dialectic and ontology are inseparable.

This conclusion may seem to have gloomy implications for our inquiry. Fortunately, however, the damage can be contained. There is, it should be remembered, a large variety of dialectical models in Hegel, a variety too large to be captured in a simple formula. In some of them, no special ontological reinforcements are needed to get the contradictions going. As a model for science, the phenomenological dialectic is the outstanding candidate among these. Consciousness, Hegel insists, is always conscious-ness *of* something. So a dialectic of forms of consciousness will have built into its structure a dualism that guarantees the complexity presupposed by relations of contradiction. Such relations will obtain in practice whenever the idea of the object by which the subject consciousness is possessed comes in conflict with the object as it is actually encountered in experience.[5] Given a subject meeting minimal conditions of rationality, the conflict brings about of itself a change in the preconceptions. This is the pattern usually taken to be classically exemplified in the opening chapters of the *Phenomenology of spirit*. That this is so is at least a happy omen. The *Phenomenology* is a key text of the Hegel-Marx nexus: it is for Marx 'the true point of origin and the secret of the Hegelian philosophy'.[6] Moreover, in its opening chapters it is forms of cognition that prove inadequate when the version of reality they project is put to the test. In the present inquiry also, it is with a form of cognition that we have to deal. It seems natural to suggest that the model for dialectical social science may be found in Hegelian phenomenology.

II

This suggestion will be developed in a schematic way at first and the details will be filled in later. In Marx's appropriation of the phenomenological theme, the subject is the social class, and so the dialectic of consciousness becomes a dialectic of class consciousness. A class may be thought of as equipped with a view of its social world which has to cope with the demands of everyday existence in that world. For a subordinate class, at least in the earlier stages of the dialectic, the essential content of this world-view is supplied by the 'ruling ideas', which, Marx tells us, are the ideas of the ruling class. In an idiom with a sharper edge to it, the class may be said to be subjected to the ruling ideology; that is, to the set of ideas and beliefs which serve the interests of the ruling class by legitimising its rule.[7] This ideology involves, like any other, cognitive claims. It purports to embody a correct picture of social reality. It is these claims which, according to the phenomenological model, will come in conflict with, and be refuted by, experience. Such experience is, of course, not unmediated. It is human social experience and, as such, highly conceptualised, not a registering of raw data. The dialectic of class consciousness is the process through which the way it is conceptualised comes increasingly to be informed by scientific insight. Thus, in Marx's version, the phenomenological dialectic is fuelled by the opposition of ruling ideas and comprehended experience. In the central case with which he was concerned this, it turns out, is equivalent to the opposition of bourgeois ideology and proletarian science.

This attempt to reconstruct Marx's conception of dialectic has, like any other, to face the difficulty posed by the reticence of the texts. These embody a practice, but without providing an explicit theory of it. The sketch that has been given seems, however, to offer a way of piecing together the major clues that are available. In the first place, it can show the exactness of Marx's favoured self-description of his work, evidenced by the titles or sub-titles of the major writings, as a 'critique of political economy'. In the terms of the preceding discussion, this is to say that it is a critique of the central, most formidable, version of bourgeois ideology. Marx evidently saw the significance of his life-work as bound up with the destruction of the cognitive core of that ideology. This is intelligible in the light of our scheme in so far as such a work of destruction serves to break the grip of the ruling ideas by exposing the gap between what they project and the reality. In doing so it exposes and activates the primary contradiction of the dialectic of class consciousness.

It should also be possible at this point to accommodate the more specific clues that Marx provides in moments of methodo-logical reflection. Perhaps the most characteristic and significant of them is the insistence that his dialectic, Hegel's dialectic 'in its rational form', is 'in its very essence critical and revolutionary'.[8] This insistence has greatly influenced later attempts to explicate his conception of his scientific work. It has been taken as confirming that its relation to its object is not to be thought of as merely explanatory or theoretical in the manner of orthodox science but as 'practical', even 'transformative', as well. In the most influential version of the idea in twentieth century Marxism, dialectical social science has been interpreted as a 'critique' or 'critical theory' of society. Such a view of its status, although all too frequently taken for granted, is open to various objections. What concerns us here is simply its ability to preserve the dialectical character of inquiry. The notion of critique that is usually taken to be involved is the familiar one of systematically elaborated negative evaluation. Some such understanding seems required if the thesis is to perform the task of explaining how theory can be 'practical'. For a negative evaluation may be thought of as yielding reasons for doing something to change what is being evaluated, and such reasons for acting are, it may be said, practical in a primitive sense. The difficulty, however, is to see what constitutes a science of social contradictions as a negative evaluation of society, and to this the literature offers no satisfactory solution. The obvious suggestion is that the exposure of contradictions is necessarily the exposure of defects, since a contradiction is, as such, a defect in whatever it appears. But this avenue seems to be blocked by the opposition of the entire dialectical tradition, formulated most trenchantly by Hegel.[9] Even if it could be overcome, the critique thesis is in other ways ill-equipped to meet the needs of dialectical thought, as adumbrated in the passage which was our starting point. The rationality of social critique, as usually conceived, is essentially the rationality of the critic: rationality on the side of the object is superfluous to its constitution. This is to say that the enterprise is constituted from an external point of view, and so fails to belong to the organic development of the matter. Marx is quite as unsympathetic as Hegel to any suggestion that the role of theory is to confront existing reality with a *Sollen*, an abstract vision of what it ought to be. Thus, he is scathing about attempts to find an intellectual basis for socialism in a condemnation of capitalism, a tendency he associates with utopian thought. His work must, it seems, achieve its practical significance in some more immediate and immanent way. If one considers the specific needs of a phenomenological dialectic, the critique thesis has other difficulties to face. There is, in particular, the problem of accounting for the unique categorial status of the phenomenological subject. The critique of society is most naturally taken as yielding considerations which are binding on all in so far as they are rational. Marx's science, however, is not addressed indiscriminately to the universe of rational beings: it is by its very nature internally bound to the standpoint of the proletariat, the subject of its dialectic. In the face of these difficulties, it is a relief to turn once again to our Hegelian model. For it then becomes clear that the critique of society thesis introduces a wholly superfluous level of mediation into the conception of dialectical science.

It will scarcely be contentious to assert that in Hegelian phenomenology transitions are not effected through negative evaluations of the successive moments.[10] The source of movement is the discovery, not that these are as such undesirable or unsatisfactory, but that they involve contradictions. This discovery is, in terms of the model, immediately practical for a consciousness meeting minimal conditions of rationality. Such a consciousness cannot rest in the awareness of its own contradictions, but is driven towards their resolution. This force exerts itself in a modality which is not that of practical judgement as normally understood, but that of conceptual necessity. For its operation is the substance of the attribution of rationality to the subject consciousness in the first place. A subject who failed to meet this condition could never begin to play a part in the movement of reason which is dialectic. It is a condition which Hegel's 'natural consciousness' and Marx's class subjects can meet without difficulty. They are at least proto-rational from the earliest stages of the movement, and their rationality develops step-by-step as it proceeds. In Marx's case, the development takes the form of the dissemination and absorption of a scientific understanding of social reality. The achievement of such understanding is itself an immanent force of change, in so far as it forms and transforms the consciousness of the subjects who make history. This perspective seems to offer a hope of grasping dialectical inquiry as an element in an organic development. But it can only be a lifeless possibility until one begins to specify how it is realised. Certain conceptual matters have first to be considered by way of clearing the ground. They concern the notions of science, of contradiction, and of the subject that are being employed here.

III

It is of some importance to guard against what may be called the élitist associations of the term 'science'. In English usage, at any rate, it tends to suggest a somewhat rarefied activity that is the prerogative of a specialised group, the scientists. Such a conception will not suit the needs of a model which postulates that scientific understanding may permeate the consciousness of class subjects. It is, moreover, foreign to Marx's style of thinking in this area. The possibility of science arises, in his view, wherever the appearances of things fail to correspond to their reality. His basic image of scientific activity is the going behind such appearances to find what they conceal. In the case of social science, the possibility of this unmasking arises for subordinate classes just in virtue of their role in social production. For the ruling ideology is never entirely successful in imposing its version of reality, or, at any rate, its success is inherently precarious. Thus, it is a persistent theme in Marx's writings from early to late that subordinate classes are in a privileged position so far as grasping the truth about their society is concerned: they are best placed to penetrate the fog of its phenomenal forms.[11] Hence it is that, in its heroic period, the bourgeoisie had access to important insights into the nature of the society it was seeking to dominate, and its ideology began to degenerate only after it had achieved power. This penetration of what is given is, for Marx, the epitome of all science. Thus, the insights of subordinate classes are significant as both the historical basis and the conceptual model for the further elaboration of social science. In this elaboration, Marx recognises, of course, a role for specialist intellectuals, and he thought of himself as playing such a role for the working-class movement. Such contributions are possible, however, only in so far as theorists adopt the standpoint of the epistemologically privileged class. Social scientific understanding is, in the first instance, the birthright of such classes. This view of the cognitive potential of the proletariat goes together with Marx's conception of its historical role: 'the emancipation of the working classes must be conquered by the working classes themselves'.[12] For this conquest to occur, the dissemination of forms of scientific understanding among the workers is indispensable.

The task of the self-conscious theorists is to articulate insights, that arise, as it were, spontaneously for subordinate classes, into fully-fledged scientific concepts. In the case of Marx's science the central theoretical concepts form a tightly-knit group whose function may be characterised, in general terms, as that of theorising the role of labour in commodity production. The group includes the concepts of class and class conflict, of value and surplus value and of labour power and exploitation. As Marx freely acknowledges, he had for the most part taken over ideas found in the work of bourgeois historians and economists. So far

169

as the main stock is concerned, he made the firmest claim for originality in the case of labour power, the understanding of the commodity status of labour which is the key to the secret of commodity production. In the work of the most advanced bourgeois thinkers such as Ricardo, the basic scheme had already served to conceptualise society as a field of class antagonism. Apart from adding some fresh elements, Marx's appropriation of it involves two related claims. The first is that the social antagonisms are treated as forms of dialectical opposition, that is, as contradictions. The second is that the entire static structure is located in history, in a process of development leading to the overcoming of class society.[13] These claims should be examined in turn.

The idea that there are contradictions in society is often regarded as paradoxical or absurd. The chief source of such scepticism is the entirely proper conviction that contradiction is ultimately a category of logic, and that, in all its legitimate applications, this logical character has to be preserved. For present purposes, however, it should be possible to achieve it in a fairly straightforward way. The primary opposition for Marx is that of labour and capital. The substance of this opposition is a network of antagonistic class relationships which find expression in conflicts of beliefs, purposes and practices. Beliefs and purposes seem readily enough conceived of as bearers of logical relationships, and the possibility of tensions of a logical kind between them is well recognised in our everyday thinking. This tendency may be given a grounding in contemporary philosophy of logic. There, contradictions are standardly explained in terms of the notion of truth. The essential pre-condition for relations of contradiction to obtain is that the items related be bearers of truth-values. Strictly speaking, of course, contradictories necessarily have opposite truth-values. However, as we shall have to encompass the traditional notion of contrariety as well, it may be permissible to work with the weaker requirement that truth on one side of the relationship excludes the possibility of truth on the other. This requirement is easily met in the case of beliefs, which are assessable as true or false, if anything is. Moreover, recent philosophy of logic has been prepared to entertain the possibility of logical opposition between items which can support features analogous to truth, such as fulfilment or satisfaction conditions.[14] This is, for instance, the crucial step towards a logic of imperatives. But purposes may be realised or unrealised, and the achievement of some goals may rule out on logical grounds the achievement of others, as is presumably the case with, for instance, parliamentary democracy and the dictatorship of the proletariat. If one is now allowed to speak of logical relations involving beliefs and purposes, it seems a short step to bring in actions as well. The step is licensed by the internal relations usually supposed to hold between these categories. It is the incorporation or expression of cognitive and volitional elements in actions that is standardly taken as distinguishing them from mere bodily movements. Thus, one may think of actions as conceptually, and at least quasi-logically, related to one another in virtue of full-strength logical relations between their corresponding ingredients of belief and purpose. If actions are brought in, there can be no difficulty, in principle, in extending the argument to include the series or complexes of actions we call activities and practices, and thence, in turn, what may be thought of as the frozen practices that comprise social institutions. None of this should prove too contentious. The idea that actions may be conceptually interrelated is both deeply grounded in Hegelian theory of action and in accordance with prominent themes in post-Wittgensteinian philosophy.[15] The entire line of thought may be seen, from one point of view, as simply reflecting the fact that human social life is so saturated with language and meaning as to be a natural extension of the scope of logic, however the heartland is defined. If this is so, it must be legitimate to speak of class society as a sphere of logical opposition; that is, of contradiction.

The discussion of the internal links between belief, purpose and action is a useful preliminary to grasping the nature of the dialectical subject. A full account cannot be attempted here, but at least the general lines it must take may be sketched. The stress on action and purpose serves above all as a reminder that the subject is not pure intellect. It is a centre not just of cognition but of will and agency, a desirer and doer as well as a knower. It is a consciousness that is both theoretical and practical, and one that is necessarily embodied in the world. This latter requirement is not usually thought to present much difficulty in the case of individual human beings, where the body in question is straightforwardly included in successful identifications of the subject. Matters are more complicated when it comes to embodiment in collective subjects such as classes and nations. It is not possible now to explor the ontological problems sometimes associated with this commitment. It will simply have to be noted as a presupposition of dialectical, as of much non-dialectical, social science. Against this background it may be thought, however, that the tendency to refer to the subject as a consciousness is misleading. The ultimate concern of dialectical social science is, after all, action which is productive of social change. It is only in the light of this preoccupation that consciousness as such becomes significant. Thus, purpose is involved in the dialectic in so far as it finds expression in, and shapes, activity. Belief is relevant as the all-pervasive medium of the formation of purpose. It may, nevertheless, still be legitimate to think of the subject as essentially a practical, embodied consciousness. For consciousness is what one most directly encounters in the dialectic as the inescapable mediator and vital element of action. Moreover, it may be permissible to continue to think of cognitive discovery as the leading edge of the movement, given that it is the discovery by the subject of what it truly wants as well as of the true character of its situation in the world. What has above all to be borne in mind is the fusion of belief, purpose and activity in the dialectical subject. With this proviso, it should not prove seriously misleading to go on speaking of a dialectic of consciousness here.

IV

The ground should now be cleared sufficiently to allow a closer look at the workings of Marx's dialectical inquiry. Its concern with social contradictions is, it was suggested, in essence a concern with relations of class opposition. At this point an important contrast has to be made explicit. However valid their title as contradictions, it is clear that those relations cannot directly provide the material of a phenomenological dialectic. The source of movement in that dialectic is the gap between what the subject posits and what it experiences. This gap finds expression through what are, in a straightforward sense, self-contradictions; contradictions arising within the unity of a single consciousness. The governing assumption is that the discovery of such contradictions is inherently transformative for subjects susceptible to reason. But the discovery that such subjects stand in relations of contradiction to one another has nothing of this dynamism. This is so even where, for instance, it is the discovery that the beliefs, goals and activities of other persons are incompatible with one's own. There is then no conceptual obstacle to carrying on just as one did before, while the presence of such an obstacle is precisely what distinguished the self-contradiction cases. The focus of Marx's inquiry is on contradictions involving classes as distinct centres of subjectivity, on what may for convenience be called 'intersubjective' contradictions. It is plain that he regards these contradictions as comprising an intelligible process of directional change; as comprising, one has to say, a dialectic. Nothing has yet been said here to indicate how such a conception might be justified. It is clear, however, that account will have to be taken of the project of an intersubjective dialectic of class conflict, and the question must arise as to how that dialectic is related to the phenomenological, or, as it may now be called, 'subjective', dialectic of class consciousness.

To raise this issue is to approach the limits of the continuity between Hegel and Marx. It is to approach the point of rupture between a dialectical tradition for which, essentially, all contradiction is self-contradiction and one which undertakes to assimilate contradictions involving separate selves. The point may be expanded by noting how the whole problem might have been circumvented in the present discussion. It would be possible to regard contradictions between classes as having the character of self-contradictions, and, hence, as directly practical, if society itself could be treated as a single subject. Marx is, however, quite explicit on the nature of the error involved in doing so. Society is indeed a structured totality, but the tendency to treat it as itself a subject is, he insists, the characteristic weakness of a Hegelian-speculative approach.[16] In taking this stance he may be said to be deliberately rejecting the possibility of guidance from Hegel on the issue under discussion here. It is indeed the case that no such guidance may be had from the *Phenomenology*'s depiction of 'the path of the natural consciousness which presses forward to true knowledge'. That process is borne throughout by the internal contradictions which the consciousness encounters and surmounts on its way. There is, it must be admitted, an episode in the text which is often interpreted in a way that would make it a counter-instance to this verdict. This is the dialectic of master and slave, which, it has been maintained, provides the model for Marx's dialectic of classes.[17] On a closer look, however, its claim to be an exception begins to dissolve. The position of each side in the relationship is shown by Hegel to be internally contradictory in a way that promotes the onward movement. But, as some commentators have noted, no significant part in the story is played by contradictions between the consciousness of the master on the one hand and the slave on the other.[18] This is most obviously so because the slave is not recognised either by himself or by the master as an authentic centre of purpose and initiative, and hence a proper human subject and potential bearer of an intersubjective dialectic. The master does not qualify as such a subject either, since, for somewhat different and more complex reasons, the element of recognition is inadequate on his side also. It seems that one should be wary of too readily appropriating the episode for Marxism. This is not to deny its tremendous resonance if it can be transposed into an appropriate framework. For the present, however, the discussion of it must reinforce the conclusion that the *Phenomenology* offers little help in getting to grips with an intersubjective dialectic.

In order to make some progress, one has to consider again the characterisations that have been given of Marx's science. These were that it is the theory of the contradictions of capitalism and that it is a critique of political economy. What has now to be shown is that these aspects are so related as to be but two sides of a single coin. To do this, one has to note the way in which, on Marx's view, political economy itself dealt with the contradictions of capitalism. There are two main tendencies to be observed, corresponding roughly to the distinction between 'vulgar' economy on the one hand and 'classical' economy on the other.[19] The hallmark of the first approach is that the contradictions are ignored or concealed, either through simple failure of insight or as part of a programme of apologetics. In the second, their existence is acknowledged, even at times insisted on, but they are taken to be natural, eternally valid features of human society as such. The remedy in each case is supplied by a dialectical inquiry which reveals them not as timeless, static forms but as historical phenomena in transition. Hence it is that the science of social contradictions is at the same time a critique of political economy: it is by its very nature the assertion of what that ideology lives to deny. In being such a critique it works to break the grip of the ruling ideas in a crucial area of their operation. Thus, it serves as the trigger of the subjective dialectic by exposing for the class subject the fundamental contradiction of preconceptions and experience. The preconceptions posit a world of natural harmony or immutable division, while the science reveals a structure of contradictions in a movement towards resolution.

It should now be possible to map in a preliminary way the relationship of the subjective and intersubjective dialectics. Social scientific inquiry engages directly with the intersubjective contradictions, and, by exposing them, sets in motion the primary contradiction of class consciousness. Viewing the relationship from the other end, it appears that, in Marx's scheme, the intersubjective dialectic is, in its later stages, worked out through the dialectic of the subject. In particular, the conflict of classes can only be transcended by a transition to a new age if the historical process becomes conscious for one of the participants, the proletariat. This class must achieve a high level of class consciousness and social scientific understanding in order to become in the full sense the subject of history. In this role the subjective and intersubjective dialectics come together and complete their course.

V

In sketching this historical vision we have, however, run ahead of the argument. For something vital is missing from it, as presented so far. It may be said to have redeemed the first of Marx's claims for his contribution to the legacy of bourgeois thought, the treatment of social antagonisms as unstable contradictions. Nothing has yet been done to redeem the second, the claim to have placed these contradictions within an intelligible historical development. At its crudest, the question that remains is what guarantees the overall shape of the story and, in particular, what guarantees its happy ending. To have a historical dialectic, it is not enough that there should be contradictions continually coming into view and going under. There must be an immanent, progressive logic to the sequence of changes. What is required is, not simply an indefinite sequence of randomly revolving contradictions but, an essentially directed movement. In the language of the dialectical tradition, the question is how one can speak of reason in history. Hegel's most dramatic pronouncements on the subject leave little doubt as to the general character of his answer. Thus, he describes the contribution of philosophy to historical study as follows:

the only thought which philosophy brings with it is the simple idea of *reason* — the idea that reason governs the world, and that world history is therefore a rational process. From the point of view of history as such, this conviction and insight is a *presupposition*. Within philosophy, however, it is not a presupposition, for it is proved in philosophy by speculative cognition that reason . . . is *substance* and *infinite* power . . . [20]

History, it appears, is rational because, as philosophy has shown, reason is at work in it as substance and subject. Clearly, a doctrine which presupposes rational subjectivity in this form is not available to Marx. It may also be said that a dialectic which requires such resources is not a phenomenology, at least on the austere pattern of the opening chapters of the *Phenomenology of spirit*. There the natural consciousness has to generate its own momentum, while reason as such is a later entrant on the stage. There is a mild irony in this. It is that in dispensing with substantive reason, Marx is committed to treating the historical dialectic in a manner more closely analogous to a strict phenomenology than Hegel himself attempted. It remains to be seen whether the commitment can be fulfilled.

At this point it may appear that the question with which we began has returned in a starker, more urgent form, and that the discussion has chiefly served to uncover the core of its difficulty. Marx's practice has been used as a base from which to explore the prospects for a social dialectic not requiring a Hegelian conception of reason. But the relative lack of discursive theorising around that practice has been felt with ever increasing, and, it may be thought, now decisive, sharpness. The situation is, however, by no means hopeless. There are at any rate, themes in Marx's work which may be drawn on to take matters further. It is true that they are scarcely ever related explicitly to each other by Marx, nor are they brought to bear individually in any sustained way on our problem. Nevertheless, they are a substantial presence in his thought, and, once the issue is raised, their significance for the problem can scarcely be denied. An attempt may therefore be made to fit them together into the outline of a solution. It remains the case that if such a solution can be achieved, it must have a unique exemplary value for an age which is incapable of the original Hegelian vision.

There is considerable room for debate as to the scope Marx envisaged for his theoretical work. Yet there are obvious features of the texts themselves which warrant some modest conclusions that may suffice for present purposes. In the first place, they contain a certain amount of argument and speculation concerning the course of history as a whole. Secondly, they display a sharp sense of the limits of what they may be said to have investigated scientifically.[21] This area is more or less co-extensive with modern capitalist society. Thus, one seems entitled to use a working distinction of a familiar kind between the social science and the philosophy of history. It is to the second of these that one now naturally turns for assistance.

The crudest, most general way in which history may be characterised, for Marx, is that it records the development of the capacity of human beings to cope with nature. The guiding thread is the growth of productive power bringing in its wake successive transformations of society. A statement usually given canonical status runs as follows:

> At a certain stage of development, the material productive forces of society come into conflict (*Widerspruch*) with the existing relations of production . . . from forms of development of the productive forces these relations turn into their fetters. Then begins an era of social revolution.[22]

In this passage, one is brought into contact with yet another domain of contradictions in progressive movement, and it seems one has, accordingly, to acknowledge another level of dialectic, a level whose terms are the forces and the relations of production. It is convenient, in spite of a rather disagreeable neatness, to refer to this as the 'objective' dialectic to distinguish it from the levels identified earlier.

Contradictions in the objective dialectic are characteristically resolved through the replacement of outworn relations of production by ones better suited to the movement of the forces. The fetters are burst asunder and succeeded by 'fresh forms of development'. This story is, for the most part, enacted in class society. The role of classes within it is as agents or representatives of tendencies within the forces, and thus as primary instruments of its enactment. This is to say, in the terms of our discussion, that transitions in the objective dialectic are accomplished through the mediation of the intersubjective dialectic of classes. The overthrow of existing relations of production will be the work of a hitherto subject class which proceeds to impose new social forms stamped in its own image. In this way, the replacement of feudalism by capitalism was achieved through the bourgeois revolution, and the replacement of capitalism by socialism will be achieved through the proletarian revolution. Such transformations require certain levels of consciousness on the part of the social actors. Hence, at this point, one may introduce the subjective dialectic. The final transition to socialism presupposes an advanced stage of this dialectic marked by a relatively high level of social scientific understanding. Thus, proletarian revolutionary consciousness is required for the achievement of socialism, and socialism is required for the development of the productive forces. That these forces tend to develop in history is the basic thesis of the entire structure of ideas.

In spite of the strategic importances of the thesis, it is difficult to find a fully articulated defence of it in the Marxist tradition. It comes as no surprise that Marx himself made no serious attempt to provide it. What is somewhat strange is that his successors have not done more to repair the gap in the system. Yet, although theory is relatively undeveloped in this area, many of the elements it will have to incorporate lie plainly at hand. It should be possible to make out the general shape it must assume, at least sufficiently to allow the argument concerning dialectic to go forward.[23] There is, to begin with, an obvious constraint on any solution that is proposed. It is that it should not offend our empirical sense of what happened in history. However elastic that sense may be, it will surely not accommodate any claims for the continuous and sustained development of the forces. On the contrary, there is unambiguous evidence of substantial progress only for certain episodes. Most significantly, there is the record of development under capitalism and also, perhaps, under other forms of organisation of industrial society, such as the 'actually existing socialism' of Eastern Europe. These considerations suggest that if one is to speak of a general tendency at all, it will be, at best, in the words of a recent writer, a 'weak impulse'.[24] Moreover, it will be one liable to be overborne by many countervailing forces and even to remain for long periods in complete suspension. This is a sobering preliminary to the discussion. Nevertheless, for present purposes, it is the prospect of being able to speak of a presumption of development, rather than the ease with which the presumption is overridden, that matters. What concerns us is not so much the frequency of exceptions, but rather the possibility of giving a theoretical account of the normal situation. A 'weak impulse' may still suffice to ground a dialectic. For between the view that history is intelligible as the workings of a rational process, however imperfect and fractured its rationality, and the view that it presents only the blank externality of a causal series, there is, one might say, all the difference in the world. It is a qualitative difference if anything is. The problem, however, is how to conceptualise such an impulse within the framework provided by Marx.

The most promising line of thought is again one that draws on a theme he found in the *Phenomenology*. The outstanding achievement of that work, according to Marx, is that in it Hegel 'grasps the essence of *labour* and comprehends objective man — true because real man — as the outcome of man's *own labour*'.[25] In developing the theme, the factor that Marx emphasises is the purposive character of the labour project. Thus, what is said to distinguish the 'worst architect' from 'the best of bees' is that he 'builds the cell in his mind before he constructs it in wax'.[26] Following clues of this kind, one might hope to place such projects at the centre of one's explanatory picture. The basic claim would simply be that they have some in-built tendency to foster the development of human productive powers. Labour is purposive, and labourers are capable of employing reason in the choice of means to achieve their purposes. They have a strong incentive to achieve them with a minimum of toil; that is, in a way that enhances their productive capacity. Given this starting point, the crucial task for theory is to establish the mediations that link such achievements to the movement of society. Even in the present state of things, it is not difficult to form some idea of what these factors are. A significant point to note is that whatever innovations arise in the course of the individual project will have some tendency to catch on more generally in the community. In a context allowing for communication between labourers, others will be able to grasp the point of improvements and to adapt them in their own practice. Another factor must be that in class society, the exploiting class has some interest in promoting and preserving innovations, not in order to ease the burdens of the exploited, but in order to enhance the rate of extraction of surplus value.

This is, of course, the barest sketch of the kind of theory that is required. Nevertheless, it affords some reason for supposing that the purposive character of the labour process may be, in and of itself, an impetus to the growth of the forces. It should therefore be possible to speak of a weak impulse grounded in the teleology of labour. Moreover, the sketch has the merit of suggesting that a difficulty often associated with attempts to link the theory of history with the dialectic of class consciousness is wholly imaginary. It is supposed that there are, in Marx's thought, two distinct levels of reality, class consciousness on the one hand and the forces of production on the other, and that these are too disparate to comprise a coherent theory. It should now be clear that there is no ontological gulf here. In invoking the forces, one is not appealing to what is radically other than consciousness. The invocation has explanatory value only in so far as it is ultimately an appeal to the efficacy of human desiring and projecting. This efficacy rests on our ability to shape means to ends and to learn from one another. Instrumental rationality, as embodied in the labour process, is thus, in terms of Marx's system, a vital part of the meaning of the ascription of reason to history. Hence, it should also be noted that our sketch serves to call in question, at least in terms of fidelity to the spirit of Marx, the tendency in the later Marxist tradition both to hold such rationality cheap and to place its exercise in sharp contrast to the world of authentic human communication.[27]

This discussion may be used to supplement the main line of argument in the following way. It bears out the claim that the forces supply the source of movement in the objective dialectic and that there is a directionality built into that movement. This formative influence may readily enough be thought of as percolating downwards to the dialectic of class conflict, given that classes are the agents of the social changes required by the forces. Moreover, it seems possible to go a step further to reach the subjective dialectic. At the very least, the changes of consciousness in that dialectic may be conceived of as occurring within a structure which exerts pressure in favour of some sorts of outcome and against others. So there may be a rational confidence that the overall movement will, in spite of lulls and regressions, have a certain determinate shape. Even if it is conceded, however, that this line of thought has some merit in general, it seems to have the unfortunate disadvantage of being least useful where it is needed most. This need arises in connection with theorising, not the main body of the dialectical transitions, but the transition which is the culmination of the entire process, the acquisition by the proletariat of a revolutionary consciousness. The question requiring an answer is what is the basis of the expectation that, at the critical moment, the proletariat will set itself in opposition to the entire existing order and seek its overthrow? This moment of decision creates a special difficulty because it can arise only when a relatively high level of consciousness has already been achieved by the subject. But now talk of structures that discipline, and forces that incline choices has less authority than at earlier stages. The tendency of the Marxist tradition has been to insist that the final step is the outcome of decisions taken in freedom and self-consciousness. How then can there be any assurance of a particular outcome? It seems necessary to look still deeper into the resources of Marx's thought.

VI

The direction in which to look is towards the elements in it of a theory of the historical subject. This is, in effect, to recognise that questions of ontology cannot be bracketed indefinitely, and that no account of dialectic can be adequate without treating them. A well-known formulation of what is, for present purposes, the central idea runs as follows:

> It is not a question of what this or that proletarian, or even the whole proletariat, at the moment *regards* as its aim. It is a question of *what the proletariat is*, and what, in accordance with this *being (Sein)* it will historically be compelled to do.[28]

It is with the character of this 'being' that one has now to come to terms. The discussion through which Marx prepared the ground for its introduction has an explicitly Hegelian flavour:

> The class of the proletariat feels annihilation in estrangement; it sees in it its own powerlessness and the reality of an inhuman existence. It is, to use an expression of Hegel, in its abasement the *indignation* at that abasement, an indignation to which it is necessarily driven by the contradiction (*Widerspruch*) between its human *nature* and its condition of life, which is the outright, resolute and comprehensive negation of that nature.[29]

With this contradiction, one reaches the deepest layer of dialectic in Marx. Its resolution has, he goes on to claim, a 'world-historic' importance, for the proletariat 'cannot abolish the conditions of its own life without abolishing *all* the inhuman conditions of life of society of today which are summed up in its own situation'.[30] The proletariat is, to borrow another expression of Hegel, used in this connection by Marx elsewhere, the 'universal class' which bears responsibility for the interests of humanity as a whole. In later writings Marx uses a less explicitly Hegelian language to convey these themes, but the significance of the themes themselves does not alter. The concept of human nature remains central to his thought, and so, more specifically, does the sense of the contradiction between the requirements of that nature and the conditions of existing society and of the resolution of the contradiction by the proletariat as signalling universal human emancipation.[31] The nature which the proletariat embodies should be considered in a little more detail.

The most convenient way to take up the question is by enlarging our understanding of the manner in which human beings are, for Marx, rational beings. So far, account has been taken of rationality as an impulse of overcoming inconsistency and of instrumental rationality in the labour project. What has now to be recognised is the human capacity, in virtue of human nature, for the life of reason in a richer sense. This richness is best spelled out by invoking once more an idea from the text which was our starting point, the idea of the internal connection of reason and freedom. For Marx too, freedom may be said to be the 'culmination' of reason and the substance of a rational society is nothing but the freedom of its members. In an early work we are told that 'free conscious activity is man's species-character',[32] and this emphasis is sustained, again with changes of idiom, throughout his intellectual career.[33] The point may be linked with the preceding discussion by noting that since the proletariat is the universal class, its rejection of the existing system is a decision in favour of freedom for humanity in general. This decision is fully expressive of the being of the decider, and may be thought of as having a logic grounded in that being. There can be a rational expectation that revolutionary consciousness will be realised once it is objectively possible, since its realisation in that circumstance is required by the nature of the subject.

The final problem that confronted us was one of seeing how the unravelling of the contradictions of class consciousness may be the basis of a historical dialectic. The resources found for conceptualising it derived from the role in Marx's thought of two major themes, that of instrumental reason and that of human nature and its fulfilment. It is worth noting how strongly even this short discussion has suggested the need to integrate the two to provide a satisfactory background of theory. For there is a tradition of disjoining instrumental reason, not only from the context of authentic communication but also, from the related one of human freedom and emancipation.[34] That this tendency is foreign to Marx's thought is shown by a representative passage in *Capital* which conveniently brings together the ideas we have been discussing. The immediate topic is 'the sphere of actual material production':

> Freedom in this field can only consist in socialised man, the associated producers, rationally regulating their interchange with Nature . . . under conditions most favourable to, and worthy of, their human nature. But it nonetheless still remains a realm, of necessity. Beyond it begins that development of human energy which is an end in itself, the true realm of freedom, which, however, can blossom forth only with this realm of necessity as its basis.[35]

Thus, a form of order incorporating the rationality of means and ends is the indispensable foundation of the kingdom of ends. In the terms of our discussion, it may be said that the instrumental rationality of the labour process is instrumental also for the life of non-instrumental reason. It would not be putting the point too strongly to say that this connection provides the basic structure of Marx's vision of society and that its elaboration is at the heart of his contribution to social theory.

VII

This paper began with the question of how social science may be conceived of as being dialectical. The discussion that followed took its theoretical bearings from Hegel and its working model of science from Marx. The model is dialectical in the obvious sense of being concerned with a dialectical reality, a reality structured by contradictions in a process of development. These are the contradictions of the 'objective' dialectic of forces and relations of production and, more immediately, of the 'intersubjective' dialectic of class opposition. A science of such contradictions might, however, be conceived of as merely explanatory and, as it were, contemplative, in regard to its object. This would not meet Marx's claims for his own work. To do so, the theory has itself to be a force of change, an element in an immanent, historical logic. It achieves this status through its contribution to forming the subject of the dialectic of class consciousness. These various levels of dialectic are to be thought of as interacting in a complex network of mediations. The 'subjective' dialectic is the essential medium through which the others have to proceed in their later stages. The movement of history must become conscious for a class subject before it can achieve the *Aufhebung* of class society. From the opposite vantage-point in the network, the role of the objective dialectic appears as one of securing, through the mediation of the intersubjective dialectic, the directedness of the movement of consciousness, of rendering it intelligible as a rational process. Movement in the objective dialectic stems from the dynamism of the forces of production, which is itself ultimately grounded in the teleology of human labour. At the other extreme of the structure of ideas, the main problem was one of conceptualising the crucial transition to proletarian revolutionary consciousness. The solution proposed was based on the concept of the human nature of the proletariat, a nature whose realisation is a society of rational freedom. It appears that, starting from Marx's acknowledgement of his methodological debt to Hegel, one arrives at a perspective from which the whole of his system may be reconstructed. This possibility has an obvious bearing on the vexed issue of the significance of the Hegelian dimension in his thought. More important for our purposes is the fact that the attempt to realise it throws into relief, as perhaps nothing else can, the contemporary prospects for dialectical science.

It will throw those prospects into still sharper relief to note where Marx's own achievement now seems most precarious. Besides, reference was made earlier to what is dead in Hegel, and it seems a little unfair to conclude without raising the same question about his successor. A curiously parallel answer suggests itself. It is one that focuses on a point likely to be vulnerable in any historical dialectic, its identification of the subject. If the times seem unpropitious for accepting the Idea in that role, they are scarcely more kind to Marx's candidate, the proletariat of what were in his day the most advanced capitalist countries. A welter of voices insists that, in the industrialised West, the speed of the proletariat's movement away from anything resembling a revolutionary consciousness is matched only by the rate of its decline as a factor in the economy.[36]

Against this background it seems difficult to see how Marx's original attribution can now be maintained unrevised by people in touch with what is going on around them. His confidence on the matter may, perhaps, be regarded as the result of, quite excusably, mistaking the place of his own society in history. This is due in turn to underestimating the vitality of capital, its extraordinary capacity to renew itself in ever fresh and vigorous forms. The most important of the resources it found is, of course, that so uncannily foreseen in the *Philosophy of right*, the development of colonialism and imperialism and, thereby, the establishing of capitalism as a truly global system.[37] A failure of identification on Marx's part has to be acknowledged. Such a failure, however, goes nowhere near the heart of the theory, and indeed, may in the end testify to its strength by being explicable precisely in terms of it, as a failure to hold to its deeper logic. The work needed to substantiate this suggestion fully cannot be attempted here. But it seems clear that anyone concerned for the fate of the dialectical tradition should at least be prepared to try again. If they do, their perspective will need to be informed by the sense, acquired by Marx from Hegel, that social forms do not perish before all their potentialities are revealed. They should also remember what is plainly the chief lesson of the master-slave episode on a Marxist reading, that the human future belongs to the labourer who through the work of fashioning the thing 'becomes conscious of what he truly is'. Putting these points together, one might suggest that the subject of history can only be taken as comprising the most oppressed and alienated producers at the point of maximum development of the system. We have no means of telling with certainty who this subject may be, though in a general way it is surely to the workers and peasants of Third World capitalism that one must look. Neither can we be sure what stage capitalism has reached in its historical life-process. On the face of things, it seems to be far from decrepit. If this is so, the tradition of Hegelian-Marxist rationalism has yet to face the true test of history, and the future has many further adventures of the dialectic in store.

Notes

An earlier version of this paper was read at the Fifth Annual Conference of the Hegel Society of Great Britain, St. Edmund Hall, Oxford, 1983.

I am grateful to all who took part in the discussion on that occasion, and, more especially, for critical comments from Chris Arthur, Susan Easton, David Lamb, Peter Osborne, Sean Sayers and Alan Spence.

1. G.W.F. Hegel, *Hegel's philosophy of right*, trans. T.M. Knox (Oxford, Clarendon, 1952), pp. 34–5.

2. See David Lamb, *Hegel — from foundation to system* (The Hague: Martinus Nijhoff, 1980), Parts 4 and 5.

3. Karl Marx, *Critique of Hegel's 'Philosophy of right'*, ed. Joseph O'Malley (Cambridge: Cambridge University Press, 1977), p. 11; *Capital*, vol. I (Harmondsworth, Penguin, 1976), p. 102.

4. The clearest example of this tendency is still J.M.E. McTaggart, *Studies in the Hegelian dialectic* (New York, Russell and Russell, 1964).

5. For an illuminating discussion, see Gillian Rose, *Hegel contra sociology* (London, Athlone Press, 1981), pp. 45–7, 83–91, 107, 122.

6. *Economic and philosophic manuscripts of 1844* (Moscow, Progress, 1974), p. 127.

7. For a fuller account of this view of ideology, see J. McCarney, *The real world of ideology* (Brighton, Harvester, 1980).

8. *Capital*, vol. I, p. 103.

9. 'Altogether it has appeared from the consideration of the nature of Contradiction that in itself it is not, so to speak, a blemish, deficiency or fault in a thing if a contradiction can be shown in it.' *Hegel's science of logic*, vol. 2, trans. W.H. Johnston and L.G. Struthers (London, Allen and Unwin, 1929), p. 70.

10. Hegel does not condemn this. To do so would be to stop outside the phenomenology and to impose another abstact definition of what the experience should be on the will. The discrepancy between the natural will's definition and its experience, the social reality presupposed by the definition, itself transforms the inequity (Rose, *Hegel contra sociology*, p. 85).

11. To get a sense of Marx's consistency on this, compare the comments of 1844 on the Weavers' Uprising in Silesia, *Early writings* (Harmondsworth, Penguin, 1975), p. 415, with those of 1880 in the preface to the *Enquête ouvrière*, quoted in *Karl Marx: selected writings in sociology and social philosophy*, ed. T.B. Bottomore and M. Rubel (Harmondsworth, Penguin, 1963), p. 210.

12. *The First International and after*, ed. David Fernbach (Harmondsworth, Penguin, 1974), p. 82.

13. See, e.g., letter to J. Weydemeyer, *Marx-Engels selected correspondence* (Moscow, Foreign Languages, 1953), p. 86.

14. See, e.g., Susan Haack, *Philosophy of logics* (Cambridge, Cambridge University Press, 1978), ch. 6.

15. Charles Taylor, 'Hegel and the philosophy of action', *Hegel's philosophy of action*, ed. Lawrence S. Stepelevich and David Lamb (Atlantic highlands, Humanities, 1983), pp. 1–18; Peter Winch, *The idea of a social science* (London, Routledge and Kegan Paul, 1958), ch. 5.

16. See, e.g. *Grundrisse* (Harmondsworth, Penguin, 1973), p. 94.

17. For discussion and rebuttal of this claim, see Chris Arthur, 'Hegel's master-slave dialectic and a myth of Marxology', *New Left Review*, *142*, Nov.–Dec. 1983, pp. 67–75.

18. See, e.g., Jon Elster, *Logic and society. Contradiction and possible worlds* (Chichester, Wiley, 1978).

19. See discussion in Bhikhu Parekh, *Marx's theory of ideology* (London, Croom Helm, 1982), chs. 3 and 5.

20. *Lectures on the philosophy of world history: introduction*, trans. H.B. Nisbet (Cambridge: Cambridge University Press, 1980), p. 27. A full discussion would have to take account of the less dramatic qualifications which Hegel immediately goes on to make. Thus, he appears to recognise another kind of proof, not derived from philosophy and brought to history as a presupposition but, lying 'in the study of world history itself', (p. 28). Moreoover, he warns that the remarks quoted above are not 'to be regarded simply as prior assumptions, but . . . as the *result* of the ensuing enquiry', and he insists that in this enquiry 'we must be sure to take history as it is; in other words, we must proceed historically and empirically' (p. 29). For the conception of two kinds of proof here, see Charles Taylor, *Hegel* (Cambridge, Cambridge University Press, 1975), pp. 219–20.

21. For a particularly clear statement, see letter of 1877 in *Selected correspondence*, pp. 378–9.

22. *A contribution to the critique of political economy* (Moscow, Progress, 1970), p. 21.

23. What follows is influenced by the discussion in G.A. Cohen, *Karl Marx's theory of history: a defence* (Princeton: Princeton University Press, 1978), pp. 150–7, and in Erik Olin Wright, 'Giddens's critique of Marxism', *New Left Review*, *138*, March–April, 1983, pp. 11–35.

24. Wright, 'Gidden's critique of Marxism', p. 28.

25. *Economic and philosophic manuscripts of 1844*, p. 131. It seems difficult not to acknowledge the master-slave episode as a significant element of the background to this verdict.

26. *Capital*, vol. 1, p. 284.

27. The main reference is to the work of Jürgen Habermas. For a useful summary, see David Held, *Introduction to critical theory: Horkheimer to Habermas* (London, Hutchinson, 1980), Part 2.

28. K. Marx and F. Engels, *The holy family, or critique of critical criticism* (Moscow, Progress, 1975), p. 44.

29. *The holy family*, p. 43.

30. *The holy family*, p. 44.

31. Doubts about the continuity here should have been finally dispelled by Norman Geras's polemic, *Marx and human nature: refutation of a legend* (London, Verso, 1983).

32. *Economic and philosophic manuscripts of 1844*, p. 68.

33. *Vide* the insistent concern in *Capital*, vol. 1, for 'the free intellectual and social activity of the individual' (p. 667) and for 'the free play of the vital forces of his body and his mind' (p. 375).

34. The main reference is to the 'Critical Theory' of the Frankfurt School. For summary, see Held, *Introduction to critical theory*, Part 1.

35. *Capital*, vol. 3 (London, Lawrence and Wishart, 1974), p. 820.

36. Representative of those voices is Andre Gorz, *Farewell to the working class* (London, Pluto, 1982).

37. *Philosophy of right*, pp. 151–2.

9

Hegel and Religion

John Walker

One of the most distinguished modern exponents of Hegel's philosophy of religion, Emil Fackenheim, has spoken of a 'legend of great longevity', according to which 'the Hegelian philosophy is not and never was to be taken seriously'.[1] There is no part of Hegel's philosophy more responsible for the birth and the persistence of this myth than Hegel's philosophy of religion; and there is no part of his philosophy which modern critics have been less willing to accept on its own terms.

Hegel is a philosopher who asserts that philosophy is the service of God;[2] that the proper object of philosophy as of religion is the contemplation of God.[3] He declares that God is to be found in thought itself,[4] that in philosophy religion is sanctioned and confirmed by the thinking consciousness of man.[5] The central religious claim of his philosophy is that we cannot speak intelligently of the reality of God without at the same time speaking of the self-interrogation and self-consciousness of the human mind, nor fruitfully pursue that interrogation itself unless we conceive our activity in doing so as one sustained and made possible by God.

Must not Hegel's philosophy of religion, which not only offers to speak about the life of faith, but claims also to be itself part of that life, ignore or avoid the most fundamental distinctions between spheres of experience? Must we not conclude that such a philosophy is of necessity debarred from establishing proper standards of clarity and evidence in its own discourse? How can Hegel's philosophy do justice to the autonomy and coherence of religious experience? For is it not Hegel's intention fraudulently to annex the province of piety to the realm of philosophy? And if that really is Hegel's intention, is Hegel's philosophy really a philosophy at all: an activity concerned with clarifying language and concepts, with making claims about the truth in such a way that they can intelligibly and publicly be discussed?

In this paper I want to argue that Hegel's view of philosophy as itself a religious activity is of crucial relevance to his philosophy as whole. The religious claim of Hegel's philosophy is no Romantic extravagance or historical anachronism which might safely be separated from Hegel's total argument on matters of epistemology and metaphysics, nor some ideological mystification which is irrelevant to the capacity of the Hegelian philosophy to give us insight into our actual experience of ourselves in human culture.[6] Hegel's claim that philosophy itself can be religious is of central importance to the epistemological legitimation of Hegel's philosophy as a whole, and in particular to the defence of Hegel's claim to have written a philosophy of 'absolute knowledge': a mode of knowledge which is not dependent upon any source of truth or evidence external to its own systematic articulation.[7] Hegel thinks that the systematic language which mediates the categories of philosophy with each other — the language of what he calls *Vermittlung* — is the only language which enables us to speak meaningfully of the categories which it mediates.[8] There is not one category of Hegel's thought which has any logical identity in abstraction from the total system of meanings which is that thought. And because it is with the *relationship* between thought and being that Hegel's thought is concerned — with precisely that which Hegel, in one of his few usages of the term, calls 'experience' (*Erfahrung*)[9] — there can in particular be no category of 'Being', referring to some source of evidence external to Hegel's own system, against which the assertions which that system leads Hegel to make could be tested.[10] I will argue that this view of philosophy can be neither understood nor defended except in the light of Hegel's vision of philosophy as a religious activity. I will argue also that the religious character of Hegel's philosophy, far from being an anachronism, is one of the main reasons why that philosophy continues to be relevant.

My argument has a limited scope, although I hope a general relevance. What is usually called Hegel's *Philosophy of religion* consists in the *Vorlesungen über die Philosophie der Religion*, lectures which Hegel delivered at the University of Berlin from 1821 onwards, and which were published posthumously in book form by a group of Hegel's friends. It is here that Hegel deals philosophically with the phenomena of religious consciousness and practice, with the particular religions of mankind and with the theology of what Hegel calls the 'absolute' religion: Christianity. This paper will be concerned only incidentally with that work. My argument will be concerned less with any of Hegel's arguments or theories *about* religion than with the way in which Hegel conceives the business of philosophical thought as itself a religious undertaking. For it is in this sense that Hegel's concept of the relationship between philosophy and religion is truly original, and of major importance to contemporary concerns both in the philosophy of religion and in philosophical theology. I will argue that Hegel conceives of religion and philosophy as modes of human experience through which what Hegel conceives as the whole truth about our experience, in each case in a different way, is articulated and understood. I will try to show that, although Hegel's total vision of experience is itself a religious one, that vision is still capable of encompassing within itself an understanding of the necessary separation, as well as the necessary connection, between philosophy and religion.

The key doctrine through which Hegel expresses the religious character of his philosophy in this sense is the doctrine of Spirit and of absolute Spirit which is expounded in the third section of the *Philosophy of spirit*. This paper will focus especially upon those doctrines in an attempt to show that Hegel's claim to have written a philosophy of absolute knowledge is both an intelligible and a defensible one.

Firstly, however, I must explain my use of the term 'experience', as it has such a central significance for my argument. I use the term 'experience', as well as the terms 'mode' and 'totality' of experience, in the sense given to them by Michael Oakeshott in *Experience and its modes*. Oakeshott defines 'experience' there as follows: '"Experience" stands for the concrete whole which analysis divides into "experiencing" and "what is experienced"'.[11] He goes on to add: 'Experiencing and what is experienced are, taken separately, meaningless abstractions; they cannot, in fact, be separated . . . these two abstractions stand to one another in the most complete interdependence; they compose a single whole.'[12]

Oakeshott argues that it is impossible for us to describe either the ways in which we experience the world, or the world which we experience, without considering both in relation to each other: 'Perceiving, for example, involves a something perceived, willing a something willed . . . The character of what is experienced is, in the strictest sense, correlative to the manner in which it is experienced.'[13]

What we call 'thought' or 'judgement' Oakeshott describes as itself 'the concrete whole of experience'.[14] This view of the relationship between thought and experience is, in Oakeshott's terms, the very opposite of an abstract one. For by 'abstraction' Oakeshott means what happens when we try to separate 'thought' from the other ways in which we experience, or to separate our experience as a whole from the thinking mind through which we know about our experience:

> All abstract and incomplete experience is a modification of what is complete, individual and concrete, and to this it must be referred if we are to ascertain its character. And thought or judgement, as I see it, is not one form of experience, but is itself the concrete whole of experience.[15]

But, when we try to understand our experience in thought, we find that our powers of coherence are limited; they are often not adequate to the whole scope of our experience, and we are forced to accept a coherent but limited consciousness of our experience. There is then an excess of experience over thought; and thought can only bring experience under mental control by viewing experience in a coherent but abstract way. It is then that what Oakeshott calls a 'mode of experience' arises. A mode of experience, therefore, Oakeshott defines as a 'homogenous but abstract world of ideas'.[16]

I will argue firstly that Hegel's doctrine of absolute knowledge is a doctrine of thought as experience in the sense which I have just outlined, that Hegel conceives of both philosophy and religion as modes of experience, and that he believes the experiential connection of philosophy to religion to be the way in which what Oakeshott calls the 'concrete purpose' of experience is satisfied:[17] the way in which our thought and our experience are one. My thesis is that it is Hegel's doctrine of the connection of philosophy to religion, as modes of experience, which is the real epistemological legitimation for his doctrine of absolute knowledge. Hegel's conception of philosophy, therefore, differs in one crucial respect from that of Oakeshott. Oakeshott argues that philosophy itself is not a 'mode of experience', for philosophy is not a specific world of abstract ideas.[18] But Hegel's philosophy, I shall argue, *is* an abstract mode of experience and knows itself to be so. It is only because of this knowledge and the consequences of it in experience that Hegel's claim to have written a philosophy of absolute knowledge is a serious and meaningful one.

To apply to the interpretation of Hegel the philosophical vocabulary of a modern thinker like Oakeshott, and especially to use that vocabulary in a way which differs enough from Hegel's own natural idiom as to describe philosophy as an 'experience', necessarily begs a lot of questions about what the proper standpoint of 'interpretation' should be.[19] My purpose is not to argue a case about what Hegel 'meant' to say (it is arguable that that might, in any case, be in principle inaccessible to us), but to suggest a way of looking at certain key elements in Hegel's philosophy which will make the communicative power of that philosophy more apparent, in particular by dispelling certain of the confusions for which Hegel's own philosophical idiom has been responsible. Nor is my intention to defend or to attack any particular thesis of Oakeshott himself, but to use Oakeshott's terms where they seem more appropriate than Hegel's own in the defence of Hegel's philosophy against certain characteristic modern objections. My argument is intended to be heuristic and apologetic rather than formal and exegetical. I want to suggest a way of looking at Hegel which will enable the specific force of the Hegelian view of what philosophy is to be *communicated* in debate with Hegel's modern opponents. Whether or not I have been successful in this intention the reader must judge whilst reading the Hegelian texts themselves.

It is above all because Hegel considers philosophy to be itself a religious activity — and not just because Hegel is a Christian philosopher who preoccupies himself with religious matters and speaks favourably of the central tenets of Christian belief — that modern commentators on Hegel have been overwhelmingly hostile to the religious claims of Hegel's thought. The challenge to Hegel's philosophy of religion has come not only from critics hostile to Hegel's general project in philosophy, but also from writers broadly in sympathy with that project. The religious dimension in Hegel's thought has been attacked by theologians and philosophers alike; by atheists, agnostics, and orthodox Christians.

Orthodox theologians have objected to the religious ambitions of Hegel's speculative thought because that thought has seemed to them to violate the most fundamental distinctions between spheres of experience: to annex the province of piety, of humility, and of faith to the realm of speculative dialectic. This is an objection which is of particular significance for theologians of the Protestant tradition such as Karl Barth. This is a tradition which Hegel himself claims to adhere to,[20] and which plays a significant part in the cultural and historical milieu from which Hegel's thought sprang. And yet Hegel's persistent polemic against any theology which affirms the hiddenness of God,[21] or the primacy for philosophy of religious emotion,[22] appears to be at odds with the central Protestant doctrine of the supremacy of grace. As Barth writes: 'Hegel, in making the dialectical method of logic the essential nature of God, made impossible the knowledge of the actual dialectic of grace, which has its foundation in the freedom of God.'[23]

The philosophers among Hegel's opponents have likewise objected to what they have seen as Hegel's unreasonable ambitions for philosophy. Karl Popper, for example, considers Hegel's philosophy to be illegitimate because Hegel gives to his own argument the kind of sanction which precludes any possibility of his theses being empirically refuted.[24] For Popper, the ambition of the Hegelian philosophy for a systematic and total articulation of experience is nothing other than Hegel's ambition to write a philosophy which can impose upon any possible opponent its own terms of reference. Such a philosophy, Popper objects, is prophecy if not sorcery.[25] Because Hegel's philosophy cannot in principle be proved wrong, it cannot contingently be shown to be right; and so it is a philosophy, Popper alleges, which disqualifies itself from philosophic debate. The 'religious' claims of Hegel's philosophy, for Popper, are merely the rhetorical clothing for this unrealisable as well as discreditable ambition.[26]

Perhaps more importantly for our present argument, philosophers broadly in sympathy with Hegel's philosophy have held the specifically religious claims of that philosophy to be philosophically indefensible. David Lamb, for example, argues that Hegel's thesis that 'the content of both religion and philosophy is God, absolute substance, absolute Spirit', does not mean that 'his philosophy of religion is inseparable from religious knowledge'.[27] Michael Rosen, on the other hand, whilst arguing that we can adequately understand Hegel only if we read him as a philosopher of Revelation, claims also that, when we do that, 'the irrational kernel of Hegel's concepts becomes apparent'.[28]

I want in this paper to argue against these interpretations: to argue not only that the *religious* dimension in Hegel's thought is an integral part of the particular kind of *philosophical* truth which Hegel has to offer us, but also that only in the light of his doctrine of philosophy as a religious activity can Hegel's concept of philosophical truth be defended against the charge of incoherence and indifference to experience.

I have spoken of Hegel's doctrine of the connection of philosophy to religion as a *legitimation* for his concept of absolute knowledge. Every philosophy must be concerned with the question of its own legitimation: the question of why we should be prepared to believe in the very possibility of the kind of knowledge which the philosophy in question offers to give us about the world. That is, the question of why we should be prepared to believe that the questions which a philosophy asks, let alone the answers which it gives, do not derive from some initial confusion about the relationship between the philosophical mind and our non-philosophical experience of the world, the experience which that mind proposes to talk about. But this is a question of quite *radical* significance for the philosophy of Hegel. Hegel frequently describes his philosophy as a science without presuppositions,[29] as a science which must constitute its own object. Hegel claims to have written a philosophy which can speak about the whole of human experience, and claims also that the way in which his philosophy talks about every particular part of experience is a necessary way, one which derives from the structure of experience as a whole.[30] When a philosophy of this kind wants to justify its own basic orientation in relation to experience, there is nothing in experience to which such a philosophy can appeal without at the same time bringing what it appeals to within the systematic framework of its own discourse.

Hegel's philosophy can only be defended on its own terms because the point of that philosophy is to show how and why there can be no 'other terms'. That is the central difficulty in the legitimation of Hegel's philosophy. That is the reason why that philosophy, for all its dialectical power, has so often appeared to be wholly dissociated from what we commonly call our experience: to be suspended, as it were, over a void. It is for this reason that Hegel's claim to presuppose nothing is also a claim to be justified in presupposing everything. In order to persuade us to believe in the central thesis of his philosophy Hegel has to persuade us to make the first step: to believe in the very possibility of a self-legitimating mode of knowledge. Thereafter the particular resources of argument which Hegel has at his disposal might be capable of persuading us that what claims to be such a mode of knowledge is at least as intelligible, as coherent, and as rigorous as its empiricist or analytic opponents. But what Hegel's philosophy appears at first to be unable to do is precisely that which it claims to do: to legitimate its *own* kind of knowledge, and not just to expose the weaknesses, contradictions, and limitations of other kinds. To show a philosophical standpoint to be limited, or even contradictory, is not necessarily to show that it is wrong. Perhaps knowledge is necessarily limited. Perhaps the truth about the world involves certain unresolvable contradictions.

The initial legitimation for Hegel's philosophy cannot be just an argument within that philosophy — for any such argument would be internal to Hegel's vision of what philosophy is, to his conception of the relationship between philosophical thought and non-philosophical experience. But neither can the legitimation for Hegel's philosophy appeal to anything in experience outside that philosophy; for any argument which did so would be a legitimation not for Hegel's philosophy, but for another philosophy altogether. The real legitimation for Hegel's philosophy is neither a speculative philosophical argument, nor an appeal to experience, but both at once: a vision of philosophy as itself a mode of experience, a description of the kind of experience which philosophy is in relation to experience as a whole.

This description, I believe, is provided by the doctrine of Spirit and of absolute Spirit which Hegel expounds in his *Philosophy of spirit*, and in particular by Hegel's doctrine of the reciprocal relationship between philosophy and religion as modes of absolute Spirit. But before arguing this case I must first explain why I have chosen to speak of the problem of legitimation in Hegel in relation to his *Philosophy of spirit* instead of in relation to the two works in the context of which that problem has most frequently been discussed: the *Phenomenology of spirit* and the *Science of logic*.[31]

We may speak of the problem of legitimation in Hegel's philosophy — indeed Hegel himself speaks of it in this way — as the problem of 'how to begin' doing philosophy. But what has to be legitimated — the particular kind of beginning which Hegel makes — is the claim that in philosophy we cannot know how to begin before we have actually *begun*.[32] This is what Hegel means to tell us when he says that 'the fear of error' is 'the fear of truth',[33] or when he says that the philosophy of his day cannot come 'to' the truth about itself because it is already 'with' that truth.[34] This is what Hegel is trying to tell us when he says that to believe we can learn, in the discipline of Logic, how to think before beginning the enterprise of speculative philosophy would be like waiting to study physiology before trying to digest.[35] Hence any argument which speaks in anything more than a metaphorical way about the question 'How to begin?' in relation to the philosophy of Hegel cannot provide the kind of epistemological legitimation which that philosophy requires. But we cannot avoid at least considering the problem in the terms which that question proposes. For to avoid doing that would be uncritically to accept Hegel's answer.

What we have to do is to ask the question in such a way that we do so without any presupposition about whether or not it is the right question for us to be asking. This is something which Hegel's *Science of logic* cannot do. Hegel's philosophy as a whole, because it claims to be a science without any presuppositions about the relationship of thought to experience, requires a philosophical foundation which does not depend upon the connection of thought to any particular kind of object in experience. That foundation must therefore be a kind of knowledge which is 'pure thought', thought trying to think, without any presupposition, about what thought, experience, and the relation between them are. This is indeed what Hegel conceives his *Logic* to be.[36] But it is just for this reason that Hegel's *Logic*, although it is the foundation *of* his philosophy, cannot provide a legitimation *for* that philosophy in relation to other alternative and incompatible philosophical views of experience. Precisely because the *Logic* is the most pure form of speculative knowledge, the central problem in the legitimation of Hegel's philosophy must apply pre-eminently to the *Logic* itself. The *Logic*, more than any other of Hegel's works, is debarred from proposing any justification for its procedure, not even a definition of terms, which is not already part of the systematic movement of its own argument.[37] Indeed, it is at the beginning of the *Logic* that Hegel most explicitly takes issue with and rejects the metaphor of 'beginning' as a way of speaking about the legitimation of philosophical knowledge.[38]

The *Phenomenology of spirit*, however, is limited in its ability to *legitimate* Hegel's philosophy (although it may work as a propaedeutic to that philosophy) for just the opposite reason. The *Phenomenology* is a work which employs the particular tools of

Hegelian philosophical argument, and yet temporarily and rhetorically abandons the one most central claim of Hegelian thought: that true or 'absolute' knowledge has no beginning external to itself, that there is no 'way in' to the truth which is not already part of the truth.[39] The *Phenomenology* is a work which tries to use 'experience' itself in order to persuade us to believe what Hegel says about experience. The *Phenomenology* tries to lead the mind, by means of a consideration of actual or 'natural' consciousness, to an acceptance of the coherence and necessity of the concept of absolute knowledge. In the *Phenomenology* we are supposed to 'watch' as the forms of the natural consciousness 'move towards' the standpoint of absolute knowledge.[40] But the fact that there could be other routes, as well as other starting points, for the journey is not relevant to the rightness or wrongness of our decision to embark upon it. (That indeed is the particular strength of the mode of argument which the *Phenomenology* employs.) Hence although Hegel in the *Phenomenology* might provide a kind of legitimation for the central theses of his philosophy, he is unable to show the necessity for the *particular* kind of legitimation which he has chosen. The *Phenomenology* cannot be said to provide a systematic legitimation for Hegel's philosophy because, in that work, Hegel's philosophy does not legitimate *itself*.

Hegel cannot, even rhetorically, legitimate his conception of philosophical thought by appealing *to* experience. He has, on the contrary, to make us believe that his thought has the right to tell us originally and independently what 'thought' and 'experience' are. We will only believe that if we also believe that Hegel can show us in his philosophy a mode of thought which *is* experience. If there is indeed such a mode of thought, then from the standpoint of that mode there will be no 'experience' which we can conceive of as absolutely separated from thought, and no thought so abstract that it is not also a kind of experience.

Because this is what Hegel conceives philosophical thought to be, his philosophy can be legitimated neither by speculative philosophical argument — such as the *Science of logic* — nor by heuristic appeal to cultural or psychological experience — such as the *Phenomenology of spirit*. Hegel has to produce a credible conception of what Oakeshott calls the 'standpoint of the totality of experience',[41] and a credible conception of philosophy as a mode of experience experientially connected to that standpoint. I will now try to show how Hegel does indeed succeed in doing this, subtly and persuasively, in the third section of the Berlin *Encyclopaedia of the philosophical sciences* which is called the *Philosophy of spirit*.

Hegel's doctrine of *Geist* or of Spirit is above all a doctrine about the relationship between thought and experience, in the sense of the term 'experience' which I outlined at the beginning of this article. 'Spirit' is the name which Hegel gives to what Oakeshott calls the 'concrete whole of experience'; and by giving the name Spirit to what whole, Hegel signals also that he considers the standpoint of the whole of experience to be also the standpoint of thought. Hegel's contention is that there is something which is not identical with the sphere of our thought, nor with the sphere of the object of our thought, which imparts an intelligible form to both those spheres. This is what Hegel means by speaking of Spirit as the mediation or middle point between the Idea (the truth in its most absolute and objective form) and Nature (the sphere of external existence which the truth is 'about'):

> Every determinateness is a determinateness only counter to another determinateness; to that of Spirit in general is opposed, in the first instance, that of Nature; the former can, therefore, only be grasped simultaneously with the latter. We must designate as the distinctive determinateness of the notion of Spirit, ideality; that is, the reduction of the Idea's otherness to a *moment*, the process of returning — and the accomplished return — into itself of the Idea from its Other. The distinctive feature of the logical Idea, however, is immediate, simple being-within-self; but for nature it is the self-externality of the Idea.[42]

By 'Spirit', then, Hegel means the kind of relationship between knowledge and being in which neither pole in the relationship has primacy. *Idea* is the term which Hegel gives to the absolute truth, when that truth is the object of pure speculative knowledge. *Nature* is the term which Hegel gives to that truth as we find it in the outward existence of the world. *Spirit*, however, is the mode of existence of the whole in which everything which is known is embodied in being; and everything which is is reflected in thought. Idea and Nature are dialectical opposites; but Spirit is the dialectical relationship between them. Hence Spirit is precisely that which Oakeshott calls experience, and it is experience as thought. Spirit is experience because it is the active synthesis of our consciousness of the world, and what we are conscious of; and Spirit is thought because Spirit is the mental form of the *whole* of our experience. Spirit is an energy, objectively as well as subjectively real, by which our minds are empowered to transmute the fact of our existence into a coherent human world. It is a form, moreover, which is just as much given to our thought by our experience as it is imparted to our experience by our thought. Hegel gives the name 'Spirit' to the way in which our thought, prompted by our experience, makes our experience ever more coherent. It is because of his doctrine of Spirit that Hegel can use the same logical term to describe the way in which we appropriate and understand experience as he does to describe the structure of experience itself. This term is *Begriff* or *notion*:

> Just as in the living organism generally, everything is already contained, in an ideal manner, in the germ and is brought forth by the germ itself, not by an alien power, so too must all the particular forms of living mind grow out of its Notion as from their germ. In so doing our thinking, which is actuated by the Notion, remains for the object, which likewise is actuated by the Notion, absolutely immanent; we merely look on, as it were, at the object's own development, not altering it by importing into it our own subjective ideas and fancies.[43]

Hegel is saying that Spirit, through what he calls the movement of the notion, is immanent in every part of our thought and experience, however partial and limited the particular parts of our thought and experience might be. But because Spirit is thus immanent in our *actual* thought and experience, our partial and limited thoughts and experiences can know about, and be in, the absolute form of experience. That is the form which, when we think of it as absolute, we call the absolute or logical idea — and which *is* absolute Spirit or God.[44] The possibility of 'absolute' knowledge cannot adequately be described by saying that the absolute is in us, but only by saying that we are in the absolute but to say that also includes the first possibility. That is what Hegel means by the participation of philosophy in the Spirit: what he means by absolute knowledge.

But what if the word *Geist*, and even more so the words *absoluter Geist*, did not correspond to anything real in our experience at all? What if they were just words?

And then, the next thing I must mention,
Is Metaphysics. Give it your close attention.
With thought profound take care to span
What won't fit into the brain of man.
But fit or not — 'tis small concern.
A pompous word will serve your turn.[45]

Clearly the kind of argument I have just outlined presupposes the conceptual framework of Hegel's philosophy as a whole. In particular it presupposes that when we talk about a Spirit which 'embodies' or 'externalises' itself in actual existence, and of that existence as something having a development akin to the movement of our thought, then we actually mean something when we do so. The very idea of a Philosophy of Spirit, moreover, presupposes the rest of Hegel's system. In particular, it presupposes Hegel's *Logic* and *Philosophy of nature*, the 'final outcome' of which, Hegel says, is 'the proof of the necessity of the Notion of Spirit'.[46] And the arguments of these works, in relation to which Hegel says that the doctrine of Spirit has to be interpreted, themselves presuppose what I have called the one fundamental premise of Hegel's thought: that there can be a kind of knowledge which presupposes nothing external to itself.

Hegel himself would appear to be aware of this difficulty at the beginning of the *Philosophy of spirit*, where he remarks that his doctrine of Spirit is a way of looking at the world the rightness of which will only be revealed by the application of that doctrine to the whole sphere of human experience which his philosophy treats. We have, so to speak, to put the idea of Spirit into the world and see what we get out:

> The Science of Spirit, on its part, has to authenticate this Notion (i.e. the Notion of Spirit) by its development and actualisation. Accordingly, what we say here assertorically about Spirit, at the beginning of our treatment of it, can only be scientifically (*wissenschaftlich*) proved by philosophy in its entirety. All we can do at the outset is to elucidate the Notion of Spirit for ordinary thinking (*Vorstellung*).[47]

The objection of course is that Hegel's doctrine of Spirit is vitiated in just the same way as all of Hegel's other doctrines: that if we see the world in the light of this doctrine, the kind of world we see will automatically confirm the doctrine's truth.

But the real reason why Hegel's doctrine of Spirit is ultimately unsatisfactory as a legitimation for his philosophy — although it is a necessary part of that legitimation — lies deeper than this. We might be able to think of the relationship between thought and experience *in terms of* Hegel's doctrine of Spirit, or *as if* Spirit really existed; and if we do so we can make a judgement about the coherence or otherwise of Hegel's philosophy without having to accept, in anything more than a formal or assertoric sense, the terms in which Hegel says that we should make that judgement. But, if we think in this way, we will understand the doctrine of Spirit in a way which — however plausible — is radically in conflict with what that doctrine actually says.

If we read the doctrine of Spirit only assertorically, then even if we find that the doctrine is confirmed by the rest of Hegel's philosophy, it will have been confirmed only *as* an assertoric doctrine: as a way of looking at the world which 'works', because it leads us to the truth about the world. Hegel's claim, however, is to describe how we can look at the world in a way which 'necessarily' leads us to the truth, because it is itself part of the truth. However Hegel's doctrine of Spirit is constructed, and however we might be able to read it, the *content* of that doctrine is an affirmation not that the world is *as if* something were true about it, but an affirmation about how the world *is*. Hegel speaks of Spirit not just as the object of his own discourse, but as an independently active principle in the world, a principle which defines the ontological status of speculative thought itself. Spirit, Hegel says, is not just something which *our* thinking shows to be true about the world; Spirit is something which shows *us* the truth.[48] Spirit has to be something like this because Hegel's doctrine of Spirit is not just the organising principle of a philosophical world view; it is the conceptual legitimation for a philosophy of absolute knowledge. If we are to believe such a philosophy, then what we have to believe is not that such a philosophy is as right, or more right, than its opponents, but that such a philosophy is *true*: true 'absolutely' because it tells us the particular kinds of truth which other philosophies possess.

If Hegel's doctrine of Spirit means what it says, then to accept it whilst regarding it only as an assertoric doctrine is a contradiction in terms. And, ultimately, even though an assertoric reading of the doctrine of Spirit might enable us to defend Hegel's conception of philosophical thought against certain of the charges which modern critics have levelled against it, such a reading cannot be successful in defending that conception of philosophy on its own terms. Hence it would seem that, if we are looking for a *relevant* legitimation for Hegel's conception of philosophical thought, we are back where we started.

What Hegel offers us in his doctrine of Spirit is a doctrine of philosophy as experience in Oakeshott's sense, and a doctrine of what Oakeshott calls the 'concrete whole' of experience. What he cannot give us, unless he gives us something more than his doctrine of Spirit, is the way in which those two doctrines are connected; and it is just this which we need. The problem is that Hegel is saying something more than that philosophy is experience. He is saying that philosophy knows how to talk about the whole of experience. If philosophy's talk, as Hegel says it is, is really absolutely necessary to experience as a whole, then there must be something *in experience* which connects philosophy to the whole of our experience. In his doctrine of Spirit, Hegel gives us a plausible argument about how philosophy can be seen as connected to the whole of experience, and so shows us one way in which we can know, in our philosophical thinking, about that connection. But knowing about something, even for Hegel, is not *automatically* the same as being it. We are not justified, on the basis of Hegel's doctrine of Spirit alone, in believing that the kind of connection which Hegel makes between philosophical thought and experience is anything more than the product of a plausible philosophical argument. There is no reason why we should believe that the connection is not just a heuristic fiction, but an objective reality which discloses to us what 'thought' and 'experience' are.

In order to believe that, we would have also to believe that there is nothing else in our experience except philosophy: God forbid! We cannot take refuge here in Oakeshott's disclaimer that philosophy is simply 'the standpoint of the totality of experience', and that such a standpoint is neither practically necessary nor conducive to the enhancement of life.[49] For Hegel, philosophical knowledge is nothing if it is not 'necessary'. Such knowledge, for Hegel, is 'necessary' not because everybody has it or has to have it in order to live; but because, being something more than the possession of our minds, it is implicit in our lives whether we 'have' it or not.

In order to show that 'absolute knowledge' is possible, Hegel has to show us that philosophy is connected to the whole of experience not by talk, but by experience. He has to show us that philosophy has the right to talk about the whole of experience, not because experience can be reduced to philosophy, but because philosophy can be enlarged to experience. He has to show us philosophy as a *mode* of experience, and he has to show us how the philosophical mode of experience is connected, by experience, to experience as a whole. And it is this which Hegel talks about when he talks, at the end of the *Philosophy of spirit*, about the connection of philosophy to religion.

In the section of the *Philosophy of spirit* entitled '*Absolute spirit*', Hegel offers two principal speculative arguments for the connection of philosophy to religion. These I will call his thesis of the *internal* connection of philosophy to religion — his thesis that philosophy is itself a religious activity; and his thesis of the *external* connection of philosophy to religion — his thesis that the mode of awareness of the world proper to philosophy is necessarily connected to the mode of awareness proper to religion. These two arguments may also be described as an argument about how philosophy is made possible by religion, and an argument about why philosophy needs religion. I will now consider each of these arguments in turn.

The internal connection of philosophy to religion

Hegel discusses, in the *Philosophy of spirit*, the three modes of absolute Spirit — art, religion, and philosophy — in turn; and says that each of these modes both is, and enables us to know about, the totality of the Spirit's life in a different way. But he also begins by describing the sphere of absolute Spirit *in general* as the sphere of religion. This description is not part of his discussion of the sphere of religion as a mode of absolute Spirit, but occurs in the section which introduces the concept of absolute Spirit itself, and follows immediately after a sentence which shows us the significance of the concept of absolute Spirit in relation to the question 'How to begin?'

> The absolute Spirit, while it is self-centred identity, is always also identity returning and ever returned into itself: if it is the one and universal substance it is so as a spirit, discerning itself into a self and a consciousness, for which it is as substance. *Religion*, as this supreme sphere may be in general designated, if it has on one hand to be studied as

coming from the subject and having its home in the subject, must no less be regarded as objectively issuing from the absolute Spirit which as Spirit is in its community.

Der absolute Geist ist eben so ewig in-sich-seyende, wie in sich zurückkehrende und zurückgekehrte Identität; die Eine und allgemeine Substanz als geistige, das Urtheil *in sich* und *in ein Wissen, für welches* sie als solche ist. *Die Religion*, wie diese höchste Sphäre im Allgemeinen bezeichnet werden kann, — ist eben so sehr als vom Subjecte ausgehend und in demselben sich befindend, wie als objectiv von dem absoluten Geiste ausgehend zu betrachten, der als Geist in seiner Gemeinde ist.[50]

Hegel only introduces his discussion of philosophy after a discussion of religion, a discussion in which he describes as part of religion the total movement of the absolute Spirit through which the question of the relation between knowledge and being is answered: the manifestation or *Offenbaren* of a spiritual principle in the external world, which at the same time discloses the way in which the mode of that manifestation can be known.[51] To be sure, Hegel says that *one* way in which this movement can be known of is by philosophy, whose element is discursive thought, just as another way is religion, whose element is the inward integrity of piety.[52] But the totality of what is known, and of the means by which it is known, is also described in the section entitled 'Religion'; and the very notion of *Spirit* in this discussion, the account of what Hegel calls the 'absolute self-mediation of Spirit',[53] is introduced in a religious context: as the third person of the Trinity or as the Holy Spirit.[54] To be sure, Spirit in this sense is described by Hegel, as it were, phenomenologically or as a category of dogma; but it is also Spirit which Hegel says is able to *talk* about the trinitarian movement of Spirit which is its precondition or *Voraussetzung*.[55] Hence Spirit can grasp the totality of the trinitarian movement of Spirit because Spirit stands within that movement.

This total movement through which finite and infinite Spirit are mediated one with the other *is* religion, although it is also the object of religion as it is of philosophy in a different mode. There is a highly significant sense, for Hegel, in which philosophy can know about this movement only because philosophy is itself inside it, and only if philosophy knows that it is inside it. The relation of religion to absolute Spirit is not only one of knowing; it is one of being. And if that is also true of philosophy, it is only so because the element of philosophy — freely self-mediating Spirit, which *knows* most adequately about itself and about the world in the medium of philosophy — has been prepared for in the element of religion. Indeed, Hegel says in the transitional paragraph which leads from his discussion of religion to his discussion of philosophy,[56] whatever it is that philosophy knows — even the result of the argument about the emergence of self-conscious Spirit which he has just expounded — if philosophy only *knows*, it knows nothing. If philosophy makes the movement of the Spirit in which it inheres into its own object — or even if philosophy knows why it cannot do so and makes that into its own object — philosophy's discourse, in knowing the reason why it is itself a necessary part of the truth, renders itself entirely superfluous to the truth. Philosophy, in knowing its own knowledge and its own being to belong together, but thinking itself alone responsible for this knowledge, causes knowledge and being in the world which philosophy experiences to be absolutely divorced. For in knowing that, philosophy does in fact know about the totality of things, and if philosophy is not prepared to put itself inside the totality of things there is nowhere for philosophy to go when it has finished philosophising. Philosophy, in Hegel's words, is empty and vain.[57]

The external connection of philosophy to religion

Hegel describes philosophy at the close of the *Philosophy of spirit* as follows:

> Such consciousness (i.e. philosophy) is thus the intelligible unity (cognised by thought) of art and religion, in which the diverse elements in the content are cognised as necessary, and this necessary as free.

> Dies Wissen ist damit der denkend erkannte *Begriff* der Kunst und der Religion, in welchem das in dem Inhalte Verschiedene als nothwendig, und dies Nothwendige als frei erkannt ist.[58]

The form of knowledge — or *Wissen* — belonging to philosophy is that of conceptual or discursive insight: the form of insight appropriate to the philosophical concept or *Begriff* through which the philosopher understands the world according to the logical form which philosophy discloses. The characteristic form of the activity of conceptual understanding or *begreifen* is to discern difference in unity, and unity in differences.[59] To understand in this way is to perceive the limits of things, and their contradictions, then in that perceiving to grasp the idea of the unity of things; and yet to know that what the mind understands as unity cannot be set beside a world of contradictions, but is in fact immanent and implicit in that world. *Begreifen* is to understand unity, and to understand difference, and to understand that the connection between unity and difference is a matter not merely of understanding, but of being.[60]

It is through their connection to philosophy, Hegel says, that the two non-philosophical modes of absolute Spirit — religion and art — cease to be particular and limited modes of experience. In philosophy, Hegel says, the particular ways in which we see the world in religion and art are unified in a single apprehension of thought, and given access to the kind of insight which comes from self-conscious thought:

> Philosophy not merely keeps them (i.e. religion and art) together to make a totality, but even unifies them into a simple spiritual vision and then in that raises them to self-conscious thought (. . . *in die einfache geistige Anschauung vereint und dann zum selbstbewussten Denken erhoben*).[61]

This self-conscious thought, Hegel says, discerns the *Begriff* or concept of religion, because it recognises that religion has an apprehension of Spirit which is different from the apprehension which belongs to philosophy, and understands that this different apprehension is *necessary* to the reality of the Spirit; and yet recognises also that this necessity does not detract from or contradict the freedom and hence the transcendence of Spirit.

Hegel is asserting that philosophy is able to understand why there is a religious mode of the Spirit which is intrinsically different from the philosophical mode, and yet discern in the religious mode of Spirit, and in the connection of that mode to philosophy, nothing other than the movement of philosophy's own thought.

This is by definition a kind of knowledge which religion, as such, cannot have. The movement of the Spirit which Hegel calls religion *is* the totality of the sphere of absolute Spirit as such. Hence whatever kind of *knowledge* religion can have of that totality — the knowledge belonging to the mode of *Geist* which Hegel identifies with the Holy Spirit — must be not only formally, but really within the totality of the Spirit which is also religion. The structure of the religious sphere of absolute Spirit means that, as far as the existence or the life of that sphere is concerned, the Spirit's knowledge and the Spirit's being must coincide. But in the case of the religious sphere's knowledge of itself — as far as the Spirit's *religious* knowledge — is concerned, the Spirit's knowledge and the Spirit's being must necessarily appear to be dissociated one from the other. And both these characteristics of the religious sphere have the same origin: the immediate identity of that sphere with the totality of absolute Spirit.

In the case of philosophy, the relationship of Spirit to itself is exactly the reverse. Philosophy knows about religion — the totality of absolute Spirit — as one particular mode of absolute Spirit. Hence philosophy's knowledge must be able to put itself 'outside' the totality of absolute Spirit, and yet by so putting itself outside, not cease to know adequately of that totality. But because the totality of absolute Spirit is the totality of knowledge and of being at once, the *being* of philosophy must be connected to that totality, and yet connected in a mode other than that of philosophical knowledge. That mode is religion. Philosophy needs religion. Philosophy needs religion because, although philosophy can know about religion, and indeed know about its own connection to religion, philosophy cannot be, and hence cannot know, as religion is or as religion knows.

Philosophy, according to Hegel, is the mode of absolute Spirit most suited to the formulation of the question, and of a certain kind of answer to the question, 'How to begin?' For philosophy can grasp, can articulate in its own discourse, the total problem of the relation between knowledge and being. Hence Hegel says that philosophy is the mode in which knowledge (*Wissenschaft*) goes back to its beginnings, and that philosophy is able to establish at the conclusion of its discourse the truth of its premise — the unity of knowledge and being:

In this way the science has gone back to its beginning: its result is the logical system but as a spiritual principle: out of the presupposing judgement, in which the notion was only

208

implicit and the beginning immediate — and thus out of the
appearance which it had there — it has risen into its pure
principle and thus also into its proper medium.
Die Wissenschaft ist auf diese Weise in ihren Anfang
zurückgegangen, und das Logische so ihr Resultat als das
Geistige, dass es aus dem voraussetzenden Urtheilen, worin
der Begriff nur an sich und der Anfang ein Unmittelbares
war, hiemit aus der Erscheinung, die es darin an ihm hatte,
in sein reines Princip, zugleich als in sein Element, sich
erhoben hat.[62]

Philosophy in this sense may be said to cause the Spirit to live
in the mind,[63] since the thoughts of philosophy are nothing other
than the pure form of the movement of absolute Spirit, which
philosophy itself discloses to be the totality of what is. Philosophy
is the mode of knowledge which creates its own object.[64] As
philosophy begins to ask the question of how to begin, it begins to
answer it — but only because philosophy knows that there is
nothing outside the movement of Spirit through which philosophy
itself begins. The doctrine of absolute Spirit shows us that
whatever we may think about Hegel's claims for philosophy, they
are ultimately claims about far more than philosophy alone; and
hence not just, and not even primarily, claims about what
philosophy can know. Hegel's doctrine of absolute Spirit is a
doctrine about why we should be doing philosophy at all. The
reason why we *are* doing philosophy, Hegel is saying, is that God
causes us to do so. The reason why we *should* do philosophy,
Hegel is saying, is that God wants us to. The point of philosophy
lies in its experiential connection to religion.

But what kind of a *legitimation* for a philosophy is this? We have
seen that the reason why Hegel has to offer us a doctrine of
absolute Spirit — of philosophy as a mode of experience
experientially connected to religion — is because of a necessary
inadequacy in his doctrine of Spirit. His doctrine of Spirit, as long
as we conceive it only as a philosophical doctrine *about* the whole
of experience, can offer us only a pseudo-legitimation for Hegel's
doctrine of absolute knowledge: an argument which provides a
legitimation for that doctrine on terms which the doctrine itself
shows to be inadequate. That is so because as long as we conceive
Hegel's doctrine as one which is about something called Spirit,
and about the relationship of philosophy to that something, we
are justified only in making a provisional or assertoric assent to it.

If Hegel's doctrine of absolute Spirit really is going to function as a legitimation for a philosophy of absolute knowledge, we have to be able to make something more than an assertoric assent to that doctrine. We have to believe that the doctrine expresses a substantive truth, a truth which defines the status of our thought and our experience alike. We cannot believe that unless Hegel does something more than tell us philosophically what 'experience' is — even if he tells us credibly what the whole of experience is. Hegel has to make us believe that philosophy *is* the whole of experience in a philosophical mode. He has to persuade us that we can hold such a belief without reducing our experience to philosophy. How does Hegel do that?

Philosophy, when it begins to formulate the doctrine of absolute Spirit, can begin to think only *as if* philosophy were connected to the whole of experience in the way which the doctrine of absolute Spirit describes. Philosophy knows that *if* the doctrine of absolute Spirit is true, then certain of the apparent contradictions in the way in which philosophy sees experience would be explained. But for the same reason that philosophy has been led to posit the doctrine — because of the fact that philosophy wants to see experience only in the mode of self-conscious knowledge — philosophy is unable philosophically to decide whether or not the doctrine is true.

Let us suppose, however, that we decide to think about the *whole* of the experience which we have when we find ourselves in this impasse. And let us suppose also that we try to do so whilst keeping an open mind about whether or not it is right for us to think *philosophically* or not about the experience we are having. Then there *might*, perhaps, be a way in which we could see the world — and could see the world whilst still doing philosophy — which would put us in a position to assess the truth of the doctrine of absolute Spirit. This would be a new way, although a way thoroughly connected to the way of speculative philosophy, for the philosophical mind to connect itself to experience. The philosophical mind, to be sure, would have to *decide* to connect itself to experience in this way; and yet such a decision would be made necessary by the way in which the mind is in any case connected to experience if it tries to do philosophy in the Hegelian way.

The kind of truth which philosophy gains by formulating the doctrine of absolute Spirit can only be called a hypothetical or metaphorical truth about the world — a truth which tells us that the world is as if certain things were true about it — if philosophy regards its own relation to experience only as a possible *object* of philosophical thought. But philosophy is *in* a relationship with experience however much philosophy thinks *about* that relationship; and it is this fact which the doctrine of absolute Spirit is itself 'about'. Hence for philosophy to think only 'about' that doctrine — to think about it as an object of philosophical discourse, without at the same time trying to think about it in any other way — would be for philosophy to make the doctrine superfluous.

When philosophy begins to think as if there were a truth in excess of the self-reflexive kind of truth about experience, and as if philosophy were necessarily connected to such a truth, then philosophy does so because it recognises that the mind which says 'as if' — the mind which is able at every point to withdraw from its own relationship to experience and to begin thinking about that relationship from the outside — is an inadequate orientation of the mind towards experience. Merely by entertaining the *possible* truth of the doctrine of absolute Spirit, philosophy has put itself into a particular kind of relationship with experience, and this act in itself means that philosophy has to do more than merely think *about* that relationship.

Philosophy has to entertain the proposition that the object of its own discourse — the relationship of the philosophical mind to experience — might have not only an objective, but also a *subjective* form; and yet a form which philosophy, by itself, does not know how to understand or control. Philosophy begins to realise that the success or otherwise of its attempt to connect itself to experience is more than its own affair. Philosophy begins to realise that its own ability to 'see through' the whole of experience, to see in experience only philosophy's own object, is not the only possible, or the only right, attitude of the mind in relation to experience. Philosophy begins to see that it might see through to nothing at all; and that its own philosophical knowledge that it is seeing nothing at all might, in relation to the totality of experience, not be knowledge at all. Philosophy begins to know that its own knowledge, which it knows can destroy the integrity of every particular mode of experience, is itself unable to become a positive form of experience — and yet that there is still experience left over. Philosophy has the experience of a *void*.

The way in which religion relates to the totality of experience is the very reverse of that of philosophy; and yet connected to the way of philosophy by a relationship of *need*. All of the philosopher's positive experience of the world — his particular and determinate experience of the world — is on the side of his philosophical knowledge. His non-philosophical experience, if he is still a philosopher when he has it, is 'negative': it is the experience that he does not know what he is experiencing, experience of the absence and lack of the content which experience requires in order to be *our* experience: experience of need.

But, for the religious believer, it is precisely the experience of self-conscious knowledge which appears absolutely lacking in content, since that particular mode of experience is wholly eclipsed, for the believer, by what is outside and beyond the domain of merely self-reflexive knowledge, and of which the religious believer has religious knowledge.[65]

In philosophy, the self-reflexive mind's experience of its own limit is that mind's need for something other than the kind of experience which it is itself able to have. In religion, that need is itself a positive form of experience: not a need for something which is absent from experience, but the reality of what is present in experience. That reality is the mind's knowledge of its own connection to its incomprehensible Ground which is God. Religion knows experientially what philosophy, when it tries to know about the totality of experience, makes manifest: that the totality of experience cannot be exhausted by the operation of the sheerly self-reflexive mind. Religion's knowledge coincides with its being, not in the mode of formal conceptual insight, but in the reverent acknowledgement of the absolute distance of the mind from its own most absolute object, the disposition of spiritual humility which is the element of piety.

Religion might well feel that awareness of the absolute distance of the spiritual energy to which it nevertheless knows itself to be connected: that anxiety or despair which is the portion also of the highest mode of philosophical knowledge.[66] But, for religion, that awareness is not incommensurate with positive knowledge of God. Religion is not, as it were, ashamed of that awareness. Indeed religion would be ashamed of not having it. Hence the religious believer may speak of being loved by a God who is at the same time incomprehensible. The infinite movement of self-reflexive thought — what Hegel calls 'the most astonishing and greatest of all powers, or rather the absolute power'[67] — is, for religion, the positive form of experience.

The reason why philosophy is able to connect itself to the whole of experience is the reason why the philosopher, if he has or thinks he has only philosophical experience, must know his experience to be absolutely divorced from the whole of experience which we call life. But the reason why religion is connected to the whole of experience is that religion knows that it is not itself which is doing the connecting. Philosophy's knowledge is the experience of ignorance. Religion's ignorance is the experience of knowledge. That is the interest of our experience in the connection of philosophy to religion.

But, it might be objected, this is all nothing more than a plausible and perhaps suggestive interpretation of what the doctrine of absolute Spirit means; it does not prove that Hegel's doctrine of absolute Spirit is a *legitimation* for his doctrine of absolute knowledge. To call a doctrine a legitimation surely implies it must be possible for there to be some commonly agreed criteria by which we can assess whether or not the doctrine works. How can an *experience* of the mind — an experience moreover which is claimed not to be identical with the experience of discursive thought — be *communicated*? How can it be spoken of in such a way that, when everything has been said, we commonly know what we have been talking about? And how can such an experience be checked or proven? For the very truth-content of the experience is the assertion that every one of our attempts to legitimate our talk about experience is encompassed by the movement of experience itself.

Every philosophy can be conceived as including both a paradigm[68] which defines its method of argument and evidence, its conception of what are the nature and limits of philosophical thought, and a framework of argument which flows from that paradigm. A paradigm defines, for a particular philosophy, what is the relationship between the activity of philosophical thought and experience as a whole. Only within such a paradigm can the framework of argument proceed to make statements or propose theories which can be tested 'against' experience, tested by the 'evidence' which the paradigm shows to be relevant in the assessment of such theories. The *arguments* of a philosophy, in this sense, may be spoken of as having an 'evidential' legitimation. Their legitimation depends upon the mind's being able to appeal to experience in a manner which the framework of argument of the philosophy itself shows to be intelligible and coherent. The paradigm of philosophy, however, cannot be legitimated in this sense, since it is the paradigm which shows us what words like 'intelligibility' and 'coherence' mean for that particular philosophy.[69] Our reasons for choosing one philosophical paradigm rather than another, therefore, can be neither exclusively philosophical, nor exclusively evidential in the sense which I have just outlined. They must have to do with experience in a sense of that word which has not been exclusively defined by any one philosophical view of experience. Those reasons must have to do with our estimate of the wavelength of philosophy in the spectrum of experience.

I want to argue that Hegel's doctrine of absolute Spirit is the paradigm of Hegel's philosophy in this sense. Clearly the particular view which Hegel has of philosophy in relation to the whole of human experience, whatever its force, cannot conclusively be shown to be the right one, or to be the wrong one, by any argument of Hegel's or by any identifiable empirical fact or connection of such facts. But it does not follow that we cannot engage in rational discussion about the worth or significance of Hegel's paradigm in relation to other alternative visions of what philosophy might be, not least those of our own time. We can, to use Michael Rosen's terms, 'interpret' and so assess Hegel's philosophy in relation to the philosophical discourse of our own time, without being able, or needing, to 'translate' Hegel into the language of that discourse.[70]

But problems of communication, which always occur when philosophies try to talk to each other, arise when we approach Hegel not just accidentally, because of the differences in cultural and conceptual idiom between our day and Hegel's own, but intrinsically and necessarily because of the kind of things Hegel is trying to talk about and to say. Hegel's philosophy, whatever the particular things it says *about* experience, is special in being a philosophy *of* experience. In the case of Hegel's philosophy, the problem of communication arises not just when we try to compare Hegel's voice with the voices of others, but when anyone, even Hegel's contemporaries, tries to read Hegel himself. It is not without significance that almost all of Hegel's works were first delivered as lectures and to students. The truth Hegel communicates becomes real only when it is consciously and actively apprehended in the experience of another mind: when it becomes true *an und für sich*.[71] Hegel's constant affirmation that his philosophy is exoteric or public[72] does not contradict this. Hegel's philosophy is 'public' precisely because it is a philosophy of communication. But communication must, in the first place, address itself to the individual mind, and we can never be wholly certain that one person has apprehended exactly the same thing as another. What we have apprehended we find out by talking to other people; and, of course, we will be disposed to say different things as our culture, language, circumstances — as our *experience* changes.

There is, I believe, of necessity a difference between the way Hegel's philosophy itself communicates truth and the way in which that philosophy must be defended in philosophical debate, and so a certain necessary inarticulateness in the Hegelian standpoint. But to say this, if we interpret the doctrine of absolute Spirit in the way I have suggested, is not to say that we have to take or leave everything in Hegel. It is not to say that there is no 'way in' to Hegel's philosophy, or that there is no possibility of communication between a mind inside the Hegelian mode and one outside. It *is* to say that we can reasonably accept what I have called the paradigm of Hegel's philosophy — his doctrine of philosophy as a religious activity and a mode of absolute Spirit — without being able to justify our decision in relation to any evidence which is absolutely independent of that paradigm. The interpretation of Hegel's doctrine of absolute Spirit which I have proposed means that, if we do accept Hegel's doctrine, we must logically do so on its own terms, which are experiential and ultimately religious ones. I hope, however, also to have shown that we can accept Hegel's paradigm of absolute Spirit without having to believe that all the things which Hegel says about our experience on the basis of it are true, still less that they are true in abstraction from the evidence which we find in experience. I hope to have shown that the conceptual framework which Hegel has given us is capable of explaining, though not of explaining away, the reasons why there is necessarily a partial failure of communication between a mind which fully accepts the Hegelian viewpoint and one which is external to that viewpoint. This capacity is one of the reasons why Hegel's philosophy remains historically vital and capable of rigorous defence in philosophical debate; and it is a capacity, I suggest, which we can only understand in the context of that dimension of Hegel's work which is explicitly and necessarily religious.

To see Hegel's philosophy in this way is not to endorse the kind of Hegel interpretation which Walter Jaeschke has called 'running away from conceptual thought' (*die Flucht vor dem Begriff*).[73] On the contrary, to do so is to point up the relevance of the religious dimension of Hegel's thought precisely to Hegel's achievement as a speculative and systematic thinker.

I have suggested one way in which Hegel shows us how we can conceive of philosophy as both required and empowered to speak of the *objects* of religious belief, and yet at the same time see philosophy as radically in need of the *experience* of religious faith. If Hegel's philosophy can in fact do this — or even if it makes a coherent effort to do so and only partially succeeds — then the Hegelian contribution is of relevance as much to contemporary disputes within Christian theology as it is to more formal problems within the philosophy of religion. One of the most urgent needs in contemporary theological discussion is for a mode of argument capable of connecting the necessary enquiry of the philosophy of religion into the *object* of religious belief — into questions of dogma, truth, and reference — to the kind of non-philosophical religious awareness which belongs to the believing community itself.

This is made strikingly apparent by the current dispute over the writings of Don Cupitt. Much of the critique of these writings has centred upon the claim that their theses do not correspond to the *experience* of religious people.[74] Cupitt's distinction, made in the interests of religious integrity,[75] between the claims of dogmatical realism and the ethical demands of religious practice itself, seems to ignore the fact that, for most people who claim to believe, religious practice cannot be conceived without reference to certain positive dogmatic claims about the truth — nor dogma conceived in abstraction from the religious practice in which it is embodied.

Hegel can help us here. Hegel's philosophy is not 'religious' in the abstract, even though it claims to articulate the 'concept' of religion as such. Hegel's is a Christian philosophy: a philosophy of Incarnation. For such a philosophy there can be no radical or absolute distinction between what we call our 'experience' and the truth about that experience. For a philosophy such as that of Hegel, the ultimate appeal is indeed to the autonomy of religious experience: to the experience of the Christian community or *Gemeinde* to whom his philosophy of religion is addressed.

At the close of his *Philosophy of religion* itself, it is indeed to the experience of the Christian community that Hegel appeals.[76] Hegel makes no claim that his philosophy can communicate a truth which will be religiously valid in abstraction from the experience of that community, still less that contradictions which are real in the life of the *Gemeinde* will disappear because they have been resolved by philosophical argument. In his own time,

Hegel says, the rationalistic theology of the Enlightenment and the reaction against it has led to a 'discordant note' or *Misston*[77] between philosophical theology and evangelical piety.[78] It is a split, as Hegel says, which is 'actually present in reality' (*in der Wirklichkeit vorhanden*),[79] and the fact that it can be dissolved by philosophical argument will not do away with it in reality. How the split is to be resolved, Hegel says, is 'not the immediate practical business and concern of philosophy';[80] it is the business of 'the actual present day world' (*die zeitliche empirische Gegenwart*),[81] the business of the kind of experience which we call Christian belief.

Decisively influenced by Wittgenstein's method in philosophy, which centres upon the analysis of linguistic usage and human practice, modern philosophy of religion in the English speaking world has often seen its task as the elucidation of the logic and the coherence, and so what it sees as the 'meaning', of religious utterances, practices, and codes of belief. Religion and philosophy are different 'forms of life' which give rise to different 'language games.'[82] The task of the philosophy of religion, therefore, can only be seen as describing the grammar of the religious language game, and acquiring such understanding of the religious form of life as is necessary in order for such a description to be provided.[83] Philosophy cannot independently make any kind of substantive statement about whether or not religion communicates truth. Philosophy can, at best, eludicate what religion means by 'truth', as well as other things which religion says and does. This is the position which D.Z. Phillips, one of Wittgenstein's disciples who has been specifically concerned with the philosophy of religion, takes up. Echoing Wittgenstein's requirement that philosophy should 'leave everything as it is' when it considers our actual use of language, Phillips asserts that the only help which philosophy can be in our practical consideration of religious questions is in clearing away possible confusions about how religious language works, or about the proper boundaries between religious and philosophical discourse.[84]

But this apparently modest view of the scope and character of the philosophy of religion is, in practice, far from modest. Hence when Phillips comes to consider a real aspect of religious practice — that of prayer — he writes as follows:

> The philosopher's trouble comes from the fact that he finds
> it difficult to give a conceptual account of a familiar

religious activity; to make philosophically explicit what is already known in a non-philosophical, that is, in this case, religious, way.[85]

But of the kind of explanation we should be seeking, Phillips writes:

> One is asking him (i.e. the religious believer) for a non-religious account of a religious activity, a conceptual or philosophical account which would give some indication of the meaning of prayer to someone for whom prayer meant little, and often, he fails to provide an adequate one.[86]

This is a kind of philosophy of religion which wants to have it both ways: to exclude, and yet covertly to answer, the question of religious truth. What Phillips is really denying is not that philosophy can have anything to say about whether or not there is a religious truth, but that such a truth is one relevant to philosophy: that when philosophy apprehends such a truth, philosophy's own *philosophical* way of understanding the world might be changed. The methodological standpoint which requires us 'to leave everything as it is', when we begin philosophically to consider the phenomenon of religion, is also a standpoint which gives to philosophy the right to *say* how things are in religion. It is a standpoint which denies to the religious mode the capacity independently to articulate any kind of truth which philosophy would have to acknowledge as capable of modifying the structure of philosophical knowledge.

Hegel, on the other hand, has to make substantive statements about religious truth, because he believes that truth is in experience and that religion and philosophy are necessarily connected as ways in which we experience the truth. But he does not presuppose that only philosophy is doing the talking when it talks about religion, or that religion never talks back. Hegel's philosophy respects the autonomy of religion not only as an object, but also as a subject of discourse. It does not presuppose that philosophy and religion can only talk either to themselves, or about each other. It opens up, although it does not fill, a space in which real dialogue can take place on the ground of articulate experience: experience which doesn't know, in advance of our categorical distinctions, exactly what 'philosophy' and 'religion' are, nor where the boundary runs between them.

Karl Barth's charge against Hegel was that a philosophy with the Hegelian ambition could only know about what it claimed to know if it at the same time destroyed the object of its knowledge: if it turned the connection of the human heart to God into an object of speculative dialectic.[87] This is the major anxiety which has attended the reception of Hegel's philosophy of religion, and it is a worry which is philosophically as well as theologically well-founded. A philosophy which tries to talk about the sort of thing which Hegel talks about can, of necessity, only speak adequately if it is also silent, only know if it is also ignorant. This is indeed the problem with Hegel's philosophy; but it is also the problem *of* that philosophy. It is what that philosophy, at its innermost core, is about.

To talk about Hegel's philosophy as an experience is not to evade the problem; it is, on the contrary, to make it explicit. Hegel's philosophy is not, as Kierkegaard alleges, about arranging the truth of Christianity in paragraphs.[88] It is about giving to philosophy, and to much else besides, the experience that Christianity cannot so be arranged. Hegel's philosophy can only give us the kind of knowledge it claims to give because there is a permanent and irrevocable tension between the kind of knowledge which it gives us about our experience, and the kind of attitude we must have to our experience if we want that knowledge to be anything other than empty and vain. This is the contradiction, I believe, which is disclosed to us when we read Hegel's philosophy of religion, and it is the one contradiction which, Hegel is trying to tell us, we cannot reasonably want *aufgehoben*. Only in the light of that contradiction can we understand what kind of an experience Hegel's philosophy is claiming to be, and so what in our own experience can help us to decide whether or not that philosophy is true.

Notes

The following English translations of Hegel's texts have been used, with very minor alterations. They are referred to in the footnotes by the abbreviations given afterwards. The full German title is given after the abbreviation:

> *The phenomenology of mind*, trans. J.B. Baillie (London, 1910)). Abbreviation: *PG* (*Phänomenologie des Geistes*).
> *The science of logic*, in two volumes, trans. W.H. Johnston and L.G.

Struthers (London, 1929). Abbreviation: *SL* (*Wissenschaft der Logik*). *The philosophy of mind* (being Part Three of Hegel's Berlin *Encyclopaedia of the philosophical sciences*), trans. William Wallace and A.V. Miller (Oxford, 1971). Abbreviation: *PM* (*Die Philosophie des Geistes*). *Lectures on the philosophy of religion*, in three volumes, trans. E.B. Speirs and J.B. Sanderson (London, 1895). Abbreviation: *PhR* (*Vorlesungen über die Philosophie der Religion*).

I have occasionally referred to other Hegelian texts; the English edition used is given in the notes.

For reasons which will be apparent from my argument. I have consistently translated Hegel's central term *Geist* as *Spirit* rather than mind. I have amended translations and refer to the English titles of Hegel's works accordingly. In my own text, therefore, I refer to *The phenomenology of mind* as *The phenomenology of spirit*; and to *The philosophy of mind* as *The philosophy of spirit*. I often use a shortened form of the full titles of Hegel's works, e.g.: *Phenomenology of spirit* = *Phenomenology*; *Science of logic* = *Logic*; *Lectures on the philosophy of religion* = *Philosophy of religion*.

The work I refer to as *The science of logic* or *Logic* is what is usually known as Hegel's 'Greater Logic', first published in German in 1812–16 under the title *Wissenschaft der Logik*. It is *not* the first part of the Berlin *Encyclopaedia*, which is usually called the 'Lesser Logic'.

The German edition used is the edition of Hegel's collected works published by Hermann Glockner (Hegel: *Sämtlich Werke: Jubiläumsausgabe in Zwanzig Bänden*, Stuttgart, 1928). In the notes, after the reference to the relevant English edition of a work of Hegel, followed where appropriate by a volume number in roman numerals, a corresponding reference to the Glocker collected works is given with the appropriate volume number (e.g. note 2: *PhR* 1, p. 20; Glockner 15, p. 37). The work I refer to as the Berlin *Encyclopaedia* (*Enzyklopädie der philosophischen Wissenschaften*) is also called by Glockner *System der Philosophie*. I have chosen English translations which seem to me to make clear the sense of the relevant passages of Hegel most effectively in relation to my own argument; the English does not necessarily correspond directly to the German of the Glockner edition. Where a quotation is especially important I have included a full German version in the body of the text; and I have sometimes included a German word or phrase after a particular English one where an adequate English translation seemed quite impossible.

In the translations I have used *Begriff* is usually translated as *notion*. In my own exposition I use the more common English word *concept*. The two terms should be taken as synonymous, and the meaning will, I hope, be sufficiently clear from the context. *Idee* is translated as *idea*.

1. Emil Fackenheim, *The religious dimension in Hegel's thought* (Bloomington, Indiana), p. 3.

2. *PhR* I, p. 20; Glockner 15, p. 37: 'Philosophy is itself, in fact, worship (*Die Philosophie ist in der That selbst Gottesdienst*); it is religion, for in the same way it renounces subjective notions and opinions in order to occupy itself with God.'

3. *PhR* I, p. 19; Glockner 15, p. 37: 'The object of religion as well as of philosophy is eternal truth in its objectivity, God and nothing but God, and the explication of God.'

4. *PhR* I, p. 132; Glockner 15, p. 144: 'God exists essentially in Thought. The suspicion that He exists through thought, and only in thought, must occur to us from the mere fact that man alone has religion, not the beasts.' But n.b. also: 'Yet not only *may* a true content exist in our feeling, it *ought* to exist, and *must* exist; or, as it used to be put, we must have God in our heart.'

5. See *PhR* III, p. 148; Glockner 16, p. 353: 'In philosophy, religion gets its justification from thinking consciousness. Piety of the naive kind stands in no need of this, it receives the truth as authority, and experiences satisfaction, reconciliation by means of this truth.'

6. See Charles Taylor in *Hegel and modern society* (Cambridge, 1979), especially Chapter 1, sections 7, 8 and 9.

7. I use the term 'absolute knowledge' in this encompassing sense; and not with any specific reference to the concluding section of the *Phenomenology* which is called *Absolute knowledge*.

For a representative formulation of this conception of philosophical knowledge, see Hegel: *Lesser logic* (the first volume of the *Encyclopaedia of philosophical sciences*), trans. William Wallace (Oxford, 1873), pp. 1–2; Glockner 8, p. 41.

8. See e.g. *PhR* III, pp. 175–6 (Third lecture on the proofs of the existence of God); Glockner 16, p. 380.

9. See *PG*, p. 86; Glockner 2, p. 78.

10. Robert C. Solomon provides an illuminating description of this view of philosophy when he writes that 'for Hegel, epistemology is the "ontology" of knowledge'. See Solomon, '*Hegel's Epistemology*' in Michael Inwood (ed.): *Hegel* (Oxford Readings in Philosophy, 1985), especially pp. 36–7.

11. Michael Oakeshott, *Experience and its modes* (Cambridge, 1933), p. 9.

12. Ibid.

13. Ibid.

14. Ibid., p. 11.

15. Ibid.

16. Ibid., p. 75.

17. Ibid., p. 82.

18. Ibid., p. 350.

19. I use this term in the sense outlined by Michael Rosen in *Hegel's dialectic and its criticism* (Cambridge 1982), Chapter 1: 'The Interpretation of philosophy'. Cf. notes 68 and 69 below.

20. See Hegel , *Lectures on the history of philosophy*, trans. E.S. Haldane (London, 1892), Vol. 1, p. 73; Glockner 17, p. 105: 'We Lutherans — I am a Lutheran and will remain the same . . . '

21. See e.g. *PhR* I, pp. 36–7; Glockner 15, pp. 53–4: 'It no longer gives our age any concern that it knows nothing of God; on the contrary, it is regarded as a mark of the highest intelligence to hold that such knowledge is not even possible . . . '

22. See e.g. *PhR* I, p. 62; Glockner 15, p. 78: 'God is not the highest

emotion, but the highest Thought. Although he is lowered down to popular conception (*wenn er auch in die Vorstellung herabgezogen wird*), yet the content of this conception belongs to the realm of thought.'

23. Karl Barth, *Protestant theology in the nineteenth century* (London, 1972), p. 420.

24. See e.g. Karl Popper, *Conjectures and reputations* (New York, 1963), p. 69.

25. See Popper, *Conjectures*, pp. 37–9. Cf. Popper, *The poverty of historicism* (London, 1957), Introduction, p. x: 'If there is such a thing as growing human knowledge, then we cannot anticipate today what we shall know only tomorrow.'

26. Popper, *The open society and its enemies* (London, 1945), vol. II, pp. 29–30, 45–6.

27. David Lamb, *Hegel — from foundation to system* (The Hague, 1980), p. 170.

28. Rosen, *Hegel's dialectic*, p. 178.

29. See e.g. *PhR* I, p. 89; Glockner 15, p. 103: 'It is not allowable in philosophy to make a beginning with "There is, there are", for in philosophy the object must not be presupposed.'

30. *PM*, p. 5(§. 379); Glockner 10, p. 15:

> In contrast to the empirical sciences, where the material as given by experience is taken up from outside and is ordered and brought into context in accordance with an already established general rule, speculative thinking has to demonstrate each of its objects and the explication of them, in their absolute necessity. This is effected by deriving each particular Notion from the self-originating and self-actualising universal Notion, or the logical Idea.

31. For a treatment of the *Phenomenology* in this way, see Robert C. Solomon, 'Hegel's epistemology'; for a treatment of the *Logic*, see Terry Pinkard, 'The logic of Hegel's *Logic*', both in Michael Inwood (ed.), *Hegel* (Oxford Readings in Philosophy. 1985). On the *Logic*, see also Klaus Hartmann, 'Hegel: a non-metaphysical view', in Alasdair Macintyre (ed.), *Hegel: a collection of critical essays* (Notre Dame, 1976).

32. See *SL* I, pp. 79–90 ('With what must the science begin?'); Glockner 4, pp. 69–84.

33. *PG*, p. 75; Glockner 2, p. 69.

34. See Hegel, *Lectures on the history of philosophy* (London, 1895), vol. III, pp. 428–9: 'Thus since the investigation of the faculties of knowledge is itself knowing, it cannot in Kant attain to what it aims at because it is that already — it cannot come to itself because it is already with itself.'

35. See *SL* I, p. 34; Glockner 4, p. 15.

36. See ibid., p. 60; Glockner 4, p. 45.

37. Ibid., p. 53; Glockner 4, p. 36.

38. Ibid., p. 84; Glockner 4, p. 77:

> We cannot extract any closer determination or positive content for the beginning from the fact that it is the beginning of

philosophy. For here at the beginning, where there is yet no philosophy, philosophy is an empty word, or an idea taken at random and not justified. Pure knowledge affords only this negative determination, that the beginning must be the abstract beginning.

39. See *PG* I, pp. 23–4; Glockner 2, pp. 28–9.
40. Ibid., pp. 85, 88; Glockner 2, pp. 77, 79–80.
41. Oakeshott, *Experience*, p. 41.
42. *PM*, p. 9; Glockner 10, pp. 20–1.
43. Ibid., p. 5; Glockner 10, pp. 15–16.
44. Cf. *PhR* I, p. 26; Glockner 15, pp. 43–44.
45. Goethe, *Faust*, Part 1, trans. Albert G. Latham (London, 1908), pp. 87–8.
46. *PM*, p. 8; Glockner 10, p. 20.
47. Ibid.
48. See ibid., pp. 16–17; Glockner 10, pp. 33–4: 'Hence the special mode of mental being is manifestation (*Die Bestimmtheit des Geistes ist daher die Manifestation*) . . . '
49. Oakeshott, *Experience*, p. 355: 'Philosophy is not the enhancement of life, it is the denial of life.'
50. *PM*, p. 292; Glockner 10, p. 446; The reference to a community (*Gemeinde*), I believe, has as much the connotation of a community of religious faith as it has of the community of human discourse by which philosophical knowledge is sustained. Cf. note 76 below.
51. Ibid., pp. 300–301; Glockner 10, pp. 456–7.
52. Ibid., § 571.
53. Ibid., ([die]absolute Vermittlung des Geistes mit sich selbst).
54. Hegel does not actually use the term 'Holy Spirit' (*heiliger Geist*) in this discussion; but the notion of Spirit is used in the part of the section 'Absolute Spirit' (*Der absolute Geist*) which is entitled 'Revealed religion' (*Die geoffenbarte Religion*) with a clear theological reference. The total movement of absolute Spirit which is the transcendental form of experience Hegel describes in trinitarian terms — in the three modes of Creator, Son, and Spirit (*Schöpfer, Sohn,* and *Geist*). Cf. *PM*, pp. 181–2 (§ 441, Zusatz); Glockner 10, pp. 297–8.
55. Ibid., pp. 299–300 (§ 566–9); Glockner 10, pp. 455–6.
56. Ibid., pp. 301–2 (§ 571); Glockner 10, pp. 457–8.
57. Ibid.

If the result — the realised Spirit in which all mediation has superseded itself — is taken in a merely formal, contentless sense, so that the Spirit is not also at the same time known as implicitly existent and objectively self-unfolding; — then that infinite subjectivity is the merely formal self-consciousness, knowing itself in itself as absolute — Irony. Irony, which can make every objective reality nought and vain, is itself the emptiness and vanity . . .

58. Ibid., p. 302 (§ 572); Glockner 10, p. 458.

59. See *SL* II, p. 219; Glockner 5, p. 16:

> Indeed to form a notion of an object (*Das Begreifen eines Gegenstandes*) consists just in this, that the Ego (*Ich*) appropriates it, penetrates it, and reduces it into its own form, that is, universality which is immediately determinateness, or determinateness which is immediately universality . . .

60. Ibid.
61. *PM*, p. 302 (§ 572); Glockner 10, p. 458.
62. Ibid., pp. 313–14 (§ 574); Glockner 10, p. 474.
63. See Iwan Ilyin, *Die Philosophie Hegels als kontemplative Gotteslehre* (Bern, 1946), p. 53.
64. See e.g. *SL* I, pp. 79–80; Glockner 4, pp. 69–70. Cf. *PhR* I, p. 89; Glockner 15, p. 103.
65. See *PhR* I, pp. 211–12; Glockner 15, p. 222:

> Since faith must be defined as the witness of the spirit to absolute Spirit, or as a certainty of the truth, it involves relation in respect of the distinction of object and subject, a mediation in fact, but a mediation within itself; for in faith as it is here defined, external mediation and that particular mode of it have already vanished.

66. Cf. Kierkegaard, *Concluding unscientific postscript*, trans. David Swenson (Princeton, 1941), pp. 202–3.
67. *PG* p. 30; Glockner 2, p. 33.
68. I take this term from T.S. Kuhn's *The structure of scientific revolutions* (Chicago, 1970). For Kuhn's definition of a paradigm in science, see Chapter 2: 'The Route to Normal Science', especially pp. 10–11. Kuhn's argument about the importance of paradigms and of paradigm change to the growth of scientific knowledge is perhaps of even greater relevance to philosophy than to science, and in particular to the problem of how we should understand and criticise the philosophical texts of the past. In philosophy, what Kuhn calls 'paradigms' define not only what *kind* of evidence is relevant and what is irrelevant in the testing of scientific theories, but also the ontological status of 'evidence' and 'proof' as such.
69. Cf. Rosen, *Hegel's dialectic*, pp. 6–7.
70. Ibid., pp. 2–3.
71. See *PG*, pp. 18–19, 22–3; Glockner 2, pp. 25, 27–8. This conception of the nature of philosophical argument is, I believe, common to Hegel's work as a whole and does not depend upon the particular rhetorical and apologetic standpoint adopted in the *Phenomenology*.
72. See e.g. ibid., pp. 9–12; Glockner 2, pp. 17–20.
73. See Walter Jaeschke, 'Die Flucht vor dem Begriff: Ein Jahrzehnt Literatur zur Religionsphilosophie (1971–1981)', in *Hegel — Studien*, Band 18 (Bonn, 1983).
74. For a powerful and representative formulation of this critique see Stephen Clark, *From Athens to Jerusalem* (Oxford, 1984), pp. 198–203.
75. See Don Cupitt: *Taking leave of God* (London, 1980), Chapters 5

and 6: 'Worship and Theological Realism' and 'Doctrine and Disinterestedness': especially pp. 68–9:

> In religion, there is no independent being whose existence validates the practice of worship, just as in morality there is no independent being whose will validates the principles of morality. There does not need to be such an independent being, for the aim of worship is to declare one's complete and *disinterested* commitment to religious values. Belief in the God of Christian faith is experience of the impact of those values in one's life.

76. See *PhR* III, pp. 145–51; Glockner 16, pp. 350–6.
77. Ibid., p. 150, Glockner 16, p. 354.
78. Ibid., pp. 147–8; Glockner 16, pp. 352–3.
79. Ibid., p. 150; Glockner 16, p. 354.
80. Ibid., p. 151; Glockner 16, p. 356.
81. Ibid.
82. See Wittgenstein: *Philosophical investigations*, trans. G.E.M. Anscombe (Oxford, 1968), pp., 11–12, 88; especially Remark 241 (p. 88).
83. See e.g. ibid., p. 116 (Remark 373).
84. See D.Z. Phillips: *Religion without explanation* (Oxford, 1976), pp. 189–90. Cf. Wittgenstein, *Investigations*, p. 49 (Remark 124).
85. D.Z. Phillips: *The concept of prayer* (Oxford, 1981), p. 3.
86. Ibid., p. 2.
87. Cf. note 23 above.
88. Cf. Kierkegaard, *Concluding unscientific postscript*, trans. David Swenson (Princeton, 1941), p. 19.

10

The Difference Between
Begrifflicher Spekulation and Mathematics
in Hegel's Philosophy of Nature

Wolfgang Neuser

If one were to attempt to say what significance Hegel's philosophy of nature plays for contemporary natural science, one would encounter great difficulties. For almost a century research about Hegel has simply ignored his philosophy of nature. It has only been in recent years that both the historical influence of the natural sciences upon Hegel's thinking and the systematic position of natural sciences in the Hegelian philosophy of nature have been researched. However, the question as to whether or not Hegel's philosophy of nature can in any way be innovative for contemporary natural science has hardly been explored.

I

One of the acknowledged capabilities of the modern natural sciences is the ability to represent processes in nature with mathematical models. Nevertheless, it would appear that the natural sciences cannot be reduced to mathematics. Instead the natural sciences — alongside mathematics — employ forms of speculation in the understanding of nature. Within this notional frame of speculation ('notional deduction') mathematics serves as an auxiliary science. The consistency assumed in mathematical deductions means that predicates are allowed which, in turn, must be interpreted within the above mentioned notional frame. In using mathematics the natural sciences, e.g. physics, possess discriminating forms of deduction. (For the 'notional deduction' the natural sciences do not have any proven method.) They are based on general ideas, intuitions or scientific experience.[1] The intention of Hegel's philosophy of nature is to achieve a dialectical formal frame for notional conclusions. In so doing, the dialectic should be formulated so generally that absolutely everything one can understand can be reformulated within it. In this context Hegel must discuss mathematics and its role in the natural sciences. In what follows we shall investigate the relationship between 'mathematical argumentation' and 'notional speculation' in Hegel's philosophy (of nature). This leads to the question whether or not Hegel's understanding makes it possible to explain the procedures used in the natural sciences.

Observe the role of notion and mathematics as exemplified in the situation that arises when a student shows his research results to a physics professor. A situation evolves in which the student believes he has attained a conclusion after a long process of mathematical deduction that yields results hitherto unknown. Under what criteria might the teacher judge whether or not the result is correct? Carl Friedrich von Weizsäcker explains such a situation, dating from the beginning of his research. Werner Heisenberg was his teacher and saw the results without having checked the mathematics involved.[2] Simply on the basis of the results and their interpretation he was able to conclude whether or not they were correct or whether a mistake in thinking or in calculation had been made. Apparently Heisenberg had at his disposal a theoretical framework within which he could undertake amplifications without depending on certain mathematical methods of deduction. Thus we can at this point assert a (notional) frame of reference within which mathematical deductions must be arranged — at least in theoretical physics. If used correctly mathematics should, in general, not conflict with this approach.

There is a rather strained relationship between experimental physics and theoretical physics. Theoretical physics is not strictly committed to the production of a monistic closed theory. On the contrary, a proliferation of theories are formulated to meet the requirements of special cases by different specialists. Competing theories cannot always be traced back to a common point of reference. There are schools of thought within theoretical physics. Yet there is a common consensus — hard to formulate in detail — that allows the experienced physicist to examine the validity of the results reached by specialists from other schools. Of course, agreement in experimental data also plays an important role here. One must bear in mind, however, that such data is already theory-impregnated the moment it has been abstracted from experience. This is the case whether or not the notion arrived at is adequate.

In addition to the abundance of (non-classical) theories, modern experimental physics has to contend with the difficult problem of carrying out experiments in the microscopic world with macroscopic instruments. In so doing classical theories have to be combined with non-classical theories (i.e. quantum theories and the theory of relativity) that are often disparate and incommensurable. When experimental physics attempts to explain its experimental findings by means of mathematically described theories of theoretical physics, reference is often made to classical and non-classical explanations in one and the same breath. The experimental physicist proves his skill by combining both the classical and the non-classical. Yet a demonstration of the consistency of both explanations is extremely difficult to produce. Often this consistency is not explicitly shown at all. For example, one frequently finds explanations of an interference experiment in quantum mechanics that is actually two-thirds classical. But the impression often left is that physics is representing — over a broad scope — a consistent method of explanation for one aspect of nature. Here it must be recognised that there is at least a belief in a notional frame of reference; a belief that guarantees the unity of the comprehended world beyond mathematics and the perceived.

In all cases mathematics appears as the guarantee of consistency for physics: whenever an experiment can be transformed into a theory, or whenever a classical theory is harmonised, in each case, the corresponding mathematical apparatus can be employed to interpret the results of one side as a mathematical approximation to its opponent. This consistency, however, is not to be found in mathematics itself since the interpretation of individual magnitudes in the approximation must be the same in the complete mathematical description and in the approximation. Here again, it is a notional structure that must be intuitively grasped in order to secure the unity of the physical conception of the world.

Can we extract an adequate explanation of this relationship from Hegelian philosophy? What does Hegel think of the role of mathematics from a philosophical perspective? Two questions are of special interest: what significance does Hegel give mathematics in the system of knowledge? Of what relevance is mathematical knowledge for the method of understanding?

Hegel discusses these problems at different places in his writings as exemplified by three cases: theory of numbers, calculus (explanation of the notion of the infinite) and arithmetic.

II

Hegel saw his philosophy as a form of science out of which the speculative notion could be attained. Our question here touches the problem of how mathematics and philosophy are related to each other.

Hegel stood in critical opposition to the numerous philosophical attempts to make mathematics the methodological model for philosophy (Plato, Pythagoras, Kant, Spinoza, Schelling). Whereas Schelling still believed that both mathematics and philosophy represented absolute knowledge, Hegel limited this to philosophy:

> But the perversity of employing mathematical categories for the determination of what belongs to the method or content of the science of philosophy is shown chiefly by the fact that, in so far as mathematical forms signify thoughts and distinctions based on the Notion, this their meaning has indeed first to be indicated, determined and justified in philosophy.[3]

Whereas mathematics merely amounts to the usage of formula, truth proves itself only in the thinking of the notion.[4] The use of mathematical structures as a symbol for thought veils and muddies the truth with the physical sensory element.[5] It is unfitting to employ the methods of geometry and arithmetic in philosophy,[6] because they depend upon 'constructions' and 'proofs' due to their abstractness. 'Construction stands by itself without its subjectivity of its notion' and 'proof is a subjective proceeding without objectivity'.[7] Hegel illustrates how the deficiency of 'construction' and 'proof' as ways of explanation are to be understood by using the example of a (mathematical) theorem proved qua construction. A theorem is a relation of real determinations that have no notional relation.[8] The theorem is proved after having related the necessity of the determinations. For this the real determinations have to be mediated. This being the prerequisite, it is not the notion that mediates; the mediating determination occurs without the notion of context;[9] the mediating moment is taken as temporary material for the proof.[10]

The mathematician has accidentally found a method of proof that will thereafter only be reproduced by memory. The goal of the proof is thus never constitutively entered into the proof actually done. Hegel consistently differentiates between 'proof'

(*Beweis*) and 'construction' (*Konstruktion*): whereas a proof is based on a successive sequence of deductions in which the goal of the proof is not known, in the case of a construction the starting point and the result are known — but the path is still sought that leads from the beginning to the goal.[11]

Hence, neither the Kantian meaning of 'construction' nor Schelling's is the same as Hegel's: for Kant the 'representation of the object' is constructed '*a priori* in intuition', but Schelling interprets this as 'equating the notion with intuition', whereby in intellectual intuition the geometrist is given the archetype of his object, which is consequently reflected into the sensation by drawing.

For Hegel, however, the 'construction' is at first limited to the geometrist's incomprehensible operations with 'temporary material'. His interpretation of Schelling is such that construction is not the equation of intuition and notion, but rather the sensed reflection of an archetype.[12] It is important for Hegel that the notion of the object of construction is not explicitly thought in its inner logical structure. 'This collection of material does not make sense until the proof happens. It appears in itself to be blind and without notion.' The material or the steps of the proof — taken by themselves — are irrelevant. Only in the context of the intention of the proof do they have relevance. Here Hegel is playing with the well-known Kantian dictum that intuition without notion is blind.

Unlike Kant, Hegel maintained that construction does not follow an *a priori* rule; one must 'blindly obey' contingent and external assertions.[13] 'On its own account, therefore, this operation is unintelligent, since the end that directs it is not yet expressed.[14] Not until later, in the result, does the secret reveal itself as the proof.

In the proof we find the connections between the determinations as articulated in the theorems. This connection retrospectively appears to be a 'necessary one'.[15] The proof did not occur by following the inner dynamics of the notional determination, but by subjective deed without objectivity. The object did not necessarily determine the course of the proof.[16]

That is to say, because the content determinations of the theorem are not at the same time posited as Notion-determinations but as given *indifferent parts* standing in various external relationships to one another, it is only the *formal, external* Notion in which the necessity manifests itself. The proof is not a *genesis* of the relationship that constitutes the content of the theorem; the necessity exists only for intelligence, and the whole proof is in the *subjective interests of cognition.*[17]

The construction, on the other hand, is the 'consequence of the nature of the object'. In the proof, however, this consequence is assumed to be the ground. The relationship between ground and consequence has been turned around in the construction, and the consequence results only subjectively from the ground. The ground is a 'subjective ground'. This description reproduces the logic of the argumentation of the geometrical construction, and it is obvious that a procedure (such as the construction) that is based on subjective ground cannot be sufficient for a philosophical argument. In Jena, Hegel used proof and construction as a method of philosophical comprehension.[18] Nevertheless, in both terms the meaning that Hegel uses in his later works is already present: proof and construction are understood as opposing structures of argumentation that are only true when they appear in combination. Hegel later calls this appearance in combination of proof and construction the 'notional constitution' (*Begriffskonstitution*) and forgoes naming construction and proof elements of the dialectical method.

The words 'construction' and 'proof' are in Hegel's *Logic* thereafter used exclusively for the type of construction and proof that are used in the mathematical sciences.

Proof and construction as a means of understanding philosophy are the link connecting Hegel to Schelling. Thereafter the universal (*Allgemeine*) constructs itself in that it divides into parts which themselves have the nature of the whole. The proof of being oneself (*Fürsichsein*) of the parts and their relationship to each other completes the construction. Thus, the universal is the unity of the parts and of their 'negative unity' and 'negative oneness' with regard to the opposing determinations contained within it. We can recognise in these opposing argumentational structures of construction and proof an early formulation of Hegel's dialectical method.[19]

In Jena it was already evident to Hegel that 'only in the proof is the necessity of the construction shown'.[20]

This first division (i.e. the construction), in itself, exists therefore through the second (i.e. proof) — or there is nothing accidental except that which appears as necessity in the proof. It is the necessary content, the determination of the concretion such that it is constructed only in so far that it is a different unity than first appears in the proof.[21]

So far as the spirit thus recognises the infiniteness it comprehends itself, for its comprehension is this: it equates it as referred to another; it comprehends itself because it equates itself to that to which it refers that is itself as the other of itself, as infinite and thus the same as itself.[22]

In the absolute spirit construction and proof are one and the same. The former part is that which presents itself in the proof as one; in the proof there exists the unity which equates itself and the infiniteness that equates itself as one, and both of these are separately also the parts of the construction. The construction itself is necessary as such, for it is itself equated with the proof. Or the spirit is in itself this that it finds itself as the spirit and that, in which it finds itself, or much more that which it finds as itself is the infiniteness.[23]

It is only in this sense that this convergence of construction and proof can be seen as valid parts of the philosophical method in Hegel's later system. Construction and proof together become the method of thinking in philosophy. Taken by themselves, however, construction and proof are limited figures of argumentation, i.e. of mathematics.[24]

From the argumentational structure of philosophy — that is from the inner structure of the speculative notion — we then learn that Kant's construction phenomenologically describes what Hegel logically thinks. The inner self-development of the notion is a concretion of thinking. Notion and intuition thereby have the same content. Schelling's construction and the mathematical proof as representations of the universal into the particular and of the particular into the universal (both of which take place in intellectual intuition and represent original knowledge — or the idea) together form the dialectical constitutive procedure for the self-determinating notion.

III

With this background we are now capable of determining the systematic position of mathematics in the Hegelian system and of describing the relationship of mathematics to the science of nature.

The location of mathematics between logic and sensation, which in Kant's philosophy becomes a mediating position between notion and intuition, has for Hegel the critical defect that it places in opposition to each other the logical 'constitutiva' of notions. This crucial shortcoming can be seen, for example, in the notion of 'number'.[25] From sensation number has the characteristic of an unarranged diversity.[26] To transfer this sensation into the notion means that we think of the notion 'being external in itself', or 'dead motionless determination'.[27]

The unrelatedness of the diverse is taken as a basis and yet at the same time ignored in the natural sequence of numbers in as much as the isolated is understood as one number. The number contains in itself — as we may paradigmatically see for mathematics — the contradiction to be thought unrelated, but as a thought to be 'thought in relation'.[28] The unrelatedness of the diverse is sometimes described by Hegel as 'the dead' (*das Tote*).[29] It is also characteristic for notions of understanding (*Verstandesbegriffe*). Should the number be transformed into 'concrete ratios' the attempt will remain futile, 'to want to still retain it in notion'.[30] When Euclid intends to prove the congruence of two figures by overlapping and comparing them, this procedure is 'a roundabout way by which the method refers to sensation', rather than thought.[31] In contrast, philosophy has to explain the relationship — including the merely postulated relationship — of the unrelated.

On the other hand mathematics does not only deal with the sensation, but by virtue of its rules and its method it is principally related to thought. Similarly a geometrist does not intend to regard a drawn triangle as a sensed one, but as an ideal one.[32] The geometrist only draws a triangle because he is unable to 'express its physical being as a thought'.[33]

Another reason for the fact that mathematical proofs are not based upon objective features of the things concerned is that the proof does not determine the object by its features. Only in retrospect can the result show whether the proof was correct.[34] This is one more difficulty, to 'think' a triangle without concrete intuition. Whereas Schelling regards sensation in mathematics as positive,[35] Hegel uses 'sensation' with a clearly pejorative meaning: mathematics does not reflect on the notion of its objects which would make possible a pure thinking of those objects.[36]

As Hegel shows, in geometry space is thought totally abstracted from the features of the bodies that constitute it. As 'space' remains in intuition in spite of abstraction, it is an 'unsensed sensation'. In this respect we find in the conception of space an analogy to the above mentioned conception of number. Space is the object of the 'separateness of sensuality'. The diverse is prerequisite in its diversity and at the same time ignored as a thought. As an unsensed sensation space is established as the intuition of the diverse abstracted from the diverse. Space is only the 'form of intuition',[37] and from its materiality it is 'thought' or 'abstraction'. It is 'the pure absence of notion of the sensation', the 'separateness of sensation'. But Hegel rejects reliance on this intuition as an 'advantage of science' and even rejects basing proofs on it with the remark that 'by intuition science does not emerge, but only by thinking'.[38] The scientific character of geometry results from its ability to abstract from objects of sense[39] and in particular to refer to the triangle thought of and not to the sensed one.

The fact that mathematics acts rationally and therefore does not question the use of notions is obvious in calculus.[40] The differential dx was regarded as 'infinitely small' in Hegel's time.[41] Therefore the features of the differentials are not quantitative (small) but have to be thought in their quality (infinite). For the infinitely small can only mean a limit which cannot be surpassed.[42] Infinity gives the small a new quality. Therefore calculus is in principle different from calculations with finite numbers.[43] In Hegel's time this difference caused much philosophical confusion. Hegel explains the notion of infinity as follows: 'The quantum is truly completed to a qualitative existence'.[44] This would require that mathematics rely on the philosophical notion of the infinitely small.

> It is this concept which has been the target for all the attacks made on the fundamental determination of the mathematics of this infinite, i.e. of the differential and integral calculus. Failure to recognize it was the result of incorrect ideas on the part of mathematicians themselves.[45]

Nevertheless it was not always a disadvantage that mathematics did not reflect on the notions of calculus, because intuitively mathematics has usually taken the correct notions of the infinitely small. 'It is announced as a triumph of science that by means of the calculus alone, laws are found *transcending experience*, that is, propositions about existence which have no existence.[46] The reason for this success is the fact, that the infinitely small is not only a quantity but has a qualitative determination in itself (for instance the transformation of a curved parabola into a straight line by differentiation).

All of this does not mean that Hegel regards mathematics as an insufficiently developed science, lacking maturity. Instead it should be seen as Hegel's attempt to characterise the very nature of mathematical knowledge. The philosophical deficit lies in the fact that mathematics is an activity of ratio and unable to prove the trueness of its notions, because pure rational activity cannot think the notion and therefore cannot think the criteria of trueness. Nevertheless, mathematics has its merits:[47]

> One could go further and work out the thought of a *philosophical mathematics* apprehended through notions, instead of the assumed determinations from which the method employed by the understanding derives ordinary mathematics. It is because mathematics is the science of the finite determinations of magnitude, which are supposed to remain firmly and consistently in their finitude, and may not go beyond these determinations, that it is essentially a science of the understanding; and since it is capable of realizing this science in a perfect manner, it has the advantage over other sciences of this kind, of not being contaminated by the admixture of heterogeneous notions or empirical application.[48]

For Hegel the intermediate position of mathematics, between sensation and thought, means that mathematics has purely mental objects but represents them as sensed because mathematics is unable to fix the notion of such an object. Thus we see how Hegel interprets Kant's 'construction' in mathematics in a pejorative way. Because mathematics is unable to rely on a controlled reflection of notions there arises a philosophically insufficient difference between the thought of an object and its notion.[49]

So Hegel opposes Wolff, who uses a measurement to illustrate why differentials of a higher order can be neglected in the representation of a function as a series. Wolff argues that the measurement of a mountain remains correct even if a grain of sand is blown away.[50] This argument combines empirical and analytical argumentation and therefore is not conclusive. Wolff's analogy is inadequate and inconsistent because it identifies two logically different arguments: mathematical inference and measurement. The limited accuracy of measurement is not a mathematical proof. Hegel's objection to the differential calculus of his contemporaries refers to a difference between logical argumentation (notion) and the object that remains unresolved.

Hegel's argument runs a similar course: differential calculus must think the opposed together, therefore it is in need of notion, which makes this possible.[51]

Hegel praises the fact that Euclid limits himself to the means of mathematics, because notional deduction was not at his disposal. Euclid did not even attempt to deduce from a rational notion of mathematics what only can be inferred from (the notion of) reason (*Vernunftbegriff*).[52]

The axiom of parallels (which according to today's understanding constitutes a plane geometry) could be proved from the notion of parallels. This, however, is not the task of mathematics, which does not rely upon the notion (of reason). It cannot undertake the deduction of its definitions, axioms and least of all its object (space and its dimensions). Euclid's outstanding scientific achievement is precisely that he exactly appreciated both the element and the nature of his science[53] and recognised this.[54]

Unlike Euclid, Schelling attempted to employ the methods of Euclidean geometry in his philosophy. But such an application was in Hegel's opinion unfitting,[55] because mathematics observes 'only quantitative determinations', from which the qualitative are abstracted. Mathematics

> treats of the merely quantitative determination and abstracts from the qualitative, and can therefore confine itself to *formal identity*, to the unity that lacks the Notion, which is *equality* and which belongs to the external abstractive reflection. Its subject matter, the determinations of space, are already such abstract subject matter, prepared for the purpose of having a completely finite external determinateness. This science, on account of its abstract subject matter, on the one hand, has this element of the sublime about it,

that in these empty silent spaces colour is blotted out and the other sensuous properties have vanished, and further, that in it every other interest that appeals more intimately to the living individuality is silenced.[56]

Hegel here addresses the fact that mathematics acts rationally.

In his later system Hegel shares Schelling's position in so far that he believes there is in mathematics an intellectual intuition that reflects into sensation.[57] Hegel calls both — reflection into sensation, and the reflection on the totality of the objective — intuition, once with the attribute 'intellectual' and once completely without any attribute.

> But if by intuition we are to understand not merely the element of sense but the *objective totality*, then it is an *intellectual* intuition; that is to say, intuition has for its object not the external side of existence, but what existence holds of imperishable reality and truth — reality, only in so far as it is essentially in the Notion and *determined* by it, the Idea, whose more precise nature has to reveal itself at a later stage.[58]

One of the differences between the respective positions of Hegel and Schelling is that Hegel does not accept intuition as a basis of proof. The content of intuition is the real material (*realer Stoff*), which in space and time does not exhibit the relationship of the diverse parts to each other. This relationship is a product of reason. On these terms the material of intuition is a disunity of the diverse (*Einheitslosigkeit des Mannigfaltigen*). With its adaption into intuition this material is tentatively arranged. This arrangement already points to the universal structure under which the material will be arranged in notion — as the construction appears in a theorem with the goal of the proof already given, but without an inner necessity. The universal structure, however, is not in itself explicitly thought. It is not yet the 'universal of the diverse';[59] for intuition the adapted material is still fixed in its sensed structure.

Kant regards intuition as that which appears between subject and object, because it appears not only in the notion but also remains glued to sensation. For Hegel this interpretation of intuition is insufficient, because intuition is still affected by sensation and therefore can be deceived by sensation.[60] The concrete form of intuition may be the totality of all the characteristics one can intuitively know; intuition remains none the less sensation.[61] This also pertains to Schelling's intellectual intuition, because it does not think the object in the notion. The thinking of the notion, however, effects the logical movement by the determination of the object. The deficiency of intellectual intuition does not lie in its material, unlike the case of sensed intuition, the material of which is the sensation. Intellectual intuition, however, acts in accordance with the unchanging reality and truth of the object.[62] The object of intellectual intuition is reality, in as much as its essence is expressed in the notion, and the object is determined by notion.[63]

There is even a relationship between the intellectual intuition and something concrete; not through perception but through reflection. It refers to the 'idea': 'The advantage which intuition as such is supposed to have over the Notion is external reality, the Notionless element, which first receives a value through the Notion.' The notion is supposed to receive the world by the lack of notion.[64] Intuition is thus the entire notion albeit as the 'dead' — without self-explication. The rational impresses upon this disunited diverse a 'fixed existence' by determining the universal — also the contents of intuition — and then applies the universal. That which is not yet impressed upon by intuition on the universal, and which is also a disunited diverse, becomes a fixed determination. The rational maintains that the intuited is none other than this. The rational also represents the 'infinite power', preparing that which is made available of the object for thinking and, on the other hand, giving spirit to the object.[65]

This universal, asserted by the rational as a determination of reflection, appears in its being solidified and fixed in the form of a reflection in itself.

The determinations are thought as unchanging. Were this universal to be understood as the notion, then the notion would have the form of an 'eternal essential'. The transitoriness of material, however, cannot come into question. Such a notion would therefore have a form that would not be adequate to its content.[66] The absorption of transitoriness into form both realises and guarantees reason. This notion must contain the unity of an 'abstractly determined' and of the universal, which expresses the 'determination of the finite' and the 'inadequacy' of the universal as a fixed being.[67]

Hegel takes up Schelling's position: Schelling believes the 'real' and 'ideal' in absolute knowledge to be identical. In Hegel's opinion Schelling's 'real' corresponds to 'determination in its finiteness', whereas the 'ideal' means the fixed determination of the universal, which at the same time reflects the inadequacy of its being fixed. Schelling based his philosophy on Spinoza's model of the absolute, in which two opposing determinations are thought under the same name.[68] Hegel clarifies Spinoza's notion of the absolute in *Logic* with a mathematical example of the infinitely small.[69]

Hegel shows that philosophical argumentation does not take place on the level of intuition; he shows that construction is a mere subjective proof of geometry and, on the other hand, that in philosophy form and content should be adequate in the notion: Hegel, therefore, cannot believe that mathematics can be a method of philosophy — as Schelling did. All that Hegel accepted was a notion that relativises the abstract determination of the universal. Hegel's criticism of mathematics amounts to this: mathematical sciences should not be allowed to observe the quantitative without a qualitative.

This criticism is also found in Hegel's discussion of the 'positive and negative' in arithmetic.[70] Hegel cites this in a 'Remark' in his *Logic*.[71] This does not represent a philosophy of 'determination' in arithmetic, because this sort of determination is indeed not an 'immanent evolution of the notion'.[72]

> However, philosophy must be able to distinguish what is an intrinsically self-external material; the progressive determining of it by the Notion can then take place only in an external manner, and its moments, too, can be only in the form peculiar to their externality, as here, equality and inequality. It is an essential requirement when philosophizing about real objects to distinguish those spheres to which a specific form of the Notion belongs, that is, spheres in which the Notion has an actual existence; otherwise the peculiar nature of a subject matter which is external and contingent will be distorted by Ideas, and similarly these Ideas will be distorted and made into something merely formal.[73]

The notion 'number' is a 'specific form' of the 'external'. In the notion 'number' the idea comes only partly to consciousness.

As for the supposed primary importance of number and

calculation in an *educational* regard, the truth of the matter is clearly evident from what has been said. Number is a non-sensuous object, and occupation with it and its combinations is a non-sensuous business; in it mind is held to communing with itself and to an inner abstract labour, a matter of great though one-sided importance. For, on the other hand, since the basis of number in only an external, thoughtless differ-ence, such occupation is an unthinking, mechanical one. The effort consists mainly in holding fast what is devoid of the Notion and in combining it purely mechanically.[74]

In the tradition of Vieta[75] and Schelling, Hegel juxtaposes geometry and arithmetic as analytical and synthetical methods.[76]

Geometry constructs a universal into a particular and arithmetic proves by attributing a particular to a universal. Geometry synthesises universal elements into a particular figurative shape. Arithmetic analyses the particular proposition with regard to its universal validity. Geometry is only synthetic from the perspective of geometry itself. In fact the construction of the triangle precedes the notion of the triangle and fulfils only the notion of the triangle. The construction is in this respect a tautology.

Hegel, who differed from Kant and modified Schelling's concept of mathematics and philosophy, saw these disciplines as sciences, whose object, structure of proof and method, exhibit fundamental differences.

For Hegel, philosophy alone is in a position to concern itself with its own proof by thinking the self-explication of the notion. It follows that the scientific character of a discipline is not defined by its share in mathematics.[77] The external representation of mathematics does not create an advantage over philosophy.[78] On the contrary what makes a science a science is its ability to make use of thought, and it is defined by its share in notion.

What is the significance of the mathematical and empirical natural sciences for Hegel? Mathematics is a rational activity, whose rationality is founded by the act of reason in philosophy. The different methods of proof in mathematics and philosophy give rise to Hegel's important criticism of mathematical natural science. For Hegel philosophy constitutes notions by relativising the originally fixed initial notion, whereby the initial notion is identically thought with the opposed notion.

Philosophy can thus build over several levels a chain of argumentations by the development of notions. Mathematics must reverse the succession of its apparently contingent construction, in order to recognise this construction as a proof. But in this case it is only subjective reason, because the argumentation is not determined by the object itself — as it is in the case of the development of notion.[79] In the mathematical natural sciences it is announced 'that by means of the calculus alone, laws are found transcending experience, that is, propositions about existence which have no existence.'[80] This occurs in the extrapolation of the directly and immediately observed. Hegel finds such proofs of things 'without real meaning' inadequate because no proof of existence can be found. In Hegel's opinion this is a systematic rebuttal: in notions one thinks of concrete objects; laws are ruled by notions. Should such a law be given referring to a non-existing object, then the notion will contain an unsolved contradiction and will thereby be formally untrue. Since a mathematical natural science states quantities but, on the other hand, interprets these specific qualitative procedures, e.g. natural phenomena, it can only be appropriate if it is based upon notions, which relate qualities and quantities in one unit.

Hegel discusses this type of inner notional relation in his *Logic* in the chapter 'measure'.[81] 'But yet a still higher *proof* is required for these laws; nothing else, that is, than that their quantitative relations be known from the qualities or specific Notions of time and space that are correlated.'[82] As argued in this chapter it is desirable that the ratios of the numbers found in nature are known. Kepler's and Galileo's merits are that they found such ratios.[83]

For the mind (*Geist*) such empirical ratios are then considered natural laws containing reason.[84] Mathematics as understood in nature is therefore not merely formal or ideal, but 'real' and 'physical'.[85] Mathematical determinations have their true notions in philosophy itself.[86] Hegel recognises that nature is written with the letters of mathematics. He expresses his regret that there is no natural science in his sense, although there are already a series of works preparing the ground for such a natural science.[87] The existing form of applied mathematics is full of a 'brew of experience and reflections'.[88]

The truly philosophical science of mathematics considered as the *doctrine* of quantities, would be the science of *measures*; but this already assumes the real nature and the particularity of things, which is first present in concrete nature. Because of the external nature of quantity, this would certainly also be the most difficult of all sciences.[89]

Here I have merely traced the foundations of a rational interpretation, as this must be employed in the comprehension of the mathematical and mechanical laws of nature within the free realm of measures. Specialists do not reflect upon the matter, but a time will come when the rational concept of this science will be demanded![90]

Might Hegel's philosophy of nature then be such a postulated mathematical natural science? Absolutely not: natural science has the task of stating the empirical finds, i.e. formulating its laws in intuition by attributing the diversity of the sensed experience to notions. Instead philosophy exclusively thinks the notion. Philosophy does not examine experience directly, but instead abstracts from experience by using the rational notions (*Verstandesbegriffe*), that are natural laws to natural sciences.[91]

Within the notion — as expressed by Hegel — the unity of form and content is always thought. Intuition contains the notion in itself, but does not think it explicitly. Intuition is not a logical category. Only logical categories contain the inner structure of notion.[92] Therefore only (Hegel's) logic can also guarantee the apodictic characteristics of scientific (philosophical) statements.

IV

Although it is compared to the method of knowledge in philosophy,[93] mathematics, because it does not think notions, is real and physical.[94]

As long as mathematics presents something as well-reasoned, these reasons are founded in notions. If mathematics describes an object of nature, its reasons are the essence of nature — as Hegel argues in his *Dissertatio philosophica de orbitis planetarum*.[95] When these reasons are recognised, he continues, they have become laws. Laws are abstractions from the perceived and have a status of notions.

In point of fact, however, the measure and the number of nature cannot be strangers to reason: the study and the knowledge of the laws of nature are based on nothing else but our belief that nature has been shaped by reason and that all the laws of nature are identical. When those who seek the laws of nature in experience and by induction happen to come across the appearance of a law, they acknowledge the identity of reason and nature and they rejoice in their discovery.[96]

According to Hegel the relationship between the natural sciences, mathematics and philosophy of nature are thus represented so that the natural sciences transform laws by attributing them to mathematical ratios. These mathematical ratios are reasonable reasons (*Vernunftgründe*), to be sure, neither the methods of the natural sciences nor those of mathematics allow a demonstration for the necessity of the reasonable reasons.[97] This can only be done by philosophy in that it constitutes the notions through self-reflection. In Hegel's point of view the relationship of theoretical physics, experimental physics and mathematics could therefore be understood as follows: Experimental physics is a form of 'comprehending perception'. By using notions it attributes the singularly perceived to a law that it considers a universal. Notions are thereby not consciously used, as in the case of philosophy which constitutes from its inner logical structure. The physicist cannot make explicit the inner structure of the notion by his own means. In physics the notion acts 'behind the back of the consciousness'.

Theoretical physics examines the lawfulness and tries to grasp the logic of its notion. However, theoretical physics makes exclusive use of mathematical inferences. It does not use any method in examining the inner dialectical structure of notions — unlike philosophy. This becomes clear, for example, in the co-existence of Newton's and Einstein's notions. The completely different theorems of addition for velocity in both 'physics' are considered valid for different ranges of velocity. Newton's physics is considered an approximation to Einstein's formula for low velocities. But then there is a limit, at which Newton's physics is valid and Einstein's is not. Even if this can be solved pragmatically, it must be unsatisfactory for thinking that reality should be understood as a mixture of two theories of physics, whose notions are completely incompatible. It can only follow, that there are some notions which are still not understood in both theories of physics.

Whether or not one wants to take into consideration the

Hegelian view of these facts as a criterion of consistency for the physical point of view depends, to a large extent, on whether one is convinced by Hegel's account of the self-constitution of the notion — as intimated here — otherwise known as the 'dialectics of notion'.

This criterion of consistency — Hegel emphasises — cannot be realised with the methods of the natural sciences and mathematics. It can only be understood through philosophical thinking.[98] Only knowledge which is conscious of itself — thus reflecting upon itself — is capable of proving the necessity and consistency of its own deeds.

Notes

In the following notes Hegel's books are cited without titles from the edition G.W.F. Hegel, *Werke* in 20 Bänden, Auf der Grundlage der Werke neu edierte Ausgabe, Hrsg. E. Moldenhauer und K.M. Michel, Frankfurt/Main (Suhrkamp-Verlag), 1970/71; references are to the volume number followed by the page number. I have also used the following abbreviations: *Real.*1 for G.W.F. Hegel, *Jenenser Logik, Metaphysik und Naturphilosophie*, hrsg. G. Lasson (Hamburg 1967); *PG* for G.W.F. Hegel, *Phänomenologie des Geistes*, hrsg. J. Hofmeister (Hamurg 1952); Gies for G.W. F. Hegel, *Naturphilosophie*, Band 1, Die Vorlesungen von 1819/20 in Verbindung mit K.H. Ilting hrsg. von M. Gies, Neapel 1982; *Habil.* for G.W.F. Hegel, *Dissertatio philosophica de orbitis planetarum*, übersetzt, eingeleitet und kommentiert von W. Neuser (Weinheim 1986). I have used A.V. Miller's translation of Hegel's *Science of logic* (New York, 1969) which is cited as *SL* followed by the page number. M.J. Petry's translation of Hegel's *Philosophy of nature* (London, 1970) is cited as Petry followed by the volume and page number.

1. W. Stegmüller, *Hauptströmungen der Gegenwartsphilosophie*, Bd. II, Stuttgart 1975, p. 531 f.
2. C.F. von Weizsäcker, *Die Einheit der Natur* (Munich 1971), p. 109 ff.
3. 5/248; *SL* 216.
4. 5/248.
5. Ibid.
6. 6/535, 537.
7. 6/534.
8. 6/533.
9. Ibid.
10. Ibid.
11. Ibid.
12. 6/286.
13. Contrary to this general tendency Hegel writes in his *Differenzschrift* (2/35, 45) that philosophy constructs something.

14. 6/534.
15. Ibid.
16. *PG*, 34 ff.
17. 6/534; *SL* 812.
18. *Real.* 1/173 ff. See Hegel's polemics in 1806: 'Statt des innern Lebens und der Selbstbewegung seines Daseins wird nun eine solche einfache Bestimmtheit von der Anschauung, d.h. hier dem sinnlichen Wissen, nach einer oberflächlichen Analogie ausgesprochen und diese äußerliche und leere Anwendung der Formel die KONSTRUKTION genannt' *PG*, 42.

['Instead of expressing the inner life and motion-in-itself of its existence now there is expressed such a simple determination of intuition by superficial analogies, that means of sensual knowledge. This external and meaningless application formula is called a CONSTRUCTION.']

19. See also: 'Die Beglaubigung des bestimmten Inhalts, mit dem der Anfang gemacht wird, scheint rückwärts derselben zu liegen, in der Tat aber ist sie als Fortwärtsgehen zu betrachten, wenn sie nämlich zum begreifenden Erkennen gehört' 6/554.

['The authentication of the determinate content with which the beginning is made seems to lie behind it; but in fact it is to be considered as an advance, that is if it belongs to philosophical (*begreifenden*) cognition.'] *SL* 828.

20. *Real.* 1, 175.
21. *Real.* 1, 174.
22. *Real.* 1, 181.
23. Ibid.
24. For correlations between mathematics and logic see B. Heimann, *System und Methode in Hegels Philosophie*, (Leipzig, 1927), pp. 444 ff.
25. See R. Baer, 'Hegel und die Mathematik', in, *Verhandlungen des 2. Hegel-Kongresses* (1931), 1932, pp. 113 ff.
26. 5/246; 8/70.
27. 5/247.
28. 5/246.
29. 5/244.
30. 5/247.
31. 6/531.
32. 5/245.
33. Ibid.
34. *PG*, 35 ff.
35. F.W.J. Schelling (1803), *Vorlesungen über die Methode des akademischen Studiums*, hrsg. W.E. Ehrhardt (Hamburg, 1974), p. 50.
36. 'In der Mathematik läßt man es gelten, die Definitionen sind Voraussetzungen; Punkt, Linie werden vorausgesetzt. In der Philosophie soll der Inhalt als das an und für sich Wahre erkannt werden.' 'Ein anderes ist es, ob dieser Inhalt an und für sich wahr sei. Solche Frage macht man bei geometrischen Sätzen gar nicht. Bei philosophischer Betrachtung ist dies aber die Hauptsache.' (20/172)

['In mathematics it is accepted that the definitions are prerequisites;

points and lines are assumed as prerequisites. In philosophy the content is to be recognised as truth in itself and with itself.' 'It is quite another question whether this content is true in itself and with itself. Such questions are not asked in geometry. In philosophical reflections this is the main point.']

37. 6/535.
38. Ibid.
39. 6/536.
40. 5/279; 5/305.
41. J. Szegetti, 'Hegel und Cantor', in, *Hegel-Jahrbuch*, 1971, pp. 283–93.
42. J.O. Fleckenstein, 'Hegels Interpretation der Cavalierischen Infinitesimalrechnung', in, *Hegel-Studien-Beiheft 11*, 1974, pp. 117–24.
43. Cf. Fleckenstein (1974), p. 117.
44. 5/296. Cf. W. Neuser, 'Hegel's approach to Euclid's theorem of parallels', in, *Explorations in knowledge, III*, 1, 35–9.
45. 5/296; *SL* 253.
46. 5/111; 5/297; *SL* 272, Cf. 20/187 ff.
47. For further information on Hegel's notion of identity in mathematics and philosophy see B. Taureck, *Mathematische und transcendentale Identität* (Munich, 1973).
48. 9/52 f; Petry I, 233f.

49. Alle Bildung reduziert sich auf den Unterschied der Kategorien. Alle Revolutionen in den Wissenschaften nicht weniger als in der Weltgeschichte kommen nur daher, daß der Geist jetzt zum Verstehen und Vernehmen seiner, um sich zu besitzen, seine Kategorien geändert hat, sich wahrhafter, tiefer, sich inniger und einiger mit sich erfassend. (9/20 f.) Cf. 5/296.

['All cultural change reduces itself to a difference of categories. All revolutions, whether in the science or history world, occur merely because spirit has changed its categories in order to understand and examine what belongs to it, in order to possess and grasp itself in a truer, deeper, more intimate and unified manner.'] Petry I/202.

50. Wolff, *Elementa matheseos universae* (1713/15), Tom I. *Elementa analyseos mathematicae*, P. II, C. I., 5. Schol. (*Gesammelte Werke* II. Abtl. Bd. 29, hrsg. J.E. Hofmannus, Hildesheim 1968):

Similiter in Astronomia diameter Telluris respectu fixarum habetur pro puncto seu infinitesima: idem enim observaretur motus primus, si tellus esset punctum individuum. Eodem etiam modo in eclipsibus lunaribus computandis terra pro sphaera perfecta, consequenter montium, multoque magis aedium ac turrium altitudines pro infinitesimis habentur: neque enim aliter nobis appareret umbra telluris super disco Lunae, si terra sphaera perfecta esset.

51. 5/296.
52. 6/529.

53. 6/528; *SL* 808.

54. 6/528.

55. 6/535. At the end of the nineteenth century there were 'mathematical' enquiries about Hegel: G. Engel, *Die dialektische Methode und die mathematische Naturanschauung* (Berlin, 1865) and C.H. Weiße, *Grundzüge der Metaphysik*, (Hamburg, 1935).

56. 6/535; *SL* 611.

57. See E. Oeser, 'Der Gegensatz von Kepler und Newton in Hegels "absoluter Mechanik",' in, *Wiener Jahrbuch für Philosophie* (1969) *3*, pp. 69–93.

58. 6/286; *SL* 611.

59. 6/286.

60. See '*sinnliches Bewußtsein*' in Hegel's *Phänomenologie des Geistes*.

61. 6/286.

62. Ibid.

63. Ibid.

64. 6/287; *SL* 611.

65. 6/287.

66. 6/285.

67. 6/287.

68. 20/172, 8/383 and F.W.J. Schelling (1803), *Vorlesungen über die Methode des akademischen Studiums*, hrsg. W.E. Ehrhardt (Hamburg, 1974) pp. 359 ff, pp. 387 ff.

69. 5/291–5.

70. 6/60 ff. Cf. M. Wolff, 'Über das Bedürfnis nach einer philosophischen Naturbetrachtung', *Dialektik*, *3* (1981) pp. 83–100.

71. 5/243.

72. Ibid. Critique: H. Schwarz, *Versuch einer Philosophie der Mathematik* (Halle 1853), pp. 36–59, 100–19, 170–93.

73. 5/243; *SL* 212. A. Bullinger, *Hegels Naturphilosophie in vollem Recht gegenüber ihren Kritikastern* (Munich, 1903).

74. 5/243; *SL* 216 and Gies, 19.

75. Hegel refers here to Vieta's attempt to connect analytical method of arithmetic to the synthetic method of geometry.

76. For example Euclid 4/34–6, 5/234 f., 6/505, 6/530 f., 6/531–8, 5/244, Hofmeister *Dokumente zu Hegels Entwicklung* (Stuttgart, 1936), p. 297.

77. I. Kant, *Metaphysische Anfangsgründe der Naturwissenschaften* (Riga, 1786), A IX.

78. F.W.J. Schelling (1803), *Vorlesungen über die Methode des akademischen Studiums*, hrsg. W.E. Ehrhardt (Hamburg, 1974), p. 50.

79. 5/318–20, 9/77, 9/248, 5/321, 6/293.

80. 5/320; *SL* 272.

81. A. von Pechmann, *Die Kategorie des Maßes in Hegels 'Wissenschaft der Logik'* (Cologne, 1980).

82. 5/407; *SL* 343.

83. 5/406 f.

84. *Habil.* 32.

85. *Habil.* 5.

86. 9/54.

87. 5/406 f.

88. 5/321.
89. 9/54. Petry I, 235.
90. 9/106. Petry I, 281.
91. F.W.J. Schelling (1803), *Vorlesungen über die Methode des akademischen Studiums*, hrsg. W.E. Ehrhardt (Hamburg, 1974), Vorlesung 11, 12.
92. See Goethe's criticism of mathematics in his *Farbenlehre, Polemischer Teil*.
93. 5/392:

> Die Entwicklung des Maßes ... ist eine der schwierigsten Materien; indem sie von dem unmittelbaren, äußerlichen maße anfängt, hätte sie einerseits zu der abstrakten Fortbestimmung des Quantitativen (einer Mathematik der Natur) fortzugehen, andererseits den Zusammenhang dieser Maßbestimmungen mit den Qualitäten der natürlichen Dinge anzuzeigen, wenigstens im allgemeinen; denn die bestimmte Nachweisung des aus dem Begriffe des konkreten Gegenstandes hervorgehenden Zusammenhanges des Qualitativen und des Quantitativen gehört in die besondere Wissenschaft des Konkreten, ... Es mag hierbei dies überhaupt bemerkt werden, daß die verschiedenen Formen, in welchen sich das Maß realisiert, auch verschiedenen Sphären der natürlichen Realität angehören.'
> Also 5/406.

['The development of measure ... is extremely difficult. Starting from immediate, external measure it should, on the one hand, go on to develop the abstract determination of the *quantitative* aspects of natural objects (a mathematics of nature), and on the other hand, to indicate the connection between this determination of measure and the *qualities* of natural objects, at least in general; for the specific proof, derived from the Notion of the concrete object, of the *connection* between its qualitative and quantitative aspects, belongs to the special science of the concrete. Examples of this kind concerning the law of falling bodies and free, celestial motion will be found in the *Encyclop. of the Phil. Sciences*, 3rd ed., Sections 267 and 270, Remark. In this connection the general observation may be made that the different forms in which measure is realised belong also to different spheres of natural reality.'] *SL* 331

94. *Habil.* 5.
95. Ibid.
96. *Habil.* 32.
97. See C. Frantz, *Die Philosophie der Mathematik* (Leipzig, 1842), pp. 3–4, 46–61, 88–114.
98. For the difficulties of consistency see G. Ludwig, *Die Grundstrukturen einer physikalischen Theorie*, (Berlin-Munich-New York, 1978), pp. 248 f.

11

Hegel's *Habilitationsthesen*:
A Translation with Introduction and
Annotated Bibliography

Norbert Waszek

Introduction

When his father Georg Ludwig died in January 1799, the twenty-eight year old Hegel was able to pursue a career of his own choice. At least in this context, the loss of his father had positive side-effects too: on the one hand, filial piety no longer committed Hegel to the 'profession of preacher' which his parents had intended him for;[1] on the other hand, his modest inheritance (just over 3,000 Wuerttemberg Guilders) provided him with a financial basis sufficient to leave his position as private tutor and to enter what was then the risky path of philosopher and academic. Hegel's awareness of this liberating break from his previous way of life was acute, as is testified in a little poem of 1801 and the 'curriculum vitae' of 1804:

Resolution

Break then, peace with thyself, break with the work of the
world.
Strive, seek something more than today or yesterday. So
wilt thou
Better not be than the time, but still be the time at its best.[2]

... after my father's death I resolved to devote myself entirely to philosophic science.[3]

However, Hegel did not rush into the new life thus opened up to him; he took his time and employed careful deliberation over his next move. He continued to work on various manuscripts in order to enter the new arena well prepared. Only in November 1800 did

249

he seek the advice of his friend Schelling who had achieved early
fame as a philosophical author and subsequently received a
position in the prestigious University of Jena. Writing to
Schelling, Hegel still appears to be thinking of going to a quiet
place, such as Bamberg, in the first instance in order to prepare
himself further, before moving on to the intellectual focus of
Jena.[4] Schelling had no patience with such overcautious planning
and he urged his friend to come straight to Jena. When Hegel
arrived in Jena in early 1801, the intellectual life of the city was
brilliant, though it could be argued that the contemporary
eminence of the University of Jena, which will for ever be
associated with the efforts of Goethe, had passed its peak when
Fichte and the Romantics departed and had entered a period of
gradual decline.

During his first year at Jena, Hegel had to bring his scholarly
and literary projects and interests in line with what was necessary
or helpful in terms of securing an academic post. His contemporary
projects may be divided into three subject areas: a) political
studies; his interest in the 'philosophy of identity' on the side of
b) the philosophy of spirit as well as c) the philosophy of nature.
In the early months of 1801, the political studies which had
hitherto taken up much of his energy continued to hold a
prominent place among his activities. However, the internal
difficulties he was bound to encounter in these early efforts in
political philosophy were aggravated by the hectic pace of the
political events at the time, which tended to outdate his studies
continually. Due to these difficulties, Hegel did not succeed in
completing the political writing he had in mind. Moreover, the
political studies, even completed, would not help him in gaining
the recognition of the philosophical establishment at Jena, a
recognition that was vital for obtaining a teaching post in the
philosophy department. As H.S. Harris puts it, 'it became
evident that he must now do something more philosophical to
make his mark before it was too late' (Harris, 1983, p. xxv).
Hegel's friend Schelling, well-known himself for the rapid pace of
his publishing, was highly prudent in such matters and may well
have urged Hegel to establish himself through the publication of
a philosophical book. At any rate, Hegel put politics aside for the
time being and used the early summer of 1801 to write his essay
Difference between the systems of Fichte and Schelling.[5] The publication
of the essay served as Hegel's introduction to the philosophical
circles of Jena, but it had the drawback of making its author

appear to be, at least in the eyes of the contemporary reading public, a mere follower of Schelling. In the hope that his essay would gain the attention of the academic community at the University of Jena, Hegel applied immediately to the Faculty for the validation of his Tübingen degree and for the granting of the '*venia legendi*', the formal permission to deliver lectures in the university. It was required — this requirement survives, to the present day, in the German and similar university systems — that the candidates undergo a procedure, called '*Habilitation*', before the '*venia legendi*' was granted. The '*Habilitation*' consists of a dissertation (then written in Latin) and a disputation (normally a defence of the written work). As he had contributed to the transcendental side of the philosophy of identity with his 'Differenzschrift', it seemed appropriate that Hegel would choose a dissertation topic from his other field of interest, the philosophy of nature. Indeed, as soon as he had finished the 'Differenzschrift', Hegel appears to have started on his Latin dissertation *On the Orbits of Planets*.[6] However, the beginning of the academic year was approaching rapidly and it seemed unlikely that Hegel would be able to submit his dissertation before then. It thus became necessary that a compromise was negotiated and, since the details of the negotiations are beyond the scope of the present article,[7] it was agreed upon to allow Hegel an early disputation based on theses and to grant him the '*venia legendi*' so that he could lecture in the autumn term on the understanding that he would submit his dissertation shortly after. The disputation was held on the 27 August and the theses Hegel presented and defended on this occasion are here presented in their original Latin and an English translation. In formal terms, the disputation resembled a debate between two teams with Hegel, seconded by Schelling's younger brother Karl who was still a student, on the defending side, and the older Schelling, Friedrich Immanuel Niethammer, and another student, Thomas Schwarzott, as the opposing team.[8]

The Jena publisher Prager printed the Latin theses for the disputation in the form of a leaflet and it is to this source and the subsequent reprint by Karl Rosenkranz — as part of his biography *G.W.F. Hegels Leben* (Berlin, 1844), pp. 156-9 — that the modern editions, e.g. *TWA*, vol. II, p. 533, go back. In his edition of Hegel's early writings, Georg Lasson provided a German translation to the Latin original of the theses, and there is now a new translation by Wolfgang Neuser.[9]

The theses are formulated paradoxically in order to provoke discussion. This characteristic makes it difficult to provide an unambiguous interpretation of the theses and the verdict of Harris on them — 'quite cryptic' (Harris, 1983, p. xxx) — is well justified. The aim of the present edition of the theses is to open up a wider discussion of them and not to pre-empt such a discussion by offering hasty conclusions about their meaning and significance. Thus, the annotated bibliography that follows the translation does not pretend to solve the problem of interpretation, rather, it should be seen as an attempt to bring together various comments on the relation of the theses to wider issues of Hegel's thought, on some parallels between the theses and Hegel's other writings, and on certain allusions to other philosophers.

Karl Rosenkranz suggested a classification of the theses according to their subject matter (Rosenkranz, 1844, p. 156). Although this classification is outdated in some respects, it may still be helpful: theses I and II are said to deal with logic; theses III, IV and V with the philosophy of nature; theses VI, VII, and VIII discuss the concept and scope of philosophy in general; finally, theses IX, X, XI, and XII contribute to the area of practical philosophy.

Notes

1. Compare Hegel's c.v. of 1804, most easily accessible in: G.W.F. Hegel, *Theorie Werkausgabe* (henceforth quoted as *TWA*). In 20 vols ed. by E. Moldenhauer and K.M. Michel (Frankfurt, 1969 ff), vol. II, p. 582 f.

2. Johannes Hoffmeister (ed.), *Dokumente zu Hegels Entwicklung* (Stuttgart, 1936) p. 388. The English translation is quoted from H.S. Harris, *Hegel's development: night thoughts* (Oxford, 1983), p. xix.

3. *TWA*, vol. II, p. 582. English translation quoted from H.S. Harris, (*Hegel's development*) p. xx.

4. Johannes Hoffmeister and Rolf Flechsig (eds), *Briefe von und an Hegel*, in 4 vols (Hamburg, 1961) vol. I, pp. 58–60.

5. G.W.F. Hegel, *Differenz des Fichte'schen und Schelling'schen Systems der Philosophie* (Jena, 1801). English translation, under the above title, by H.S. Harris and Walter Cerf (Albany, 1977).

6. G.W.F. Hegel, *Dissertatio Philosophica de Orbitis Planetarium* (Jena, 1801); cf. the references to Lasson (1928) and Neuser (1986) in the bibliography.

7. The documents are reproduced in Heinz Kimmerle, 'Dokumente zu Hegels Jenaer Dozententätigkeit (1801–1807)', *Hegel-Studien*, vol. *4* (Bonn, 1967) pp. 21–100.

8. Cf. the Protocol of the Faculty, in Kimmerle 'Dokumente', p. 43.

The notes of Hegel and Schelling for the disputation have also survived: Hoffmeister (*Dokumente*) pp. 312 ff (Hegel's notes); Wolfgang Neuser (1986) pp. 142–5, 163 (Schelling's notes).
  9. Lasson (1928) pp. 404 f; Neuser (1986) pp. 74–7.

Translation

I

Contradictio est regula veri, non conradictio, falsi.
Contradiction is the rule for the truth, non-contradiction for falsehood.

II

Syllogismus est principium Idealismi.
Syllogism is the principle of Idealism.

III

Quadratum est lex naturae, triangulum, mentis.
The square is a law of nature, the triangle [is a law] of the mind.

IV

In Arithmetica vera nec additioni nisi unitatis ad dyadem, nec substractioni nisi dyadis a triade, neque triadi ut summae neque unitati ut differentiae est locus.
In true arithmetic there is no place for addition other than of unity to a dyad, nor for substraction other than of a dyad from a triad, nor for the triad as a sum, nor for unity as a difference.

V

Ut magnes est vectis naturalis, ita gravitatio planetarum in solem, pendulum naturae.
Just as the magnet is a natural lever, so the gravitation of the planets to the sun is a pendulum of nature.

VI

Idea est synthesis infiniti et finiti, et philosophia omnis est in ideis.
An idea is the synthesis of the infinite and the finite, and philosophy exists totally [in the sphere of] ideas.

VII

Philosophia critica caret Ideis, et imperfecta est Scepticismi forma.
Critical philosophy lacks ideas and is an imperfect form of Scepticism.

VIII

Materia postulati rationis, quod philosophia critica exhibet, eam ipsam philosophiam destruit, et principium est Spinozismi.
The matter of the postulate of reason, which critical philosophy exhibits, destroys that very philosophy, and is the principle of Spinozism.

IX

Status naturae non est injustus, et eam ob causam ex illo exeundum.
The state of nature is not unjust, and that is why one must depart from it.

X

Principium scientiae moralis est reverentia fato habenda.
The principle of moral science is [the] reverence that should be observed towards fate.

XI

Virtus innocentiam tum agendi tum patiendi excludit.
Virtue excludes innocence of both action and suffering.

XII

Moralitas omnibus numeris absoluta virtuti repugnat.
Morality that is absolute in every respect conflicts with virtue.

At various stages in the preparation of my translation, I consulted the following Latinists and Hegel scholars, who kindly responded to my queries: Dr Jon Edmondson (Dulwich College, London); Prof. H.S. Harris (York University, Toronto); Dr Stephen Hinds (Girton College, Cambridge); Dr David Sedley (Christ's College, Cambridge); Dr David Simpson (Westfälishce Wilhelms-Universität, Münster). While thanking them for their help, the five scholars are absolved from any responsibility for my shortcomings.

Annotated bibliography

Baum, Manfred, *Hegel's philosophische Methode I: Die Entstehung der Hegelschen Dialektik* (Bonn: Bouvier, to appear shortly).
    Prof. Baum perceives two allusions in thesis XII: (a) to the doctrine of the Pythagoreans, as transmitted by Aristotle (*Metaphysics* 985 B 29; *Magna Moralia* 1182 A 11–14), according to which virtues such as justice are defined as numbers; (b) to Shaftesbury's *Characteristics* (as edited by J.M. Robertson. In 2 vols London, 1900; vol. I, pp. 90 ff) in which it is stated that 'the men of harmony' are inspired by their 'love of numbers, decency and proportion'. In the context of defining his ideal of balance and measurement — 'the thought of numbers and proportion in a life at large'; ibid. vol. I, p. 92, Shaftesbury quotes Horace approvingly: 'Et verae numerosque modosque ediscere vitae' (*Epistulae* II. 2, 144). (I am grateful to Prof. Baum for making his typescript available to me prior to publication.
Düsing, Klaus, 'Spekulation und Reflexion. Zur Zusammenarbeit Schellings und Hegels in Jena', *Hegel-Studien*. vol. 5 (1969) pp. 95–128.
    Prof. Düsing provides a comprehensive survey of the co-operation between Schelling and Hegel at Jena, a survey which is obviously relevant to our present purposes given the active rôle of Schelling in Hegel's '*Habilitation*'.
Haering, Theodor L., *Hegel: Sein Wollen und sein Werk. Eine chronologische Entwicklungs-geschichte der Gedanken und der Sprache Hegels*. In 2 vols (Leipzig, 1929 and 1938) vol. I, pp. 759–62.
    In the context of this broad survey, Prof. Haering offers a brief interpretation of the thesis which emphasises continuities with earlier manuscripts.
    Theses I and II are seen as reflecting a new study of logic stimulated by Aristotle or Bardili. Theses III, IV, and V are

described as following Schelling's keen interest in the philosophy of nature. Thesis V, in particular, is related to the mechanics of Hegel's later system (cf. Haering, vol. II, pp. 296 f). Thesis VI is regarded as echoing the 'Systemfragment' of 1800 and as criticising Kant's notion of 'synthesis' with the help of Fichte's and Schelling's discussion of 'idea'. Haering's comments on theses VII and VIII emphasise Hegel's critical perspective on Kant further. Thesis IX is considered to be critical of Hobbes' account of the state of nature, and both thesis IX and thesis XII are said to express Hegel's views on 'ethical life'. Theses X and XI are characterised as condensing principles from Hegel's 'Spirit of Christianity'.

Harris, H.S., *Hegel's Development II: Night Thoughts (Jena, 1801–1806)* (Oxford, 1983) pp. xxx, 18 n, 48 n, 49, 87–9, 125–6, 157–9, 393.

Prof. Harris' comments on the theses are easily the best-informed account of them in English. He provides a summary of the *'Habilitation'* procedure (pp. xxx f), and then concentrates on theses III and V, VII and VIII, IX, and X.

Ad thesis III:

> The four dimensions of the absolutely resting motion are the 'squareness' of Nature . . . The dimensions of nature are four, three spatial and one temporal; the dimensions of Spirit are but three, the three inner dimensions of time, past, present, and future. (p. 87)

> Hegel's thesis about the 'laws' of nature and of mind was formulated in terms of Schelling's Spinozist parallel between thought and extension as equally complete images of the Absolute Identity. Thus each side forms its own order, the order of things and the order of ideas. But the Trinitarian theology makes intelligence more fundamental than nature. Nature was created. Translating this into Spinozist terms, there are two aspects of Nature, and they do not have the same law. The square is only the law of 'natura naturata'; 'natura naturans' is the absolute spirit of the whole, and as such it obeys the law of Spirit even while laying down its own law for the manifest world of natural phenomena. (pp. 158 f)

Cf. Kimmerle (1980) and Schneider (1973 and 1975).

Ad thesis V: Prof. Harris ascribes Hegel's effort 'to bring the mechanical conception of the pendulum under the more organic sway of the concept of magnetism' (p. 88) to the direct influence of Schelling's *Darstellung meines Systems der Philosophie* (1801, Sect. 95, Addition 1).

Ad theses VII and VIII: Hegel's criticism of Kant is spelt out (pp. 48 f).

Ad thesis IX:

> The justice of natural ethics is perfect reciprocity. The criminal must suffer what he did. His own inward consciousness of this creates a sense of guilt. Hegel's view that one who is conscious

of guilt must go on provoking attack until his debt is paid, is one of the most interesting anticipations of modern depth psychology produced by his conception of our universal human nature as an inwardness that must utter itself.

The whole conception of nature as an external fate that is just one's own attitude to the world reflected back upon oneself was developed at Frankfurt and is unchanged here. What is new is the concentration upon the workings of individual fate, and the consequent awareness of how the fear of death dissolves all natural relationships, including the bond of guilt. It is the fact that there is a form of conscious life which does not give way before the fear of death which makes it necessary, in terms of natural justice itself, to pass over to the political condition founded upon a constitution that is publicly established, generally recognized, and impartially maintained. (pp. 125 f)

Ad thesis XII:

That is what the ultimate identity of the Metaphysics, the identity of absolute spirit with absolute matter, asserts too. When we read that 'the simple absolute self-to-self connecting Spirit is the *Aether*, or absolute Matter' [G.W.F. Hegel, *Gesammelte Werke*, vol. 7, ed. by R.-P. Horstmann and J.H. Trede (Hamburg, 1976) p. 178] we have only to remember that 'absolute Spirit' was first identified as Fichte's practical Ego, in order to see this [ibid., p. 165]. (p. 393)

Hoffmeister, Johannes, *Dokumente zu Hegels Entwicklung* (Stuttgart, 1936) pp. 312–14, 475.

Hegel's notes for the disputation are here published for the first time. These Latin notes are mainly phrases of politeness and gratitude which Hegel might have used during the disputation; they throw no light on the content of the theses. What might be gathered from these notes is the highly formal character of the disputation and its marked absence of spontaneity.

Kimmerle, Heinz, *Dokumente zu Hegels Jenaer Dozententätigkeit (1801–1807)*, *Hegel-Studien*, vol. 4 (1967) pp. 21–99.

This article provides the most extensive and most reliable edition of all surviving documents with regard to the *Habilitationsvorgang*' (pp. 28–44). There is also an introduction on the contemporary situation of the University of Jena (pp. 21–7) and further sections deal with Hegel's appointment as professor (pp. 45–52), his lectures at Jena (pp. 53–65), Gabler's report on Hegel's Jena years (pp. 65–73), and Hegel's membership in learned societies (pp. 74 f).

—— 'Hegel's Naturphilosophie in Jena', in *Hegel in Jena*, ed. by Dieter Henrich and Klaus Düsing (Bonn, 1980) pp. 207–15.

Ad thesis III: Prof. Kimmerle sees thesis III in the context of the fragments of Hegel's lecture notes of 1801/2, which will be published in the new critical edition [G.W.F. Hegel, *Gesammelte Werke*, vol. 5. Edited by M. Baum and K.R. Meist (Hamburg, to appear shortly)].

For this early stage in Hegel's development, Prof. Kimmerle claims a priority of nature over spirit (p. 207). According to him, the 'square' (*quadratum*) consists of 1) the 'system of sky' (*dem himmlischen System*), i.e. the pure appearance of the idea in its full movement; 2) the 'mechanical' and 3) 'chemical' phenomena (*das Mechanische und das Chemische*); and 4) the 'organic' (*das Organische*) in which the idea returns to its complete structure (pp. 211 f). The 'triangle' (*triangulum*) of spirit on the other hand is said to consist of 1) 'imagination' (*Vorstellung*); 2) 'desire' (*Begierde*); and 3) 'a free people' (*ein freies Volk*).

Lasson, Georg (ed.), G.W.F. Hegel, *Erste Druckschriften* (Leipzig, 1928) pp. XLII, 404–5.

In his edition of Hegel's early writings, Lasson publishes Hegel's theses and provides the first German translation of them. In his introduction (p. XLII), he emphasises Schelling's contribution to the theses: in his view, the theses are more characteristic for the friendship and co-operation of Hegel and Schelling than for the specifically Hegelian way of thinking.

Neuser, Wolfgang (ed.), G.W.F. Hegel, *Dissertatio Philosophica de Orbitis Planetarium, Philosophische Erörterung über die Planetenbahnen*. Bilingual edition, with introduction and commentary (Weinheim, 1986) pp. 176, here pp. 1–6, 74–7, 142–5, 163, 165–76.

In his bilingual edition of Hegel's 'professorial thesis' (*Habilitationsschrift*): *De Orbitis Planetarium*, Dr. Neuser also reprints Hegel's theses for the disputation and provides a new German translation of them (pp. 74–7). In his introduction (pp. 1–6), he gives a brief account of the '*Habilitation*' procedure (pp. 2–3). Dr. Neuser's edition contains a facsimile, a first transcription, and his own translation of Schelling's Latin notes for the disputation (pp. 142–5). Although the transcription does not appear flawless — given their content, I am unconvinced that the notes refer to thesis VII as Dr. Neuser assumes on the basis of a doubtful reading of the figure '7' at the beginning of the manuscript — Dr. Neuser must be given credit for making this document available to the scholarly community. A brief note on Schelling's manuscript draws attention to certain parallels with Schelling's published work: 'Fernere Darstellungen aus dem System der Philosophie', *Zeitschrift für speculative Physik*. vol. *I*, No. 2 (1802) pp. 63 f. There is also a good bibliography on the relevant period of Hegel's development, the writings of his contemporaries, and Hegel's possible sources (pp. 165–76).

Pöggeler, Otto, *Hegels Idee einer Phänomenologie des Geistes* (Freiburg and München, 1973) pp. 141 f.

Ad theses VI and VII: Prof. Pöggeler places theses VI and VII in a developmental account of Hegel. According to his view, the last manuscript of Hegel's years at Frankfurt (G.W.F. Hegel, *Theologische Jugendschriften*, edited by Hermann Nohl (Tübingen, 1907) p. 146) does reveal the intention of transforming a theological inquiry into the relationship of the finite and infinite into a metaphysical inquiry. Soon after, Hegel is convinced that metaphysics alone can succeed in raising the finite to the infinite. Thesis VI is an expression of this conviction. That the reference to the 'idea' has to be seen as an acceptance of older metaphysical positions and implies a criticism of Kant can be taken from thesis VII. As further support for his view, Prof. Pöggeler quotes a passage from an early lecture of Hegel in which Hegel speaks of 'recreating the oldest old' (*das älteste Alte wiederherzustellen*) and of 'burying the non-philosophy of recent times' (*die neueren Zeiten der Unphilosophie begraben*). (The passage can be found in Karl Rosenkranz (1844) p. 192).

Rosenkranz, Karl, *G.W.F. Hegels Leben* (Berlin, 1844) pp. 156–9.

Apart from suggesting a classification of Hegel's theses (cf. Introduction), Rosenkranz provides a few notes the more important of which will now be summarised.

Ad thesis I: Rosenkranz presents Wolff's views on identity as Hegel's starting-point: every definition has to exclude the opposite of the defined object. Contrary to the apparent meaning of the thesis, according to Rosenkranz, Hegel never denied Wolff's view, but felt the need to go beyond it. The difference is as essential for the comprehension of the whole as the identity which Wolff had insisted upon. The truth cannot exist without its opposite, but it is also the negation of the opposite. The underlying principle seems to be derived from Spinoza's '*Verum est index sui et falsi*' (*Ethics*. Part II, 43). In Rosenkranz' opinion, the stimulus which induced Hegel to go with Spinoza beyond Wolff is essentially Kantian.

Ad thesis II: again, Rosenkranz regards Hegel's thesis as a consequence of Kant's philosophy — especially the threefold nature of Kant's categories — of Fichte's deduction — with its thesis, antithesis, and synthesis — and of the implicit syllogism of Schelling. Hegel's achievement is characterised as showing the necessity of syllogism.

Ad thesis III: Rosenkranz directs his readers' attention to Baader and Plato as Hegel's most probable sources. The 'square' (*quadratum*) of nature is said to consist of fire and water, earth and air. The 'triangle' of spirit is called 'truly Platonic' (*ächt Platonisch*) in so far as it echoes the threefold structure of Plato's *Republic*.

Ad thesis V: the contrast between a natural lever and a natural pendulum is drawn in order to distinguish between immanent and external movement.

Ad thesis IX: once again, Hegel is said to extend rather than to oppose the view of a predecessor, in this case Thomas Hobbes. The state of nature is only the possibility of positing 'just' and 'unjust'; the will must leave its natural character behind and thus constitute 'justice' and its 'opposite'. The thesis is then related to Hegel's later criticism of the presupposition of a state of nature. Cf. Tuschling (1987).

Rosenkranz, Karl, 'Hegels ursprüngliches System 1798–1806', *Literarhistorisches Taschenbuch*, edited by R.E. Prutz, vol. II (1844) pp. 157–64. This actually appeared in September 1843; cf. Schneider (1975, pp. 135–7). Rosenkranz' article is subsequently referred to as '1844a'.

In this article, Rosenkranz publishes a fragment which may throw light on thesis III. For details, see Schneider (1975).

Schneider, Helmut, 'Zur Dreiecks-Symbolik bei Hegel', *Hegel-Studien*, vol. *8* (1973) pp. 55–77. 'Anfänge der Systementwicklung Hegels in Jena', *Hegel-Studien*, vol. *10* (1975) pp. 133–71.

Ad thesis III: in his 1975 article, Dr. Schneider presents and discusses Hegel's so-called 'divine triangle' fragment, a manuscript first published by Rosenkranz (1844a) and which has been lost since then. For an English translation, with notes, see: Harris (1983) pp. 184–8.

Dr. Schneider provides an analysis of the text, a survey of the relevant secondary literature, and a critical discussion of Hegel's sources with special reference to Plato (pp. 134 ff) and various modern authorities (Baader, pp. 143 f; Böhme, pp. 159 ff; Schelling, pp. 164 f; Goethe, pp. 167 f; and others). The details of this article go beyond the scope of the present inquiry, but the fragment it presents shows reflections on the triangle as '*lex mentis*' which resemble thesis III. In a more general sense — as revealing Hegel's interest in triangles and squares as representations of the philosophy of spirit and nature respectively — the same holds true for an otherwise unrelated drawing in Hegel's literary estate which is edited and annotated in Dr. Schneider's earlier article (1973).

Tuschling, Burkhard, 'Reason, Actuality, and Ethical Life', article circulated at the 1986 meeting of the HSGB (to appear in 1987). (I am grateful to Prof. Tuschling for making his article available to me prior to its publication.)

Ad thesis IX: the decisive claim of Prof. Tuschling's lucid analysis is that thesis IX documents the last step towards Hegel's concept of 'ethical life' (*Sittlichkeit*). In this context, Hegel's relations to Hobbes and Kant are carefully examined.

Index

Alienation 8, 9, 135–8
Antigone 16, 17, 21, 22, 27,
    37–40
Aristotle 28, 30, 112, 132, 133,
    255
Aufheben 120–9, 139, 163, 184
Aveling E. 120

Bahro, R. 153, 159
Barth, K. 194, 218, 222
de Beauvoir, S. 32, 35
Boehm-Bawerk, E. 114
Bradley, A.C. 38, 40, 54, 159

Camus, A. 52
Carr, E.H. 159
Cavell, S. 83
Clark, M. 72–3
Clark, S. 225
commonsense 60, 65, 92–100
Croce, B. 162
Cupitt, D. 216, 225

death 28, 38, 130
Delphy, C. 50
Descartes, R. 78, 81
dialectic 7, 11–13, 24–5, 57, 61,
    72–4, 82, 98, 103–4, 121,
    123–7, 132, 139, 145–7, 149,
    151, 157, 161–88, 194–5, 199,
    226–7, 231–2, 243, 244
divorce 33
Dobash, R. 55
Dobash, R.E. 55
Dworkin, A. 54

Einstein, A. 243
Elshtain, J.B. 32, 48, 53, 55
Engels, F. 48, 151, 159, 160
Enlightenment 2, 23, 28
error 5, 6, 196
Euclid 233, 236

Fackenheim, E. 189, 221
family 30–8, 42–50, 103, 122

fear 43, 44
Feuerbach L. 137
Fichte, J.G. 124, 250
formalism 2
freedom 3, 30, 31, 40–52, 115,
    148, 181–3

Gadamer H. 26, 28
Galileo, G. 241
Geach, P.T. 80, 88, 101
God 5, 27, 51, 63, 137–8, 148,
    150–1, 155, 189, 194, 200,
    203, 209, 212, 219, 221–2
Goethe, W. 246, 248, 250, 260
Gorz, A. 188

Habermas, J. 26
Harris, H.S. 117, 250, 252, 256
Heidegger, M. 26
Heisenberg, W. 227
Heraclitus 62, 66, 67, 69, 75
Hobbes, T. 259–60
Hume, D. 72, 78
Hunt, P. 55

infinity 234–5
Inwood, M.J. 60, 61, 69

Kant, I. 3, 25, 35, 53, 59, 61, 62,
    70, 83, 121, 133, 137–9, 144–6,
    159, 223, 229, 230, 232–3,
    235, 237, 240, 247, 250, 256,
    259, 260
Kaufmann, W. 27, 69
Kepler, J. 241
Kierkegaard, S. 219, 225
Kimmerle, H. 257–8
Knox, T.M. 53, 104, 112, 117,
    118
Kuhn, T.S. 94–5, 101, 224–5

Jaeschke, W. 215, 226
justice 49

labour 43–4, 49–51, 110–11, 115,
    130–1, 135–6, 179, 180

Lefebvre, H. 119, 120, 132
Lenin, V.I. 125, 127
Lloyd, G. 32, 35
Loewenberg, J. 75, 81–2, 100
lordship and bondage (also
    mastery and slavery) 12, 28,
    40–52, 130–2, 140, 174, 185
love 35, 39, 40
Lukács, G. 39, 40

MacIntyre, A. 28
McTaggart, J.M.E.M. 58, 59,
    64, 69
Marcuse, H. 159, 160
marriage 33–5, 41
Marx, K. 26, 28, 48, 49, 70,
    105–12, 114, 116–42, 145–8,
    152–60, 163–87
Marx, W. 1, 26
Mead, G.H. 101
Mill, J. 116
Mill, J.S. 30
Miller, A.V. 53, 104
Montesquieu 2
Moore, G.E. 76

nature 1, 2, 3, 36
needs 102–6, 108, 128, 133, 140,
    211
Newton, I. 243
Niethammer, F.I. 251

Oakshott, M. 191–3, 198–9, 203,
    221, 223
Ogilvy, J. 82–3, 101
Okin, M. 30, 31, 52, 53, 55
Orwell, G. 31

paradigms 94–5, 213–14, 224–5
Parmenides 61–2, 66
Pelczynski, Z.A. 117
Phillips, D.Z. 217–18, 225
physics 227–8
Plant, R. 82, 101, 108, 117
Plato 30, 57, 58, 146, 147, 229,
    259
Poggeler, O. 258–9
Popper, K. 194, 222
poverty 48
proof 229–33, 241

Pythagoras 229

Rand, A. 154, 160
recognition 24, 25, 52
reification 134–5
Revolution, French 15, 48
    social 177–8
    scientific 94–5
Ricardo, D. 102, 107, 109, 115,
    170
Rose, G. 29, 186
Rosen, M. 194, 216, 222, 225
Rosenkranz, K. 251–2, 259
Rousseau, J.J. 2, 30
Russell, B. 70–2, 75, 76, 78, 88

Santayana, G. 79, 101
Sartre, J.P. 26, 35
scepticism 8, 9, 51, 75, 170, 254
Schelling, F.W.J. 229–34, 248,
    250, 251, 256
Schneider, H. 260
Schopenhauer, A. 70
Schwarzott, T. 251
Simpson, G. G. 101
Smith, A. 102, 107, 109, 115
socialism 153, 154, 167, 178

Taylor, C. 27, 59, 60, 69, 100,
    186, 187, 221
teleology 48, 57, 179
terror 15
tragedy 8, 9, 22, 37, 39, 40
truth 5, 21, 63, 85, 149–51, 170,
    196–9, 211, 217–18, 229, 235,
    238
Tuschling, B. 260

utopian 141, 146, 167

value 111–16, 135

Weizäcker, von, C.F. 227
Westphal, M. 27
will 128–30
Winfield, R.D. 108, 109, 115,
    117, 118
Wittgenstein, L. 70–101, 217,
    225